Neighbors,
Friends,
or Madmen

Neighbors, Friends, or Madmen

THE PURITAN ADJUSTMENT TO QUAKERISM IN SEVENTEENTH-CENTURY MASSACHUSETTS BAY

JONATHAN M. CHU

Contributions to the Study of Religion, Number 14

Greenwood Press
Westport, Connecticut • London, England

Library of Congress Cataloging in Publication Data

Chu, Jonathan M.
  Neighbors, friends, or madmen.

  (Contributions to the study of religion, ISSN 0196-
7053 ; no. 14)
  Bibliography: p.
  Includes index.
  1. Quakers—Massachusetts—History—17th century.
2. Puritans—Massachusetts—History—17th century.
3. Massachusetts—History—Colonial period, ca. 1600-
1775. 4. Massachusetts—Church history. I. Title.
II. Series.
F75.F89C47 1985   974.4'02   84-29035

ISBN 0-313-24809-5 (lib. bdg.)

Library of Congress Catalog Card Number: 84-29035
ISBN: 0-313-24809-5
ISSN: 0196-7053

First published in 1985

Greenwood Press
A division of Congressional Information Service, Inc.
88 Post Road West
Westport, Connecticut 06881

Printed in the United States of America

The paper used in this book complies with the
Permanent Paper Standard issued by the National
Information Standards Organization (Z39.48-1984).

10 9 8 7 6 5 4 3 2 1

Copyright Acknowledgments

Grateful acknowledgment is given for the use of the following:

Extracts from ''The Social and Political Contexts of Heterodoxy'' by J. M. Chu, which first
appeared in the September 1981 issue of the *New England Quarterly*, pp. 365-84, are reprinted
by permission of the publisher.

''The Social Context of Religious Heterodoxy: The Challenge of Seventeenth-Century Quakerism
to Orthodoxy in Massachusetts'' originally appeared in the April 1982 number of the *Essex
Institute Historical Collections* published by the Essex Institute, Salem, Massachusetts, and is
reprinted here with the kind permission of the Essex Institute.

To My Grandparents

for their dreams on the Sandlewood Mountain

Contents

Series Foreword

The commonplace understanding of Quakers in Puritan New England is that they represented an unacceptably radical religious position and received uniformly heavy suppression at the hands of authorities. Some Puritan reaction to the Society of Friends in the mid-1600's lends credence to this sterotype, and documentation limited to selected Massachusetts divines has perpetuated a facile viewpoint to our own day. This important study, however, goes beyond such easy generalizations and carefully surveys a wider range of evidence in Puritan plantations over a more extensive period of time. The author shows that New England Puritan response was more complicated, less rigid, and more discriminating than was previously thought.

Professor Chu has produced a benchmark study that will have to be reckoned with in subsequent inquiries into this area. He is the first scholar systematically to examine local court records regarding Quakers, and he has performed yeoman service in researching wills, tax lists, and legislation to shed light on his subject. He significantly expands current usages in local history to supplement general Puritan studies, and moreover he has pioneered ways of showing who New England Quakers were and where they fit into colonial social structures. His work is the most inclusive and thorough interpretation of Quaker-Puritan relations that pertained in Massachusetts before it became a royal colony in 1690.

Puritan ministers influenced magistrates of the same faith in cooperative efforts to regulate a righteous society. Religious uniformity was a desideratum, but heterodoxy was not a crime. How could orthodox Calvinists, in a context that poses difficult questions about church and state, prevent heresy within the law? By equating religious error with sedition and by accusing theological

dissenters of attempting to overthrow the authority of the
state. This was the sequence of ideas and events that led
to the executions of four Quakers in Boston by 1661. Professor Chu shows that practical problems complicated the
situation thereafter, because solid citizens at Salem and
Kittery, not interlopers or unknown firebrands, converted
to the Society of Friends. Faced with either persecuting
dissenters on religious grounds or compromising doctrinal
uniformity, Puritans experimented from 1660 to 1690 with
rudimentary forms of religious toleration.

It is important to see how this study stresses the
value of practical exigencies over principle. The author
points out that local magistrates did not consistently
execute policies of the central colonial government. Toleration of local, law-abiding Quakers was grudging in
light of ideals about religious uniformity, but it was a
minor triumph of English Common Law in view of what criteria were permissible in civil court. So toleration
that developed in the Puritan colony recognized domestic
tranquillity as more important than orthodoxy, social
practicalities more weighty than religious conformity.
To substantiate this observation the present study explains variations among towns and regions of the Bay
Colony. It shows how the down-to-earth dynamics of local
life slowly counteracted preconceived prejudices about
Quakers. In a carefully limited and thoroughly analyzed
focus, it helps us understand the beginnings of religious
freedom in America. Forces at work on a small scale in
the limited setting of Puritan Massachusetts served as an
early example of tendencies that gathered momentum in other
American colonies over the next century. Reluctant acceptance of Quakers in orthodox New England laid the founda-
tion for later growth of religious pluralism along the
whole Atlantic seaboard. Chu's analysis of practical
judgments in the seventeenth century helps explain the
basis for similar pragmatic decisions made by federal
legislators in the eighteenth century.

Preface

Few have as much admiration for the Society of Friends as
I.   Throughout their history, Friends have stood for many
of man's finest ideals at great personal cost. One of my
regrets is my inability to share their fortitude, courage,
character, and faith. Where, however, some have seen
strength of character, others saw obstinance. Where some
have seen an idealism born of Truth; others, madness. The
distinctions, like beauty, rest in the eye of the beholder.
Should we declare religious idealism a species of madness
curable by the gallows, we would deserve, quite justly,
universal condemnation. We do not consider Quakerism a
form of madness, nor do we claim, as seventeenth-century
Puritans did, the right to hang Quakers because their
defense of conscience appears to be mad. But that is our
judgment, and we should be extremely circumspect in
forcing seventeenth-century Englishmen to live by our
standards of rectitude. When the Puritans hanged Mary
Dyer, William Robinson, Marmaduke Stephenson, and
William Leddera, they believed that they were defending
the interests of the state. In this, Puritans were not
unique. Order is, after all, a convenient justification
for many state actions. What follows is not intended
to be an excuse or apology for the treatment of Friends
in seventeenth-century Massachusetts. Rather, it is an
attempt to establish that the response of the Puritans
was more than a simple persecuting reflex of the
narrow-minded, bigoted populace. Moreover, to limit one's
focus to the executions ignores the contributions of resident Quakers who ultimately convinced Puritan authorities
that toleration was preferable to persecution.

   All quotations have been transcribed as they appeared in the source cited with minor alterations. Individual
letters were changed to conform to modern practice, and
ampersands and diphthongs were written out in full. Dates

were changed to reflect the modern practice of beginning the new year on 1 January.

Portions of the book have previously appeared in print. The publishers of the New England Quarterly have kindly granted permission for reprinting the parts of chapter five that originally appeared in the September 1981 issue under the title "The Social and Political Contexts of Heterodoxy: Quakerism in Seventeenth-Century Kittery." Portions of chapter six have also been published previously as "The Social Context of Religious Heterodoxy: The Challenge of Seventeenth-Century Quakerism to Orthodoxy in Massachusetts." The article originally appeared in the April 1982 number of the Essex Institute Historical Collections published by the Essex Institute, Salem, Massachusetts, and is reprinted here with the kind permission of the Essex Institute.

Many librarians and archivists guided uncertain steps through the maze of documents. The staff of the James Duncan Phillips Library of the Essex Institute allowed me access to materials at inconvenient moments and treated me with unfailing courtesy and kindness. I also learned a great deal about early Salem from the staff and especially from Irene Norton. Louis Tucker and the staff of the Massachusetts Historical Society provided a pleasant place to work and were helpful in finding documents from my often obscure and illegible notes. The staff of the Massachusetts State Archives provided copies of microfilm that enabled me to do much of the research away from Boston. Thyra Jane Foster, former head of the Archives of the New England Yearly Meeting provided me with a microfilm of the early record books of the Salem Monthly Meeting and arranged access for me to the original manuscripts when she could not be present at the Rhode Island Historical Society.

The book has benefitted from the personal encouragement and support of many people. Students and graduate fellows at the Yale Law School expressed constant concern and interest in the project. Martin Stone, Carole Randolph, and Jonathan Band probably heard more than they cared to about seventeenth-century Quakers and still gave me frequent encouragement and advice. Ed Kohn, Charles Hallinan, and David Fraser confirmed my thoughts on the limited range of acceptable forms of religious belief in America. They also instructed me, as did Professor Charles L. Black, in the limits of the First Amendment. I am most grateful for the early interest of Professors Arthur Worrall of Colorado State University and Richard Gildrie of Austin Peay State University. Professor Worrall has been a frequent source of counsel and reassurance. Professor Gildrie kindly shared his thoughts on early Salem and taught me how to read the town's records carefully. Professors Sidney James and Pauline Maier also read portions of the manuscript and offered suggestions that strengthened the final product.   At the University of Massachusetts-Boston, many colleagues too numerous to mention read drafts and gave important criticism and welcome support.

To Professors Richard R. Johnson and Fred J. Levy, advisors and friends, my debts are beyond reparation.   To them fell the unenviable task of making sense of my early forays into seventeenth-century English and American history.   Their patience and counsel have helped immeasurably, and I have profited by their thoughtful suggestions and gentle criticism.   Richard, especially, witnessed the birth of this project and watched its growth.   I am fortunate to have had him as an advisor and to have him as a friend.   None of the above should, of course, bear any responsibility for any errors remaining in the book; that responsibility is mine alone.

Two people made important, though indirect, contributions to this book.   The late Professor Samuel Hurwitz, formerly of the University of Hawaii, went out of his way to help a beginning graduate student with interests outside his own.   He taught me much about the impact a good, demanding teacher can have, and I will always remember him fondly.   I would also be remiss not to acknowledge the assistance of Mrs. Lucretia Burns.   "Lukie" has provided a haven for many students of early Salem.   I was fortunate to have been one of many to have shared her hospitality and friendship.

Maryann Brink and Michael Chesson deserve special thanks for their friendship and support.   They read drafts of the manuscript when they should have been doing their own work.   They offered solace in dark moments and added much good cheer in light.   They made an important difference, and they should know how fully Matthew 25:35-36 describes their importance to me.

I wish my father, David S. Chu, my maternal grandfather, Wong Buck Hung, and paternal grandparents, Mr. and Mrs. Chu Fook Ting, could have lived to see the completion of the book.   I am sure that they did not expect the first doctor in the family to be an American historian. While I did not achieve the dreams they had for me, I suspect they would still be pleased.   My mother, Sau Kum Chu, and grandmother, Mrs. Wong Buck Hung, do not understand how anyone born and raised in Honolulu could have such a passion about, much less actually live in, Massachusetts. I think they know who the real madman is.   Words cannot express the profound sense of gratitude I feel for the sacrifices and support of my parents and grandparents. Their efforts made possible the progress of this particular pilgrim; and if the book shows that I have seen a little more, it was because I traveled on the shoulders of giants.

Neighbors,
Friends,
or Madmen

1
New England Judged by the Spirit of the Law

The Puritan hanging of four Quakers in Massachusetts ad-
dresses a common American preoccupation: the extent to
which matters of religion ought to be free from state coercion. The episode has proven useful either in demonstrating how courageous some Americans were in advancing
the cause of freedom or illustrating how far we have come
since the seventeenth century. Episodes like these seemingly convinced Americans of the virtue of erecting barriers between church and state. Yet the presumption that
Americans wisely chose to separate church and state in
the interest of freedom is a partial conceit that over-
simplifies reality and overestimates the strength of prohibitions against state intervention in matters of conscience. William Holdsworth, the noted legal historian,
once observed that even when a state declares absolute
religious freedom it does not abdicate the right to suppress opinions inimical to its welfare merely because
those opinions claim to be religious.[1] Toleration did not
emerge in Massachusetts because Puritans realized freedom
would be advanced or the state had no business favoring
one form of belief over another. Rather, toleration, at
least in the case of Quakerism in seventeenth-century
Massachusetts, became convenient in the context of the
arrangement of institutions and dynamics of Puritan life.
 When historians looked at the treatment of Quakers
in Massachusetts, they saw the explicit use of state power
to suppress dissent. They then rushed to establish the
moral lesson of the evils of persecution or to justify the
state's action. Either Quakers were friends of religious
freedom or madmen threatening to destroy society. Understandably, the separate lines of analysis have their origins in Puritan and Quaker explanations for the confrontations. Quaker George Bishop charged the Puritans with
hypocrisy. Having claimed the right to oppose the English

church for conscience sake, Puritans in Massachusetts denied Quakers the same liberty.[2] Puritan apologists like
John Norton justified the magistrates' actions as attempts
to preserve the larger community from the disorder caused
by a few madmen. Nineteenth-century historians who followed Norton's reasoning became anachronisms in a world
where religious freedom had become a virtue and Quakers
less demonstrative. Respecting the faith that had steeled
Puritan wills, these historians had to justify an idealism
that persecuted Quakers.[3] Characterizing early Quakers as
mad was one means of circumventing the issue of religious
freedom and making it irrelevant. Also, the theory had
an additional benefit: Friends themselves considered the
possibility that early Quaker behavior could be considered
mad. In 1791, Moses Brown, prominent Rhode Island Quaker
and merchant, rebuked a correspondent, Jedediah Morse, for
his characterization of the activities of early Friends in
Boston. Morse, according to Brown, had observed that "the
conduct of Quakers at several times render[ed] them proper subjects of a madhouse." Brown criticized Morse not
on the grounds that Friends were incapable of acting mad
but that the total context of the persecutions had to be
considered. Brown's implication was that Quakers could
have exhibited traits of madness.[4]
     More recent historians attempting to be fair to both
sides tried to place the episode in a larger context.
Still, they defined Quakers as outsiders or deviants--a
more sophisticated and genteel way, perhaps, of calling
them madmen--who attacked the foundations of Puritan society. Perry Miller escaped, somewhat, the problem of
criticism or apology by his general focus upon an intel-
lectual world attempting to cope with new social conditions. The persecutions from Miller's perspective were
one of many responses to the forces of change. Having
created a New World Zion, intolerance in defense of the
godly administration of rights and liberties was an understandable, though regrettable, characteristic. Quakerism
provided an index of change that illustrated Puritanism's
growing inability to define reality.[5] Yet while he tried
to be more understanding and less judgmental, Miller still
looked at the episode in Puritan terms. Similarly, Kai
Erikson's attempt to present a more dispassionate understanding of Puritan motives still viewed the world in
their terms. Ironically, Erikson made the Puritans seem
less sympathetic. According to Erikson, Puritans used
Quakers, along with witches and Antinomians, to define
deviance. Thus, the perservation of a Puritan world required the punishment of scapegoats like the Quakers.[6]
     While Erikson extended Miller's conceptual framework
in a specific examination of actions purportedly arising
out of Puritan ideas, he, like Miller, presumed that policies established by the central government were carried
out consistently at all institutional levels. Such a view,

however, assumed a homogeniety that has been challenged in
other areas by the recent spate of town and regional
studies. Examinations of English Quakerism and of Cam-
bridgeshire illustrate considerable variation in the
treatment of religious dissidents.[7] In seventeenth-
century New England, variations in the development of
towns or regions are explained in terms of English origins, geography, or the peculiar dynamics of local life.
Timothy Breen especially has warned against presuming
that the General Court's will could be enforced precisely
at all levels of Bay Colony society.[8] Taken into consideration with the recent work of Arthur Worrall and Richard
Gildrie, Breen's caution points to the necessity of
placing the Puritan treatment of Quakers in a context
that considers not only the actions and justifications
of the General Court but the particular conditions of
local life. Both Gildrie and Worrall indicate the presence of complex, varied sets of human and institutional
factors, Puritan and Quaker, locality and General Court,
that shaped the treatment of religious dissidents in
Massachusetts Bay.[9]
    Thus, an understanding of the motives that influ-
enced the treatment of Quakerism must also consider the
extent to which the dynamics of local life may have altered the Puritan view of the sect and its believers.
Because it provided an issue compelling action, the prosecution of Quakers illustrates the ability of central
authority in Massachusetts to enforce its will in the
localities. Moreover, the episode arose when Bay institutions were subject to particularistic forces from below
and more general, imperial ones from above. As such, an
examination of the Puritan prosecution of Quakers provides
an opportunity to synthesize the Miller view of Puritanism
with the new local history. The issue cuts vertically
across institutional lines and requires an examination of
the motives shaping treatment at each level as well as the
relationships of the parts to the whole. In more specific
terms, Puritans had to consider the extent to which they
defined Quakers as deviants at each separate institutional
level.
    As Puritans learned to cope, however reluctantly,
with the presence of resident heterodoxy, they also revealed an important lesson in the origins of religious
toleration in America. Ultimately, local Puritans moved
the state to become more tolerant, but tolerance also
emerged from within the structure of their institutions.
In moving from intolerance to tolerance, the Puritans'
desire to sustain their unique ecclesiastical and civil
polity significantly affected the definition of Quakers'
place. In spite of the Puritan's initial fear of Quakerism, they chose to keep civil peace at the expense of
orthodoxy. When they did so, they revealed not only important changes in the perception of the central nature

of Quakers but values Puritans held most dear in the last
quarter of the seventeenth century.

On the eve of the Quaker invasion of Massachusetts
Bay, Puritans believed that they had developed an effective balance between ecclesiastical and temporal power in
a way that maintained peace and orthodoxy. Crucial to the
Puritan enterprise in the New World had been the attempt
to balance church and state. Scarred by their recent experiences in England with Charles I and Archbishop William
Laud, Puritans in Massachusetts Bay established ecclesiastical and civil institutions with separate, limited areas
of jurisdiction. Both church and state were, in theory,
equal partners in the quest for a godly commonwealth, and
neither was supposed to interfere in the affairs of the
other. There was one exception: magistrates were supposed to suppress corrupt forms of religious worship.
Intent upon balancing church and state in an organic unity,
Puritans saw a potential for civil disorder that inhered
in heterodoxy. Chaos, confusion, and anarchy would reign
without the intervention of the state in behalf of orthodoxy. Still, this particular extension of civil power
into religious affairs had to be sharply limited; magistrates could not perform ecclesiastical functions, interfere with the election of church officers, or, most
important, resolve matters of conscience or issues of
faith.[10]

When Puritans used civil authority to suppress
Quakers, they merely followed precedent. Bay Puritans
had learned to use secular authority in religious affairs
when they faced heterodox people like Roger Williams,
John Wheelwright, the Antinomians, and other religious
dissidents.[11] The state was forced to act when ecclesiastical institutions seemed incapable of restoring orthodoxy and order in the face of heterodoxy. But because of
the avowed limitations upon the state's ability to act in
matters of conscience, Puritans in their proceedings
against the Quakers had to go beyond a simple determination of whether heterodoxy existed. Heterodoxy alone was
an insufficient ground for punishment by temporal institutions. Instead, Puritans justified state intervention
in ecclesiastical matters when mad dissidents posed threats
to peace.[12]

But the application of secular institutions to the
task of suppressing heterodoxy introduced peculiar struc-
tural and functional requirements potentially at odds with
the desire to preserve religious conformity. Using civil
courts undermined the original justifications that permitted the civil enforcement of orthodoxy. Either magistrates applied ecclesiastical criteria and infringed upon
the prerogatives of the church, or they used purely secular evidence of good citizenship. As long as the heterodox were openly disruptive, the bar to state action was
not insuperable. There was no fundamental disagreement

over the state's need to act with Quakers visiting from
abroad.   To Puritans, they were openly contemptuous of
all authority and confirmed the intimate connection of
heterodoxy and civil disorder.   But courts faced an impossible dilemma when they had to try religious dissidents
for whom evidence of disorder, aside from the fact of
their heterodoxy, was lacking.   Magistrates had to choose
between civil and ecclesiastical criteria when evaluating
the threat posed by local converts to Quakerism who were
heterodox in belief and peaceful in demeanor.

Once magistrates decided to punish Quakers on the
grounds of the threat they posed to the temporal world,
they then had to use requirements associated only with
their special, limited jurisdiction.   Civil courts had to
use secular, not ecclesiastical, evidence of disorder, and
admissions of heterodoxy had to be set aside in favor of
evidence of behavior that threatened civil peace.   As long
as local Quakers sustained their beliefs, they made magistrates consider the threats posed in secular terms; that
is, the terms of the particulars of individual circumstances, place, character, and past behavior.   Once these
secular criteria assumed precedence over the simple fact
of heterodox belief--as they had to because of the Puritan
insistence upon maintaining the barrier between church
and state--then the central question in determining
Quakers' punishment had to shift.   The civil imperatives
justifying the suppression of Quakers changed the ·funda-
mental legal question because of the very application of
secular courts; it did not matter whether one was Quaker
but whether his or her punishment was warranted in light
of purely secular needs.

Thus, the peculiar nature of Puritan church-state
relationships and the decision to use temporal courts to
suppress heterodoxy brought about the adoption of a regime
that permitted the emergence of a reluctant, grudging toleration of religious dissent.   For if the city upon a hill
found that it could not consistently enforce orthodoxy, or
if secular authorities found it preferable to follow lines
of argument that originated in the initial rationale for
allocating jurisdiction between church and state, they
allowed variations in treatment where it might well be
more convenient to tolerate some forms of heterodoxy.   This
would be especially true when the costs of preserving orthodoxy seemingly required the destruction of the Puritans'
balanced civil and ecclesiastical polity.   Thus, the emergence of toleration in Massachusetts did not take place
because Puritans learned to appreciate it as an end in
itself but because circumstances made it preferable to
sacrifice religious conformity for other social ends.[13]

NOTES

1.   William G. Holdsworth, A History of English Law, 20 vols. (London, 1903-75), 18:420.

2.   George Bishop, New England Judged by the Spirit of the Lord (1661; rept. London, 1703).   See especially pp. 247-49.

3.   John Norton, The Heart of New England Rent (Cambridge, Mass., 1659), p. 40.   George E. Ellis, The Puritan Age and Rule in the Colony of Massachusetts Bay, 1629-1685 (Boston, 1888).

4.   Moses Brown to Jedediah Morse, 23 April 1791, Moses Brown Materials Relating to the History of Friends in New England, Rhode Island Historical Society Library, Providence.

5.   Perry Miller, The New England Miñd: From Colony to Province (Boston, Mass., 1961), pp. 35, 65, 77, 123-25. See also Carla Gardina Pestana, "The City upon a Hill under Siege: The Puritan Perception of the Quaker Threat to Massachusetts Bay, 1656-1661," New England Quarterly, 56 (1983):323-53.

6.   Kai T. Erikson, Wayward Puritans: A Study in the Sociology of Deviance (New York, 1966), pp. 188-95.

7.   See, for example, Hugh Barbour, The Quakers in Puritan England (New Haven, Conn., 1964), pp. 54-55, 232-33. Margaret Spufford, Contrasting Communities: English Villages in the Sixteenth and Seventeenth Centuries (Cambridge, England, 1974), pp. 289-90.

8.   Timothy H. Breen, "Persistent Localism: English Social Change and the Shaping of New England Institutions," William and Mary Quarterly, 3d. ser., 32 (1975):3-27. See also David Grayson Allen, In English Ways: The Movement of Societies and the Transferal of English Local Law and Custom to Massachusetts in the Seventeenth Century (Chapel Hill, N.C., 1981), and Darret Rutman, Winthrop's Boston: A Portrait of a Puritan Town, 1630-1649 (New York, 1965).

9.   Arthur J. Worrall, Quakers in the Colonial Northeast (Hanover, N.H. and London, 1980), pp. 9-15. Richard P. Gildrie, Salem, Massachusetts: 1626-1683: A Covenant Community (Charlottesville, Va., 1975), chapters 7-9.

10.   George L. Haskins, Law and Authority in Early
Massachusetts: A Study in Tradition and Design (New York,
1960), pp. 62-64.

11.   Edmund S. Morgan, Roger Williams: The Church and
the State (New York, 1967), pp. 83-86.   Thomas J. Buckley,
"Church and State in Massachusetts Bay: A Case Study, the
Baptist Dissenters, 1651," Journal of Church and State, 23
(1981):309.   Ronald D. Cohen, "Church and State in Seventeenth-Century Massachusetts: Another Look at the Antinomian Controversy," Journal of Church and State, 12
(1970):489-90.

12.   David D. Hall, The Faithful Shepherd: A History
of the New England Ministry in the Seventeenth Century
(Chapel Hill, N.C., 1972), pp. 122-23.   See also Edward A.
Johnson, The Wonder-Working Providence of Sion's Saviour
in New England, ed. J. Franklin Jameson as Johnson's
Wonder-Working Providence...(Original Narratives of Early
American History) (New York, 1910), p. 140.

13.   For a discussion of the emergence of religious
toleration in Western Europe generally, see Herbert
Butterfield, "Toleration in Early Modern Europe," Journal
of the History of Ideas, 38 (1977):573-84, especially
pp. 583-84.

2
An Upstart Branch of
the Anabaptists

In July 1656, Mary Fisher and Ann Austin landed at Boston.
Learning that the two women were Quakers, the magistrates
of the Massachusetts General Court ordered them seized,
deprived of their books, searched--according to other
Quakers, in a shameless fashion--and cast into the Boston
jail to await deportation. While they congratulated themselves on their prompt actions, the Bay magistrates were
unaware that other Quakers were en route to join Austin
and Fisher. Indeed, the two women were the advance guard
of a crusade that was supposed to carry the Quaker message
of the inner light to an unbelieving Massachusetts. In
response to this assault upon its peace, Massachusetts
would hang four Quakers, whip and banish over a devil's
dozen more, and levy large fines upon still others. In
short, it appeared, according to one historian of the
period, that the Bay magistrates were "inspired to prodi-
gious feats of persecution" in their efforts to suppress
Quakerism and to preserve Puritan orthodoxy.[1]
     Bay magistrates justified their actions by more than
the mere fact of Quaker heresy. When Austin and Fisher
rejected the right of the magistrates to jail them and
when other Quakers refused to abide by their sentences of
banishment, Puritans justified the intervention of civil
authorities in religious matters. During the first half
of the seventeenth century, few Englishmen questioned
that, despite all the religious controversy of the time,
there could be only one true church and that the state
had to support its demands for conformity. Fundamental
to this belief was confidence in one's ability to discern
religious truth and a conviction that heresy undermined
the public welfare and hence was a form of sedition. Because heresy subverted religion and, therefore, morality,
it disturbed the public peace and was punishable at common
law.[2]

In relying upon civil authorities to suppress Quakers,
Puritans illustrated the concerns of their recent past.
Having suffered in England at the hands of a hostile and
effective system of ecclesiastical courts, Bay Colony
Puritans were understandably reluctant to recreate instruments of government that could be turned against them. In
place of an episcopal hierarchy and church courts, Puritans
created a dispersed congregational polity in Massachusetts
that insulated local churches from supervision and, hence,
from regulation by a central ecclesiastical authority that,
as had happened in the English church, could be all too
easily captured by forces opposed to true religion. To
shield the congregation, Puritans kept church and state
institutionally separate. By maintaining barriers between
ecclesiastical and civil jurisdictions, the magistracy and
clergy hoped to prevent the state from sponsoring irreligion.[3] However, the need to pereserve order in the
church while building a New World Zion blurred the distinctions between civil and ecclesiastical authority and
lowered the institutional barriers between the two jurisdictions in practice. The congregational polity required
that individual theological dissent still be suppressed,
albeit in a churchly way. If no immediate correction were
forthcoming, there was no further ecclesiastical sanction
short of excommunication and with it the loss of all
church control over the dissident. The problems of discipline were further complicated by the separation within
the church of the elect from the unregenerate. In the
case of the former, presumably no discipline would be
necessary; and in the case of the latter, churchly sanctions operating through sweet reason would be expected to
have little effect.[4]

There was a practical and traditional solution to the
problem caused by the separation of church and state: the
application of temporal discipline by a godly magistracy
called to office by a virtuous people and advised by a
learned, reformed clergy. Through the requirement of full
church membership for holding political office or voting,
the colony expected to incorporate religion into civil
institutions. Godly magistrates would be expected to
respond to the imperatives of true religion and to coop-
erate with its practice, the state would be based more
firmly upon moral virtue, and the unregenerate would be
more willing to obey duly constituted authority. By
joining religion and government in this indirect manner,
observed Boston selectman John Hull, all would be better
served as "the churches and civil state thus mutually
succoring each other, the Lord hath been pleased to bless
with great prosperity and success, increasing and multi-
plying, protecting and defending all from mischievous
contrivances."[5]

That the task of suppressing heterodoxy fell to civil
magistrates illustrates the attempt to put this assumption

into practice and the attendant difficulties that the
separation of church and state engendered for the suppression of religious dissent. For while the clergy supported
the magistrates in their actions against the Quakers, the
desire to use civil institutions to enforce conformity
subtly altered the relationship between church and state.
Because they used the state to suppress heterodoxy, Puritans treated religious dissidence within the context of
institutions that were deliberately designed to avoid
religious tests thereby permitting the existence of religious dissent in the colony. It was not that the state
was unwilling to act in the case of the Quakers but that
the peculiar arrangement of church and state and of central and local government, the demands to respond to
royal pressure, and the ways in which precedents for
action had been established allowed considerable variation in the treatment of Quakers. So varied was the
treatment of Quakers that a rudimentary form of religious
toleration was able to arise in the third quarter of the
seventeenth century.

This declension of Puritanism within secular institutions was the result of the necessity to respond to
heterodoxy in ways that were circumscribed by the impulse to separate ecclesiastical and secular authority.
Magistrates did not punish the Quakers because they
were heterodox; rather, they punished the Quakers because their heterodoxy led to the disturbance of public
tranquillity. Although subtle, the distinction had
significant consequences. By limiting the discretion
of civil magistrates in the determination of what constituted heterodoxy while asking them to suppress cases
that led to disorder, Massachusetts compelled its civil
guardians of orthodoxy to use criteria in the determination of punishment that allowed one form of obvious
heterodoxy, Quakerism, to exist in the colony.

Quakerism should have been an unquestioned example
of a heinous and seditious heterodoxy that required immediate suppression. Few doubted its dangers. More
significantly, there were ample precedents empowering the
state to act in matters of religious controversy where
the claims for the right of dissent were far more acceptable in orthodox Puritan terms than those made by the
Quakers. Both Roger Williams and John Wheelwright had
had better claims to orthodoxy, and both had been silenced
by the intervention of the state. The rationale for state
involvement was that only the timely, though reluctant,
application of temporal power had prevented the seditious
activities of Williams and Wheelwright from wreaking havoc
upon the colony.[6]

Williams's advocacy of a complete separation of civil
and ecclesiastical authority was a direct challenge to
the attempt to link moral virtue to civil government in
Massachusetts Bay. Concerned as he was with the purifi-

cation of conscience, Williams did not see, as the magistrates and his fellow ministers did, that to prohibit
the enforcement of the first four comandments would have
permitted the toleration of ecclesiastical crimes seemingly
so profound in nature that they had the potential to subvert any society and especially one supposedly founded
upon Christian virtue. Moreover, because of the assumption of the autonomous nature of each congregation, no
legitimate pressure could be brought to bear upon Williams
so long as he retained the support of the Salem church.
Congregational autonomy was never intended to be a bul-
wark for heresy or a sanctuary from which one could cause
the destruction of the Puritan polity. Yet Williams's
desire to purify the church by separating it completely
from the state, from his opponents' perspective, would
have caused the rise of irreligion. This possibility,
coupled with his comments about the nature and extent of
royal authority, could have destroyed the very institutional structure that had initially provided Williams a
refuge for the practice of a purer form of religion and
that had permitted him to speak with impunity.[7]

Throughout its difficulties with Williams and the
Salem church, the magistrates and the clergy had been
careful to preserve the appearance of separate jurisdictions despite their fundamental agreement that Williams
had to conform. Williams's opinions were "erroneous and
very dangerous" and his calling to office "a great contempt of authority." In the determination of the danger
of Williams's ideas, Governor John Winthrop noted that the
magistrates had been careful to defer to the wisdom of
the clergy.

> It being professedly declared by the ministers,
> (at the request of the court to give their advice,)
> that he who should obstinately maintain such opin-
> ions, (whereby a church might run into heresy,
> apostacy, or tyranny, and yet the civil magistrate
> could not intermeddle,) were to be removed and
> that the other churches ought to request the
> magistrates so to do.[8]

Indeed, the decision to banish Williams came only after
Thomas Hooker had been unable to reduce his errors, his
congregation had repudiated him, and all but one of the
colony's ministers had approved the General Court's
actions.[9]

The most significant factor, however, had been the
stripping away of the support of the Salem congregation,
thereby denying Williams both a political base and a theological defense behind which he could be free from retribution. In view of the resistance of the Salem congregation to the persuasions of the colony's remaining ministers, the means for separating Williams from his church

lay in the General Court. Unfortunately for Williams, the
political reality was not that of an idealistic congregation solidly arrayed behind its embattled pastor for conscience' sake. The town and the congregation needed the
General Court more than it needed Williams. Concurrently
with the problems caused by Williams, the town petitioned
the General Court for a grant of land on Marblehead Neck.
Because of the imbroglio, the Court had postponed the
awarding of the grant until Salem resolved her differences
with the rest of the colony. Outraged at this blatant
application of secular pressure in what were supposed to
be purely ecclesiastical concerns, the town protested and
urged that other towns and churches join with it in ad-
monishing the General Court. The rest of the colony had
no intention of protesting an action with which it, no
doubt, fully concurred and stood silently by as the Court
suspended the Salem deputies for the town's rebellion.[10]

    In Williams's case, the magistracy and clergy recog-
nized the advantage and necessity of using state power
when religious errors threatened the well-being of church
and state. Williams's dissent, however, only posed the
possibility of danger; the activities of John Wheelwright
and his Antinomian supporters in the Boston church graphically seemed to illustrate the correlation of religious
dissent and sedition. The reaction of a sizable portion of
the Boston congregation to the rejection of Wheelwright's
appointment to the ministry bordered upon open rebellion.
Because of the theological division within both the congregation and the ministry, there were no means for ending
the dispute and restoring harmony to the church. Vastly
outnumbered in the congregation, John Wilson, the church's
senior minister, and John Winthrop, its most prominent
layman, turned to the General Court and the rest of the
colony to arbitrate the dispute. By calling upon the
Court, both Wilson and Winthrop probably realized that they
were using a mechanism that would favor their position.[11]

    By allowing Wilson to give a sermon before it, the
General Court had implicitly endorsed his observations
that internal division was the cause of the sad state of
Bay Colony churches. When the Antinomians attempted to
have Wilson censured for the contents of his sermon, the
General Court declared that it had found the sermon "a
seasonable advice." The Court then used the occasion of
the Antinomians' request against them by asking the clergy
to consider what powers the Court had in resolving ecclesiastical disputes. The ministers responded in a somewhat
contradictory manner: that actions taken by clerics under
the auspices of civil authority were not subject to ecclesiastical review, thereby affirming Wilson's immunity
from censure by the Boston congregation and the principle
of the separation of church and state, and that, where
church members were acting in a manner that was clearly
dangerous to the state, civil government "may proceed

without tarrying for the church."[12]
    The Court then considered a sermon given by Wheel-
wright that it alleged tended toward sedition. While
Wheelwright had been offered a post in nearby Mount Wollas-
ton as a compromise measure, he continued to attack Wilson
on doctrinal grounds. The specific form of the sermon
seemed highly inflammatory and seemed to urge open rebellion.[13] In convicting Wheelwright of sedition and contempt, the General Court made no attempt to determine if
Wheelwright intended to diminish the authority of either
it or Minister Wilson, only whether he had, in fact,
threatened to disturb public tranquillity. The charge was
easily proved. Since Wheelwright freely admitted to what
he had preached, the crux of the Court's case against him
rested upon its perceptions of the impact of the sermon
upon an already volatile situation. Labelling his opponents as enemies of religion and refusing to compromise
as John Cotton had done, Wheelwright had "purposely set
himself to kindle and increase" the divisions within the
Boston church.[14]

> This course of Mr. Wheel. did tend directly to
> the great hinderance of public utility, for when
> brethren shall looke one at another as enemies
> and persecutors etc. and when people shall looke
> at their Rulers and Ministers as such,...how shall
> they joyne together?...How shall it hinder all
> affaires in Courts, in Townes, in Families, in
> Vessels at Sea, etc., and what can more threaten
> the dissolution and ruine of Church and
> Commonwealth?[15]

    Although the Court found Wheelwright guilty of sedi-
tion, it still stopped short of banishing him immediately
and hoped for a reconciliation between the Boston dissidents and the rest of the colony. Despite this conciliatory approach, the Court was still unable to secure harmony. With the election of Winthrop as governor, the
Antinomians "raised the great danger of tumult." Indeed,
Wheelwright's supporters "went on in their former course,
not onely to disturbe the Churches, but miserably inter-
rupt the civill Peace, and that they threw contempt both
upon Courts and Churches, and began now to raise sedition
among us to the indangering the Commonwealth."[16] For
seven months, from March to November, the Court delayed,
hoping that informal pressure by the ministers would reduce tensions and end the dispute. By 2 November 1637,
however, Winthrop and the General Court found that the
two parties could not coexist. The Antinomians remained
adamant in their support of Wheelwright to the "hazard of
ruin to the whole."[17]
    Thus, if peace were to be restored, it could be
achieved only by the active and forceful intervention of

civil authority. When the supporters of Wheelwright continued their attacks upon Wilson, Winthrop, and the remaining magistrates and clergy, they fitted into a pattern
of seditious disorder that imperiled the entire colony.
Having refused to respond to the guidance of the gathered
ministers, the Antinomians were very clearly falling into
a category of religious error compelling state intervention. As Winthrop later observed in his defense of the
Bay Colony's actions against the Antinomians, "In every
place we find that the contentions began first by dis-
putations and sermons and when the minds of the people
were set on fire by reproachful terms of incendiary
spirits, they soone set to blows and had always a
tragicall and bloudy issue."[18]
   The quieting of Williams and Wheelwright established
a precedent for using the state to quash forms of religious dissent that had the potential to affect both ecclesiastical and civil institutions adversely. Both incidents seemingly had threatened order in church and state
under the guise of conscience and had illustrated the inability of ecclesiastical institutions to resolve internal
conflict. Notwithstanding the assumption of the invio-
lability of congregational autonomy, the General Court,
with the consent of the ministry, came to see it had the
power and obligation to suppress opinions that, while
claiming to be religious in nature, were both dangerous
to the church and subversive to the colony. In working
out the Court's response to Williams and Wheelwright,
Winthrop came to see that there were crimes against
religion that, like murder and robbery, were obviously
dangerous and required punishment by temporal authorities
needing no prior ecclesiastical advice or sanction.[19]
   When the Quakers arrived in Boston, they immediately
fell into this category of persons that used claims to
speak for religion to mask their seditious intentions.
The fact that Massachusetts Puritans so readily placed
arriving Quakers within this model of disorderly behavior
was not particularly strange in light of the Quakers'
reputation. When Englishmen like Richard Baxter and
Ephraim Pagitt described Quakerism as a recent strain of
Anabaptism, they placed the movement squarely within a
tradition of religious dissent that had been disruptive.
Baxter, Pagitt, and other critics of Quakerism had been
repelled by the proliferation of religious movements that
followed the collapse of royal authority during the Interregnum. These critics blamed the radical and more enthusiastic sects in general and the Quakers in particular
for the political instability and disorder of the 1650's.
The activities of the radical sectarians seemed to signal,
as they had at Muenster, that quintessential example of
European religious radicalism, the end to all discipline
and moral restraint.[20]

By their questioning of what constituted saving
faith, Quakers George Fox and James Naylor were part of
the Reformed Protestant tradition that, like Puritanism,
had opposed Rome and Canterbury. Still, they seemed
qualitatively different. In such differences, opponents
of the Quakers found a basis for bitter criticism, and
Bay ministers and magistrates found justification for
punishment. Critics of Naylor and Fox believed that
Quakers made their tests of virtue too simple and by so
doing subverted the abilities of the clergy to enjoin
moral behavior. Where Puritans searched diligently for
the slightest assurance of their salvation, which, if
found, only convinced them of their damnation, Quakers,
from the Puritan perspective, seemed to relish in the
ecstasy of the discovery of their alleged salvation, a
characteristic that seemed dangerously susceptible to the
delusions of depraved men lusting to be among the elect.
Once they presumed to have discovered the inner light,
Quakers seemed to exhibit in their false pride and arrogance a horrifying confidence in their abilities to carry
out the impulses of what they believed was the Holy
Spirit. Puritans had no quarrel with men wanting to do
the will of God, but when someone like Rowland Bateman
declared himself the new Abraham as the justification for
his wish to kill his son or when Mary Adams announced that
she had given birth to Jesus Christ, there seemed good
reason to doubt the supposedly divine origins of the inspiration that prompted such statements. While these were
isolated cases of what Christopher Hill has called holy
imbeciles, there was little confidence among Bateman's
and Adams's critics that Naylor, Fox, and other Quakers
had been more careful in testing the origins of their
visions.[21]
In stressing the primacy of faith over good works,
Quakers tended to emphasize spiritual criteria in their
determination of faith. In this regard, Quakers remained
within the Reformed traditions that included their critics.
Clearly, sanctified men could operate independently of
Scriptural warrant in a manner similar to Biblical prophets. Scripture, after all, was a secondary account of
God's will, a relation of men who in their own time had
been favored by God. One could not deny the possibility
that God might choose to repeat the process of revelation
or that Quaker idealism was privy to His will.[22] Richard
Baxter conceded that it was theologically possible for
regenerate men to operate outside of Scripture as the
Quakers claimed they could, but the probability that their
revelations justified such strange and radical departures
from Scripture was nonexistent. According to Baxter, one
was far more likely to see false pride in the Quaker presumption that their eccentric behavior denoted new Biblical prophets. Furthermore, in the Qaukers' insistence
that they were "perfect and without sin, yea some of them

say they are Christ and God." Baxter saw only one conclusion to be drawn from such positions: Quakers were
men made mad with spiritual pride. "Is it possible that
any man in this life, that is not mad with spiritual
pride can indeed believe that he has no sin?"[23]
     From the point of view of their Puritan critics, the
Quakers had no claim to being regenerate men. No one in-
fused with grace or moved by the impulses of the Holy
Spirit would act like the Quakers. Regenerate men, according to Massachusetts minister Edward Breck did not
"speak nonsense, idle rediculous and foolish things...
false doctrines and contradictions." It was absurd to
think that the Holy Spirit prompted men "to speak blas-
phemously against the Lord Jesus Christ, crying downe his
Institutions, as Magistracy, Ministry, Sacraments, Sabbaths, etc."[24] The willingness to commit blasphemy and
the denunciation of Christ's institutions could be explained not as divine inspiration but as the activities
of that supreme architect of disorder, the Devil. Moreover, the bizarre manifestations of faith that the Quakers
claimed were divine in origin seemed to prove their depraved natures. "Where," Thomas Weld asked George Fox,
"he could shew me for the swelling of the body or foaming
at the mouth or where did he ever reade of any in those
postures, save onely such as were possessed with Devils?"[25]
By requiring grotesque, hysterical posturing as evidence
of their possession of the inner light, Quakers proved the
satanic origins of the alleged inspiration. "I do heartily
believe," wrote Francis Higginson, "these Quakings to be
Diabolicall Raptures proceeding from the power of Satan."[26]
     What made Quakerism even more dangerous was the de-
termination of Quakers to act upon their delusions and to
encourage other men to behave similarly. Be freeing all
other men from moral restraints, the Quakers encouraged
unregenerate and depraved men to follow their passions
and "to obey and not obey as they shall see cause."[27]
Indeed, Quaker practices indicated that they were trying
to make everyone abandon all restraints and follow their
passions to their terrible ends. To critics, Quakers,
under the guise of conscience, made it their duty to de-
mean both civil and ecclesiastical authority, to violate
God's commandments, and to live lives of lasciviousness,
indolence, and vagrancy.[28]
     To Puritans, Quakers seemed to strike at the insti-
tutions that most men assumed were fundamental to any
structured and ordered society. Their attack upon the
family seemed to summarize the insidious nature of the
sect. Refusing to doff one's cap before a stranger might
be mere rudeness, but to do so before one's parents
demonstrated the depth of the Quakers' perfidy. "A son
if turned Quaker will not use the usual civility of the
world that is Christian in putting his hat to his Father
or Mother will give them no civil salutations. To bid

him good morrow that begat him or farewell that brought
him forth is accounted a wickedness." Such expression of
obvious contempt toward those for whom one might assume
that all men should have expressed affection suggested
that the Quakers were prepared to dispense with the most
elementary bonds of social order. Furthermore, the
Quakers' contempt for their parents confirmed their
"savage incivilities and their irreligious bloody, bar-
barous and turbulent practices."[29]

The rejection of parental authority was one of the
many turbulent practices Quakers used to subvert order.
The use of an itinerant ministry further strained the
capacities of family and society to maintain economic and
social order. In their journeys to spread the message
of the inner light, Quakers abandoned callings and families to flit about the countryside "living upon those of
their fraternity where they light to their excess charge."
Families abandoned by missionaries all too often became
the public charges of more industrious fellow townsmen
and villagers who remained faithful to their social responsibilities.[30] Furthermore, Quaker itinerancy corrob-
orated the perception of Quakers as agents of disorder.
Seventeenth-century civil authorities presumed that geographic mobility denoted vagrancy, and itinerant Quaker
ministers appeared to be sturdy beggars and vagabonds
who roamed the English countryside with little to do except to disturb well-ordered churches and communities.
Under such circumstances, Quakers at their best were
"notorious for idleness in their callings working not at
all for whole weeks and months together."[31]

The large number of Quaker women on the road bear-
ing witness to their faith compounded the evils of
Quaker itinerancy. When these women visited a non-Quaker
congregation and called the minister a devil's mouth-
piece, they denied the minister the deference owed his
office and violated the Pauline injunction to keep silent in the church. In this kind of action, the itinerant Quaker women attacked both Scriptural warrant
and the due order of society. To whom were such harri-
dans responsible, why were they not caring for hearth
and home, and why were they trying to destroy other
stable and ordered institutions?[32]

The answers to these questions, according to English observers, lay in the wild, ungovernable passions
that moved all Quakers in general but seemed most apparent among their women. Itinerancy coincided with
sexual license in both sexes, but promiscuity among
Quaker women seemed more blatant. While both men and
women used public nudity as a form of protest, critics
of the Quakers singled out women for their immodesty.[33]
Francis Higginson assumed that Quakers claimed that such
behavior was religious to justify sexual perversion. One
example of this, according to Higginson, was a Wrighton

Quaker woman. Claiming that she had been guided by the
impulses of the Holy Spirit, she went to the bedroom of
the husband of her friend and "bid him open his bed unto
her." At the time, however, the man was already in bed
with another man who, nonetheless, sensing the urgency of
the woman's impulses, quickly surrendered his place to
her. To Higginson, there could be no question that such
sexual practices originated in the passions of depraved
and unregenerate men.[34]

The fact of such dissoluteness was of less concern
than the determination of the Quakers to encourage similar behavior among others. In their unruly practices,
Quakers seemed intent upon encouraging unregenerate men
to destroy the existing order of society in the name of
their supposedly religious duties. When they attacked
ministers and magistrates who attempted to stop their sin-
ful behavior, Quakers affirmed that they recognized no
limits upon their actions just as they refused to allow
any regulation of their faith. Scripture obligated all
men regardless of their state of grace to render unto the
state that which was its due. Quakers, by refusing to
allow Christian magistrates to rule contrary to their
wishes under any conditions, ignored the possibility that
their depraved natures led them astray. Furthermore, by
allowing anyone to determine the level of obedience due
the state, the Quakers permitted the unregenerate and the
depraved to wreak havoc upon orderly communities in the
name of religious duty. If one could not be restrained
from abhorrent or criminal activity whenever he claimed
to speak for conscience' sake, as the Quakers did, then
asked Weld, "Who shall make the laws? Who shall preserve
the peace?" Higginson agreed: What kind of social organization was possible "when Conscience is seared and takes
tumultuousness for duty?"[35]

The questions posed by Weld and Higginson were easily
answered in light of the historical model of the Anabaptist rising at Muenster. Like the Quakers, the Anabaptists had justified their subversion of the existing
social and political order by their claims of a superior
knowledge of God's will.[36] The results had been heresy,
moral abomination, and anarchy. And to their critics,
the Quakers seemed intent upon recreating Muenster in
England. In his preface to A Brief Relation of the
Irreligion of Northern Quakers, Higginson warned that
Quakers were merely a new form of Anabaptism. The
evidence was overwhelming. Did the Quakers not meet
suspiciously in the secrecy of private homes in the
dead of night? If these meetings were as innocent as
the Quakers claimed, why were magistrates so concerned
about their seditious nature? Although Higginson was
wrong about the conspiratorial attributes he projected
onto the Quakers, he was nonetheless convinced that the
parallels between them and the Anabaptists meant the real

possibility of the Quakers establishing a second Muenster.
"When you have read it [A Brief Relation], you will be
ready to dream (if you are acquainted with the history
of the last century) that you behold the turbulent
Excorcists redivive in England and acting their Tragic
parts over again."[37]
     To the ministers and magistrates of Massachusetts,
Quaker actions confirmed the predictive nature of the
Muenster model. Austin, Fisher, and the remaining Quakers in 1656 and 1657 deliberately had gone out of their
way to defy Bay authority. In December 1658, the General
Court commissioned Boston minister John Norton to explain
the reasons for the colony's treatment of Quakers and to
justify its punishment of them. The results of Norton's
efforts, The Heart of New England Rent, earned him a
grant of land and the gratitude of the General Court but,
more crucially for our purposes, illustrated the transfer
of the Quaker image across the Atlantic. Norton repeated
the points made by the English critics of Quakerism like
Weld and Higginson who had personal connections to the
Bay Colony. To Norton, however, and presumably to the
General Court, the lessons of Muenster were far more
potent as a predictive model because Quakers in Massachusetts seemed more inclined to act upon their heretical
beliefs.[38]
     Because Norton saw that Quakers were part of an
anarchistic heterodoxy, he interpreted their attacks
upon Puritanism as a more general attack upon the Bay
Colony.[39] By pretending that they spoke for true religion, Quakers, according to Norton, masked their intentions; in fact, they intended to destroy the very
institutions that God had given man to allow him to live
in relatively peaceful, civil societies. Civil society
muted human passions and minimized the dangers of a
natural order where human depravity might run rampant.
God had allowed man to create civil societies because
"order is God's way of lapsed man's wel-doing and wel-
being, it is the forms of societies. Formes are essen-
tial without which things cannot be." Yet Quakers used
"a superscriptual reformation guilded over with specious
pretences," fed tumultuous and discontented spirits, and
disrupted the orderly arrangement of civil societies.
Their refusal to allow the natural arrangement of superiors and inferiors was one means of opening "an opportunity to the irregenerate and hungry multitude of changing places with their Superiors." Wanting to abolish all
the forms of civil and ecclesiastical discipline, the
Quakers placed themselves in a category of obviously mad
men who had to be restrained by the very mechanisms that
they decried. "The very light of nature teacheth all
nations, that madmen acting according their frantick
passions are to be restrained with chains when they cannot be restrained otherwise."[40]

Simply claiming that they spoke for conscience' sake and, therefore, were immune to civil prosecution did not exempt the Quakers from punishment. The precedents established in the cases of Williams and Wheelwright had permitted church and state to act in concert to suppress kinds of religious dissidence whose claims to orthodoxy were far more substantial. Quakerism was so clearly a threat to order in church and state that Quakers could not be permitted to use the unique separation of ecclesiastical and civil jurisdiction to destroy the Bay Colony, Puritans saw the demands of the Quakers for liberty to speak their conscience freely as disguises for sowing discord and destroying an ordered society. No society, especially a New World Zion or a model of Christian charity, could countenance its own destruction because of legalistic subterfuges. "Should the people not of Athens, but of Sion suffer themselves to be abashed by heretical deceivers and destroyers into a persuasion that whilst it is Lawfull for them under a pretence, it is unlawful for Civil Power to defend Religion?"[41]

Norton argued that civil regulation of the Quakers did not entail any violation of the separation of civil and ecclesiastical jurisdiction that characterized Bay life. In suppressing the evil of Quakerism, Puritan magistrates were not attempting to compel orthodoxy in belief. To have tried to do so would have been fruitless, requiring an ability man did not possess, the capacity to alter the fact of predestination. As long as individuals kept their own consciences, there could be no basis for magisterial interference. "Whilst a man keepeth his heterodoxy to himself, he is doubtless out of reach of the magistrate. We know that it belongeth not unto the Magistrates to compel any man to be a believer nor to punish any for not being a believer."[42] In this argument, Norton elaborated on the precedents established in the Williams and Wheelwright cases and confirmed elsewhere. While the magistrates' powers in defining heterodoxy had been sharply limited in 1647 in the Cambridge Platform, they were still obligated to act in the most obvious manifestations of heterodoxy. The justification for this action rested upon the obvious assumption that the state had to preserve civil peace. The magistrates, according to Edward Johnson, could not "exercise civil power to bring all under their obedience to a uniformity in every Poynt of religion but to keepe them in the uniformity in spirit and the bond of peace."[43]

But the Quakers, as Williams and Wheelwright had before them, clearly violated norms of public order in a profound and significant manner and, therefore, could not be exempt from civil regulation. While, as Bay minister Thomas Whalley noted, "a well-bonded Toleration might be desired, neither ought any Error to be tolerated that hath a tendency in its own nature to Profaness or the disturbing of Peace and Order in Church and State."[44] By

disturbing the tranquillity of the colony, insisting upon
speaking before the Bay's churches without the permission
of either ministers or congregations, and rejecting the
right of magistrates to punish them for their actions, the
Quakers demonstrated that they were a threat to order in
the manner predicted by critics of the sect. They seemed
to fit perfectly into the categories of religious heterodoxy that all right-thinking Englishmen agreed ought to
be regulated.[45]   In Massachusetts Bay, that task fell to
the civil magistracy.

Punishment of Quakers in Massachusetts, thus, was no
infringement upon the prerogatives of the ministry; it was
the suppression of a bald, flagrant threat to the ordering
of church and state. Both Williams and Wheelwright had
had better claims than the Quakers to immunity from civil
prosecution because of their ecclesiastical offices and
their more orthodox beliefs. In the Quakers, the General
Court saw a variety of obviously turbulent heretics, and
in this instance it was the only institution capable of
defending both religion and society. "Here is a season,"
declared Norton, "wherein it is the duty of the Civill
Magistrate to put forth his coercive Power as the matter
shall require in defense of Religion, Order, Church and
Commonwealth."[46]

Norton's defense of the actions of the General Court
was neither remarkable nor original in its concern for
order.[47] He had inherited a tradition of perceiving
religious enthusiasm as a profound threat to the kinds of
moral discipline that checked human depravity in civilized
societies, and he had witnessed the efficacy of using
civil power to suppress such ecclesiastical crimes as had
escaped the regulatory mechanisms of local congregations.
Nothing in the Bay Colony's first confrontations with
the visiting Quakers altered these first opinions for
Norton. By persisting in their defiance of duly constituted civil authority, by exempting themselves from any
kind of restraint, the Quakers threatened to make Francis
Higginson's predictions of a new Muenster a reality in
Massachusetts Bay.

The involvement of the state in the suppression of
Quaker heterodoxy, however, required the application of
different criteria of proof and justification. Massachusetts civil magistrates, as they had done with Williams
and Wheelwright, had had to determine guilt on the basis
of sedition rather than heresy to comply with isolating
the church from the state. But sedition is a much more
ambiguous crime than heresy. Whereas the latter depends
upon an examination of belief, the former depends upon the
understanding that because of their ideas individuals
threaten the fundamental ordering of the state. To determine guilt, Quakers and their beliefs had to be linked
with a series of extraordinarily destructive, overt acts
that sustained the predictive characteristics of the
Muenster model. While the activities of Quakers arriving

from England may have provided ample evidence supporting
the model, the General Court also faced Quakers who were
local residents and had personal histories indistinguish-
able from their neighbors save for their sustained expression of a peculiar religious belief. While they too
might be liable to charges of fomenting disorder, resident Quakers introduced additional ambiguities to the
problem of regulating Quakerism. What would happen if
these residents believed in dangerous heresies but kept
those beliefs to themselves? Was their heterodoxy then
of sufficient difference from other apathetic absentees
from orthodox church services to warrant their being
charged with sedition, or were they significantly more
dangerous than the religiously faithful but socially un-
reliable individuals within the several towns and villages
to warrant being treated as felons rather than petty
criminals? Sustaining the original judgment that Quakerism was seditious came to depend upon the abilities of
local magistrates to see significant dangers in the practice of Quaker heterodoxy among residents and to believe
that the dangers warranted the continued practice of intolerance.[48]
    Having chosen to use the civil state to suppress an
ecclesiastical disorder, Massachusetts Bay then had to
contend with the dispersed institutional mechanisms of
civil authority and a pattern of imperial politics that
in turn made the country courts crucial forums for the
suppression of Quakerism. The county courts had been
created to reduce the burden of petty cases heard by the
General Court while providing a more efficient and immediate system of justice to the residents of the colony.
By so doing, the General Court relieved itself of the
responsibilities of adjudicating lesser civil cases and
misdemeanors while it allocated the operations of justice
to those most affected by it. Juries were selected from
townsmen familiar with the details of most of the county
court's cases and with the character of those involved
while the judges were either General Court magistrates
residing in the county or other local residents appointed
by the Court. Also, because of the local origins of
jurymen, there was a tendency for each town to dominate
the particular session of the court held there. This also
coincided with the natural tendency to present one's case
before one's neighbors rather than travel to a distant
town to resolve litigation. While judges might sit on the
bench in court sessions other than their home towns,
juries of one's neighbors usually decided on questions
of fact.[49]
    While the General Court theoretically controlled the
operations of its lower courts by its powers of appointment, in practice the county court was an intermediate
layer of authority that could filter or insulate a minority faction from the political influence of the General
Court. The bulk of the magistrates lived in the most

populous counties of Middlesex and Suffolk, and there was
probably little desire there to deviate from the majority
opinions of the Court. Unlike the other two Bay counties
of Middlesex and Suffolk, Essex, York, and Norfolk were
farther away from Boston, and, for them, the county court
was a much more significant mechanism for resolving local
conflict. At times when interest in the General Court
seemed to favor the more populous counties to the disadvantage of the less populated more distant ones, the
administration of the dissident counties often remained
in the hands of men opposed to the will of the General
Court.[50] Ironically, this characteristic of the county
took on increased significance as the General Court sought
to insulate its policies governing religious dissidence
from royal interference after the Restoration and opened
up opportunities for variation in the treatment of Quakers
in the counties.

Lastly, the use of county courts introduced further
ambiguities regarding the local Quaker converts. Because
county courts resolved conflicts and thus presumably promoted civil peace at the local level, their evaluation of
the threat Quakers posed was crucial.[51] It was to the
county courts that the initial judgment of local Quakers
fell, and, if the courts could not sustain the image of
the Quakers as a cause of sedition or even petty disorder, they permitted the erosion of the perceived connection between the existence of heterodoxy and the continued
need for policies of intolerance. Constrained by the
decision to treat Quakerism by means of civil government,
the county courts respected the prohibitions against using
the consciences of local Quakers as evidence of disorder
and rested their decision on secular behavior. But when
evaluating the local converts, the county courts came to
see that their behavior was often virtually indistinguish-
able from other valued members of the local community.
Punishment under the circumstances would have violated
the prohibitions against civil interference in matters
of conscience or have entailed serious disruptions in the
lives of members of the community. Either alternative
would have been inconsistent with the function of local
legal institutions and would have caused more disorder in
the process. Moreover, once the courts had judged the
local converts and found that there was no threat posed
by them, they, as courts of inferior jurisdiction, made
it more difficult for superior courts to purge Quaker
heterodoxy. To do so required contradicting the finding
that those persons most affected by the local Quakers saw
no threat to the public's well-being.

When Austin, Fisher, and the other visiting Quakers
convinced residents to join their protest against the Bay
Colony's ecclesiastical and political structure, they
forced the colony to test its assumptions regarding Quakers and the separation of church and state through all
the layers of the civil institutions of government. With

the involvement of town, county, and General Court, the
existence of variations in the patterns of punishment of
Quaker heterodoxy should not be surprising in light of the
ambiguous nature of the crime, the diversity of the Quakers and of the institutions entrusted with their suppression, and the peculiar circumstances in which Quakers,
Puritans, and Bay institutions found themselves. What had
to be weighed was the assumption that Quakerism was subversive to order against the threat posed by members of
the sect as perceived by Puritans and as could be proven
over time. For Massachusetts Bay to quash Quakerism effectively in the seventeenth century, it had to decide
that all the sect's adherents were seditious. That decision would have to be made not only by the General
Court in Boston but at every layer of enforcement in the
several counties and towns in which Quakers were to be
found. That judgment then would have to be made repeatedly in the face of Quaker persistence from abroad and
within, under a host of different circumstances, and
would be subject to a wide range of influences only one
of which was religious in nature. Indeed, the ascription
of criminality, much less of seditious intent, uniformly
to all Quakers would not prove to be an easy task.

NOTES

1. Kai T. Erikson, Wayward Puritans: A Study in the
Sociology of Deviance (New York, 1966), p. 121. Also see
Vernon L. Parrington, Main Currents in American Thought:
The Colonial Mind (New York, 1927), p. 150, and Thomas
Jefferson Wertenbaker, The Puritan Oligarchy: The
Founding of American Civilization (New York, 1947),
p. 340.

2. William G. Holdsworth, A History of English Law,
20 vols. (London, 1903-75), 4:497; 6:399-400; 18:322.
William Haller, Liberty and Reformation in the Puritan
Revolution (New York, 1955), pp. 153, 236-37. There is
also, of course, the problem of the connection of
political allegiance and religious belief. Leonard W.
Levy, Origins of the Fifth Amendment: The Right against
Self-Incrimination (Oxford, England, 1968), pp. 83-87, and
Christopher Hill, Society and Puritanism in Pre-revolu-
tionary England, 2d ed. (New York, 1967), pp. 249-50.

3. Levy, Origins of the Fifth Amendment, pp. 272-73;
Hill, Society and Puritanism, pp. 333-34; and Timothy H.
Breen, Puritans and Adventurers: Change and Persistence
in Early America (Oxford, England, 1980), pp. 9-20.

4. Emil Oberholzer, Jr., Delinquent Saints: Disciplinary Action in the Early Congregational Churches of Massachusetts (New York, 1955), pp. 30-31. For the willingness of the ministry to have the state assume the functions of ecclesiastical discipline, see David D. Hall, The Faithful Shepherd: A History of the New England Ministry in the Seventeenth Century (Chapel Hill, N.C., 1972), pp. 125-30, and Timothy H. Breen, The Character of the Good Ruler: A Study of Puritan Political Ideas in New England, 1630-1730 (New Haven, Conn., and London, 1970), pp. 34-41. Also see Hill, Society and Puritanism, chapters 8, 9, 10, and Levy, Origins of the Fifth Amendment, chapter 1.

5. George L. Mosse, "Puritanism and Reason of State in Old and New England," William and Mary Quarterly, 3d ser., 9 (1952):70-76. John Hull, "Diary," Archelogia Americana, 3 (1857):168.

6. Stephen Foster argues that Wheelwright, Anne Hutchinson, and the Antinomians are further removed from Puritan orthodoxy than has been traditionally held. "New England and the Challenge of Heresy 1630-1660: The Puritan Crisis in Transatlantic Perspective," William and Mary Quarterly, 3d ser., 38 (1981):651-53. William B. Stoever, A Faire and Easie Way to Heaven: Covenant Theology and Antinomianism in Early Massachusetts (Middletown, Conn., 1978), pp. 107-10, 170.

7. John Winthrop, History of New England, ed. James K. Hosmer as Winthrop's Journal, 1630-1649 (Original Narratives of Early New England) (New York, 1908), 1:154, 163 (hereafter cited as Winthrop's Journal). Edmund S. Morgan, The Puritan Dilemma: The Story of John Winthrop (Boston, 1958), pp. 126-27.

8. Hosmer, Winthrop's Journal, 1:154.

9. Ibid., 1:163.

10. Ibid., and James D. Phillips, Salem in the Seventeenth Century, (Boston, 1933), pp. 105-7.

11. Hosmer, Winthrop's Journal, 1:204-6. According to Winthrop, only four or five opposed the Antinomians in Boston; however, all but two of the ministers in the colony, and all but three of the magistrates supported his position.

12. Ibid., 1:206-7, 210.

13. For example, in his sermon, Wheelwright urged, "If we do not strive, those under a covenant of works [i.e., Wilson] will prevail. We must have a speciall care therefore to shew ourselves courageous, all the valient men of David and all the men of Israell, Barak and Deborah and Jael, all must fight for Christ." David D. Hall, ed., The Antinomian Crisis (Middletown, Conn., 1968), pp. 158-59.

14. Hosmer, Winthrop's Journal, 1:211, 216.

15. John Winthrop, "A Short Story of Antinomianism," in Charles Francis Adams, ed., Antinomianism in the Colony of Massachusetts Bay, Publications of the Prince Society, vol. 21 (1894; rept. New York, 1967), p. 214.

16. Ibid., p. 8 Hosmer, Winthrop's Journal, 1:218. Emery Battis, Saints and Sectaries: Anne Hutchinson and the Antinomian Controversy in the Massachusetts Bay Colony (Chapel Hill, N.C., 1962), pp. 213-16. Ronald D. Cohen, "Church and State in Seventeenth Century Massachusetts: Another Look at the Antinomian Controversy," Journal of Church and State, 12 (1970):484-89.

17. Hosmer, Winthrop's Journal, 1:239.

18. Winthrop, "A Short Story of Antinomianism," pp. 206-7.

19. Hosmer, Winthrop's Journal, 1:210.

20. Richard Baxter, One Sheet against the Quakers (London, 1657), p. 2. Christopher Hill, The World Turned Upside Down: Radical Ideas during the English Revolution (New York, 1973), pp. 200-1. Barry Reay, "The Quakers, 1659, and the Restoration of the Monarchy," History, 63 (1978):193-213. See also Carla Gardina Pestana, "The City upon a Hill under Seige: The Puritan Perception of the Quaker Threat to Massachusetts Bay, 1656-1661," New England Quarterly, 56 (1983):323-53.
Anabaptists assumed control of Muenster in 1534. An absolute dictatorship infamous for its excesses in the name of religion ensued. The town, following the religious precepts enunciated by Jan Bockelson, abolished private property, seemingly encouraged promiscuity, and staged elaborate pagents and fantastic amusements. Bockelson's first important act in the town illustrated what critics found so appalling about the episode. Bockelson ran naked through the town and fell into a fit of silent ecstasy for three days. After he recovered, Bockelson declared that God had instructed him to form the government that ultimately gave him the virtually absolute powers which in turn led to the excesses. Norman Cohn, The Pursuit of the Millennium: Revolutionary Millenarians and

Mystical Anarchists of the Middle Ages, rev. ed. (Oxford, England, 1970), pp. 251-80.

21. Hill, _The World Turned Upside Down_, p. 200. Brian S. Capp, _The Fifth Monarchy Men: A Study in Seventeenth Century English Millenarianism_ (London, 1972), pp. 40-44. Geoffrey F. Nuttal, _The Holy Spirit in Puritan Faith and Experience_ (Oxford, England, 1946), pp. 41-42, 50-52. For the Puritan version of the process, see Perry Miller, _The New England Mind: The Seventeenth Century_ (Boston, 1965), pp. 382-96. Also see the relationship of heresy and disorder in Roger L. Emerson, "Heresy, the Social Order, and English Deism," _Church History_, 37 (1968):390.

22. Nuttal, _The Holy Spirit_, pp. 30-33. Also see Foster, "New England and the Challenge of Heresy," pp. 658-59.

23. Richard Baxter, "Quakers Questioned," in Hugh Barbour and Arthur O. Roberts, eds., _Early Quakers Writings, 1650-1700_ (Grand Rapids, Mich., 1973), p. 273. Baxter, _The Quakers' Catechism_ (London, 1655), p. C5. Thomas Weld et al., _A Further Discovery of That Generation of Men Called Quakers_ (Gateside, England, 1654), p. 20.

24. Breck to the Church at Rainforth, 17 August 1655 in _An Answer to a Scandalous Paper, Wherein were Some Scandalous Queries Given to Be Answered_ (London, 1656), pp. 4-6.

25. Weld, _A Further Discovery of That Generation of Men_, pp. 91-92.

26. Francis Higginson, _A Brief Relation of the Irreligion of Northern Quakers_ (London, 1653), p. 16.

27. Weld, _A Further Discovery of That Generation of Men_, p. 20. For a similar accusation made against Anabaptists, see Ephraim Pagitt, _Heresiography or a Description of the Hereticks and Sectaries of These Latter Times_, 3d ed. (London, 1646), p. 108. In his fifth edition (London, 1654), Pagitt placed the Quakers within the Anabaptist tradition.

28. Baxter, _One Sheet against the Quakers_, pp. 4-5. Weld, _A Further Discovery of That Generation of Men_, pp. 13-14. Richard T. Vann, _The Social Origins of English Quakerism, 1650-1750_ (Cambridge, Mass., 1969), pp. 173-79. Also see Hill, _The World Turned Upside Down_, pp. 161-63.

29. For a discussion of the functions of the family
and its relationship to government, see Edmund S. Morgan,
The Puritan Family: Religion and Domestic Relations in
Seventeenth-Century New England, rev. ed. (New York,
1966), especially pp. 133-51, and Gordon Schochet,
"Patriarchalism, Politics, and Mass Attitudes in Stuart
England," Historical Journal, 12 (1969):413-41, and
Patriarchalism in Political Thought: The Authoritarian
Family and Political Speculation and Attitudes Especially
in Seventeenth-Century England (Oxford, England, 1975),
pp. 39-42, 64-68, 72-114. Higginson, A Brief Relation,
pp. 27-28. Also see Pestana, "The City upon a Hill under
Seige," pp. 348-52.

30. Higginson, A Brief Relation, p. 25.

31. Ibid., pp. 26-27. For a more detailed description of the Puritan attitude toward the geographically
mobile, see Michael Walzer, The Revolution of the Saints:
A Study in the Origins of Radical Politics (London, 1965),
pp. 208-19, and Hill, Society and Puritanism, pp. 125-28.
The fear of vagabonds roaming the countryside was also
long standing and commonplace. See William Lambarde's
charge to the jury at Maidstone in 1582 in Conyers Read,
ed., William Lambarde and Local Government (Ithaca, N.Y.,
1962), pp. 169-70.

32. Nuttal, The Holy Spirit, pp. 86-87. Keith Thomas,
"Women and the Civil War Sects," Past and Present, 13
(1958):42-62.

33. Weld, A Further Discovery of that Generation of
Men, pp. 83-84. Richard Blome, The Fanatick History or
an Exact Relation and Account of the Old Anabaptists and
New Quakers (London, 1660), p. 30.

34. Higginson, A Brief Relation, p. 30.

35. Ibid., p. 33. Weld, A Further Discovery of That
Generation of Men, p. 89. Hill, The World Turned Upside
Down, p. 200.

36. Pagitt, Heresiography, pp. 3-12. Cohn, Pursuit
of the Millenium, pp. 87-88. Claus Peter Clason, Anabaptism: A Social History, 1525-1618 (Ithaca, N.Y., 1972), pp.
255-59. James M. Strayer, Anabaptism and the Sword
(Lawrence, Kan., 1972), pp. 41, 139, 211-12.

37. Higginson, A Brief Relation, pp. A2, 12.

38. Resolution of the Massachusetts General Court,
4 November 1659, Massachusetts Archives, 10:260A, State
House, Boston.

39. John Norton, The Heart of the New England Rent (Cambridge, Mass., 1659), pp. 2, 5-6, 42-44.

40. Ibid., pp. 30-31, 40.

41. Ibid., pp. 4-5, 56. Also see Holdsworth, History of English Law, 18:420 and Deuteronomy 13:5.

42. Norton, The Heart of New England Rent, pp. 52-53.

43. Edward A. Johnson, The Wonder-Working Providence of Sion's Savior in New England, ed. J. Franklin Jameson as Johnson's Wonder-Working Providence...(Original Narratives of Early American History) (New York, 1910), p. 140. Williston Walker, ed., The Creeds and Platforms of Congregationalism (New York, 1893), pp. 189, 237.

44. Thomas Walley, Balm in Gilead to Heal Sion's Wounds... (Cambridge, Mass., 1669), p. 15.

45. Thomas G. Barnes, ed., The Book of the General Lawes and Libertyes Concerning the Inhabitants of the Massachusetts (1648; rept. San Marino, Calif., 1975), p. 20. Norton, The Heart of New England Rent, p. 2.

46. Norton, The Heart of New England Rent, pp. 31-32.

47. W. H. Greenleaf observed that the primary fear of all seventeenth-century political theorists was not tyranny but anarchy. Sir Edward Forset used the same metaphor for disorder that Norton used: a disease of the body politic capable of metastasizing rapidly and destroying all basis for communal life. Order, Empiricism and Politics: Two Traditions of English Political Thought, 1500-1700 (London, 1964), pp. 76-78, 91-92.

48. Oliver Wendall Holmes argued that the essence of criminality is gauged by the harm done in the past or "the degree of danger shown by experience to attend that act under those circumstances." Sedition under these criteria is difficult to prove since its danger lies in the perception that its participants will do grievous harm to the state in the future. To sustain proof over an extended period of time, the body of ideas or activities in support of those ideas must be clear, obvious, and profound enough to confirm the original charges. Oliver Wendall Holmes, Jr., The Common Law (Boston, 1923), p. 75.

49. On the county court system, see David T. Konig, Law and Society in Puritan Massachusetts: Essex County, 1629-1692 (Chapel Hill, N.C., 1979), pp. 29-33.

    50.   Robert E. Wall, Jr., Massachusetts Bay: The
Crucial Decade, 1640-1650 (New Haven, Conn., 1972). pp.
37-40.

    51.   Konig, Law and Society in Puritan Massachusetts,
pp. 133-35.

3
To Put Away Evil: The General Court and Visiting Quakers, 1656-61

The year 1656 was not auspicious for Massachusetts Bay. The instability of the Protectorate and its apparent difficulties with Ranters, Quakers, and other notorious heretics gave the General Court a heightened sensitivity to its own seeming drift toward moral decay. To demonstrate its concern for the growing religious anarchy in England, to prevent the spread of religious confusion, and to fortify Massachusetts institutions so that "the ordinances of Christ may be more effectual," the General Court ordered a fast day to be held on 11 June 1656.[1] Within a month of the fast day, Quakers Ann Austin and Mary Fisher arrived in Boston harbor and in doing so marked the beginning of what the Court came to see a premeditated, broad-gauged assault upon its spiritual and secular institutions.

The outspoken nature of the two Quaker women did nothing to allay the magistrates' initial suspicions that the two women intended to harm the colony. When questioned by the magistrates about their reasons for being in Boston, the women responded in manner showing that their purpose was "to oppose the ministry and also to breed in people contempt of magistracy."[2] Soon afterward, another group of eight Quakers arrived and demonstrated that Austin and Fisher were not isolated cases of sedition and disorder. Interrogation of the second group of Quakers confirmed their troublesome nature. The Suffolk County Court reported that one of the Quakers, Thomas Thirston, had come to the colony solely to blaspheme.[3] The General Court had other evidence of the Quakers' intent to subvert Bay institutions. In a detailed letter to the General Court, William Brend objected to his and his companions' imprisonment on the grounds that the body that ordered it was illegitimate. Threatening the Court with forms of divine judgment that he suggested he alone was capable of calling forth, Brend demanded the release of all the Quakers.[4]

Puritans, however, considered Brend's reasoning absurd. Quakers were, declared Boston merchant and Selectman John Hull, "persons uncivil in behavior, showing no respect to any, ready to censure and condemn all; themselves would be thought the only knowing persons and their spirit infallible: carrying a semblance of humility but exceedingly proud."[5] Justification for the state's intervention in controlling these Quakers required no logical leap of faith. The uncivil character of the visitors, the absence of ecclesiastical institutions with powers to regulate heresy and dissent outside the congregation, and the existence of legal precedents governing the unwanted immigrants demanded that the state act.

Because the magistrates had no specific laws regarding the Quakers, Quaker contemporaries like George Bishop characterized their actions as arbitrary and persecuting.[6] The magistrates, however, had acted according to the tradition in English law that allowed civil authorities to regulate the movements of strangers within their jurisdictions. Five years before the first Quakers arrived, the General Court had used the English precedents in forming procedures that were to be applied to visitors. Every stranger immediately upon his arrival would report to the governor, deputy governor, or any two magistrates for permission to remain in the colony. The Court also required shipmasters to post bonds of twenty pounds to insure that they would provide authorities with lists of arriving visitors. Should there be any cause for action, any of the magistrates could bind strangers over to the next session of the county court or take whatever discretionary steps were needed.[7]

The only exception to the statute in treating the first Quaker arrivals in 1656 had been the requirement that ship captains post bonds of 500 pounds each. The absence of trial procedures designed to deal specifically with Quakers was not a violation of the principle of ex post facto and was well within the limits of magisterial discretion. In light of their dangerous nature, the Quakers had to be jailed and deported immediately. The Court of Assistants would not be convened until September, nearly two months later, and the degree of disorder was clearly beyond the misdemeanor jurisdiction of the county courts. Furthermore, since no one in the colony was prepared to offer financial or personal sureties to guarantee the Quakers' good behavior and since the Quakers had been deliberately antagonistic, the magistrates had compelling reasons for acting in summary fashion.[8]

While the size of the bonds required of shipmasters Symon Kempthorne and Robert Locke was the only apparent deviation from past practice, the large surety demanded indicated the magistrates' fear of Quakers. Kempthorne apparently accepted the levy without argument. Locke, on the other hand, petitioned for relief on the grounds that he had complied with all the regulations governing

his responsibilities for strangers. Both the Court of
Assistants and the House of Deputies denied Locke's request, citing the obvious dangers that Quakers posed and
the need for guarantees that Locke would take them out of
the colony.[9]
     The combination of Locke's objection to the size of
his bond and the obvious lack of Quaker remorse prompted
the General Court to define the Quakers' offenses against
the state and to establish new procedures specifically
treating the phenomenon. The best solution seemed to be
to isolate the colony from these Quaker agents of disorder. The Court forbade Quaker entry to the colony and
placed responsibility for enforcing the law upon ship
captains. Any master who brought a Quaker into Massachusetts would be fined 100 pounds and be responsible for
removing him as soon as possible.[10]
     With these regulations the Court felt it had prohibit-
ed the presence of Quakers. Surely Quakers would see by
their specific legal exclusion that they were not wanted
in the Bay Colony. But here was the principal bone of
contention between Puritan and Quaker in Massachusetts.
Where the former was willing to render unto a Puritan
Caesar that which was his due, the latter was not. Quakers did not see, as the General Court later argued, that
men were subject to higher powers ordained by God and
that to resist these powers was to resist His holy ordinances.[11] Indeed, while Quakers, like Puritans, looked
to God's righteousness for the criteria of law, their
denial to others of the right of judgment and the insistence upon the supremacy of their judgment in Massachusetts placed them outside the boundaries of the legal
structure and doomed them to punishment.[12]
     In the confrontations that followed the deportations
and the first anti-Quaker laws, Quakers confirmed their
reputations to Puritans as revilers of law and sowers of
discord. Despite their supposedly superior moral authority, the Quakers seemed willing to commit any sin to
evade the legal barriers erected against them. Puritan
magistrates might well have questioned the divine origins
of a moral authority that justified lying as a form of
virtue. When he was fined 100 pounds for bringing two
Quakers into the colony, ship Captain Thomas Bond petitioned for the reduction of his fine to two barrels of
gunpowder valued about twenty pounds. Bond based his
appeal upon claims that the Quakers had lied about themselves in order to secure passage. Had he known their
real sympathies, he explained, he would never have been
party to their scheme. What caused Bond to grant passage
to the Quakers mattered little to the General Court; it
clearly expected execrable behavior from them. Also,
Bond's appeal for relief contrasted his respect for
Puritan mechanisms of due process with the Quakers' lack
of it, and the Court reduced Bond's fines as he requested.[13]

The Quakers, despite the cooperation of shipmasters like Bond with the Puritans, still found ways to evade prohibitions against their presence in Massachusetts Bay. Finding regular shipping channels closed to them, they found other means of transportation. Friends like Robert Fowler who owned their own ships placed these vessels at the disposal of the missionaries. In 1657, Fowler carried eleven Quakers to New Amsterdam and Newport. From these two cities, nine of the eleven found their way to Massachusetts. Of the five who landed at New Amsterdam, two were arrested and deported by Dutch authorities. The two then headed for Boston. Two others eluded the Dutch and slipped into Massachusetts. Five of the remaining six landed at Newport and went directly to Boston. There could be no excuse that these particular Quakers were ignorant of the Bay Colony's laws: six of the nine had been expelled the previous year.[14]

To the Puritans, the second year of visits illustrated the perverse nature of the Quakers. Far from deterring them, legal prohibitions seemed to inspire them to find new ways to defy authority. Their return could only be understood as the manifestations of profoundly corrupt natures. Some men could not help but trouble authority; Quakers seemed to look for ways to express their defiance of it. As Hull noted, they took a perverse joy in it. "They seemed to suffer patiently and take a kind of pleasure in it. In those parts of the country where they might with freedom converse (as in Rhode Island and Providence and Warwick), they take no pleasure to be."[15]

Although Massachusetts led the English colonies in establishing anti-Quaker regulations, it only expressed commonly held sentiments in doing so. In New Amsterdam, Peter Stuyvesant and the Dutch Reformed dominies also saw Quakers as being dangerous to public peace. Stuyvesant's heavy-handed punishment of Quakers found within his jurisdiction soon prompted their departure. Religious leaders Johannes Megapolensis and Samuel Drisius informed Amsterdam that Quaker activities were the product of the devil's work. "The same instruments which he [the devil] uses to disturb churches in Europe, he employs here in America. We trust our God will baffle the designs of the devil and preserve us in the truth and bring to nothing these machinations of Satan." One example of the dominies' concern was a young Quaker woman who began to preach on a public street. Unable to understand the woman's English, Dutch citizens presumed her animation was a fire alarm, and they panicked. When they discovered that the woman's actions were the result of her responses to an inner light and not external flames, the Dutch deported her.[16]

Like the Dutch, other English colonies generally agreed that Quakers had to be expelled. Connecticut banished all the Quakers found in its jurisdiction. New Haven not only banished them, it also branded one,

Humphrey Norton, with an "H" to denote his heresy.[17]   New
Plymouth was also disturbed by the increasing number of
disorderly incidents in Sandwich, Duxbury, Marshfield, and
Scituate caused by Quakers en route to Boston from Rhode
Island.   In Scituate, Arthur Howland and the sons of John
Rogers stopped Constable John Phillipes when he tried to
arrest a visiting Quaker.   While other members of the two
families helped the Quakers escape, Howland warned
Phillipes that if he tried to give chase, "he would have
either a sword or a gun in the belly."[18]
     Even Rhode Island shared the common apprehension of
the Quakers.   Asked by the commissioners for the United
Colonies to close its ports to the Quakers, Rhode Island
demurred.   Conceding "that their doctrines tend to the
very absolute cutting downe and overturning relations and
civil government," Rhode Island's response to the commissioners asserted that toleration would be a more practical measure since Quakers "delight to be persecuted by
civil powers as they might gain more adherents."[19]   Somewhat lamely, the Rhode Island General Assembly reported
it could not bar Quakers from entering the colony without
violating the charter guarantees of freedom of conscience.
A far more significant factor in Rhode Island's rejection
of the United Colonies' request was the fragile nature of
the compromise that bound the colony together.   To pass
any anti-Quaker legislation would have required the
agreement of influential Antinomian exiles in Newport
like William Coddington and John Coggeshall, who were
about to become Quakers.   The imminent conversion of such
men suggested not only sympathy for the sect but dramatic
illustration that Quakers were not inherently destructive
to order.   Even if any legislation had passed, it would
probably have been unenforceable.   Still, in asserting
freedom of conscience, the Assembly recognized the seditious tendencies of the sect.   Some Quakers, observed the
Assembly, those who refused to participate in "all duties
aforesayd as trayninge, watchinge, and other ingadgements
as members of civill societies," required strict supervision and control.[20]
     The failure to close Rhode Island to the visiting
Quakers and the sense that it had been singled out for
concentrated visitations forced Massachusetts to find a
solution independently.   No other colony seemed to suffer
so much.   From the first visits in 1656 to the first
hangings in 1659, thirty-three Quakers entered the Bay
Colony, a figure unmatched by any other colony except
New Plymouth over which many of them traveled.[21]   Moreover, Quaker visitors seemed to take special delight
encouraging others to go to Massachusetts.   Writing to
Margaret Fell in 1658, John Rous noted that local converts in Salem and Sandwich held out the promise of
success in Boston and Plymouth.   In addition, the determination of the colony to purge itself of Quakerism inspired others, like Marmaduke Stephenson, to abandon
traditional callings for lives as missionaries.[22]

Thus, as it attempted to cope with the problem of visiting Quakers, the General Court faced an increasingly more stubborn, idealistic, and hence, from its point of view, a more seditious kind of Quaker. After the initial policy of isolation seemed to fail, the Court turned to corporal punishment. While a few Quakers had been whipped before October 1657, the number of lashes inflicted remained consistent with those meted out for petty disorder. Sarah Gibbens and Dorothy Waugh received ten lashes for disturbing one Boston church at worship. The number of lashes was within that permitted the president of Harvard College for students' "misdemeanours of youth."[23] After October 1657, magistrates were empowered to whip Quaker women at their discretion for second or third offenses of the prohibition law.[24] This new discretionary power implied more rigorous forms of punishment to control what appeared to be increasingly provocative forms of criminal behavior. Encouragement of more frequent and severe use of the lash was intended to stop women like Sarah Gibbens and Dorothy Waugh from making repeated trips into the colony after the previous policy of deportation had failed.[25]

Whipping was also applied to male Quakers. Used in place of earcropping, for which there was English precedent, the application of the lash here may have been intended to demonstrate the Bay Colony's mercy and to avoid obvious parallels between Puritan punishment of Quakers and the Laudian punishments of English Puritans like William Prynne. When William Brend was arrested in Salem in July 1658, he was, under the same law that prescribed whipping for second and third visits by women Quakers, liable to the loss of an ear. Instead, the magistrates of the General Court gave him a reprieve in the form of a sound scourging in the hope that he would be deterred from returning to the colony. While it is possible that he received more than the forty lashes maximum permitted by law, Brend was not disabled by his punishment and was able to travel to the West Indies shortly after being whipped.[26]

By resorting to corporal punishments, the General Court expected that the pain and humiliation of whipping or ear cropping would outweigh the pleasures of defiance and convince the Quakers to stay away. Some Quakers did as the Court wished; Gibbens and Waugh returned in the early spring of 1658 but left never to return. Other Quakers, however, demonstrated their perversity by returning with the full knowledge that increasingly severe punishments awaited them. To Bay Puritans such actions were proof that these Quakers were an obstinate lot determined to defy authority in Massachusetts and that a temperate and gradual course of action was foolish. These Quakers clearly proved the depth of Quaker sedition, and they stood convicted of their deep criminal nature by their very presence in the colony. Temporizing had only attracted hardier and more virulent strains of the seditious disease of Quakerism.[27]

Having given Brend a sound whipping, the Court expected that Quakers would have learned from his example and taken the threats of physical punishment seriously. Yet, Brend's example seemed to encourage Christopher Holder, John Rous, and John Copeland to come to the colony in the summer of 1658. After arresting the three, the magistrates threatened them with the loss of their ears on their next visit and escorted them to the border. Once their escort left them, the three Quakers simply turned around and entered the colony again. Arrested in Dedham, they were taken to Boston, where their ears were removed on 7 September.[28]

Though the magistrates had had to resort to physical multilation, some Boston residents still felt that the remedies were too lenient, that the magistrates seemed timid and indecisive, that the anti-Quaker legislation was ineffective, and, therefore, that the Quakers were encouraged to return to vex the colony. These hardliners urged harsher punishments to end the problem of the Quakers' threat to public peace. In a petition to the General Court, these men argued that since the lesser physical punishments had failed to end Quaker "incorridgibleness," Quaker recidivists should receive banishment upon pain of death. That is, the Court should banish any Quakers found in the colony and threaten to hang them if they dared return. The threat of hanging would deter most from returning, and any who did clearly demonstrated the habitual nature of his criminality and the need for his permanent neutralization through execution.[29]

The solution had a certain logical neatness. On 19 October 1658, the General Court ordered that all visiting Quakers found in the colony be banished on pain of death. Any Quaker who returned after the sentence of banishment had been passed upon him was to be hanged. To the magistrates, the justifications for their actions were obvious. The Quakers were clearly seditious and their presence posed a threat to public peace. They maintained opinions that encouraged public disturbances, they threatened the operations of orthodox churches, and they attacked the legitimacy of civil authority. Also, they actively attempted to spread their subversive beliefs by insinuating themselves into the midst of the simpler sort "such as are less affected to the order and government in church and commonwealth whereby diverse of our inhabitants have been infected and seduced." In view of the Court's failure to control Quaker activities with its previous legislation, no other alternative seemed likely to keep the peace.[30]

Notwithstanding the considerable support for capital punishment, there was still some resistance to it. Most of this rested in William Hathorne, a Salem deputy and member of the Essex County Court bench (as well as father of John, a judge during the 1692 witchcraft trials and ancestor of Nathaniel, the novelist). Although orthodox

in belief, Hathorne had a reputation for more liberal
sentiments with regard to Quakers and had voted for the
capital punishment measure only when it appeared that
popular opinion was overwhelmingly against him and that
the measure was sure to pass.[31] Hathorne's reluctance
probably rested upon a perception that applying religion
as a test of normative civil behavior was problematical.
During the previous two years, a group of reasonable law-
abiding Salem residents had ceased to attend the regular
church meetings and had given the visiting Quakers shelter
when they passed through the town. Many of these Salem
residents had lived in the town longer than Hathorne, had
been integral parts of the political and social life of
the town, and had never been in more than the most trivial
of legal difficulties. Part of the reason for their
withdrawal from regular services may have been the result
of their dissatisfaction with the unsettled nature of
Salem's orthodox church. More critically, from Hathorne's
perspective, it would appear that despite their hereodoxy
the Quakers were valuable friends. The group of incipient
Quakers comprised a significant proportion of the agrarian
constituency that usually supported Hathorne in his
political battles in the town. To alienate these generally peaceable, would-be local Quakers because some others
seemed to believe in similar kinds of heterodoxy and were
disorderly would have jeopardized a key component of
Hathorne's political strength.[32] In any event, the conversion of generally peaceable residents to Quakerism introduced a degree of ambiguity regarding the extent of
the danger all Quakers posed to civil peace.

However ambiguous the Salem Quakers might have appeared to Hathorne, the visitors were to confirm their
image as dangerous and unrepentant criminals. In the
spring of 1659, William Brend returned to Boston openly
acknowledging that he was "one of those the world in
scorne called Quakers." The Court immediately ordered
him jailed until 16 May. On that day he was to be released and to leave the colony. If he were found in
Massachusetts forty-eight hours after his release, he was
to be hanged. This time Brend left never to return.[33]
Yet while the Court had rid itself of one affliction, it
had little time for rejoicing. A month later, 15 June,
there was a disturbance during a fast day at a Boston
church. Upon investigation, the Court discovered three
visiting Quakers, Nicholas Davis, Marmaduke Stephenson,
and William Robinson, "indeavoring to make a disturbance
before the congregation.... After their owning themselves
Quakers by their words and behaviour and considering their
bold and abusive carriages," the three men were jailed
until the next session of the Court of Assistants. At
that session, the Assistants sentenced the men to death
but suspended the sentences if they would leave the
colony.[34]

While none of the three had visited the colony previously, they each represented a facet of Quakerism that
seemed to threaten peace in Massachusetts. After learning of his election at his plow in Yorkshire to be a
"prophet unto the nations," Stephenson spent a year as a
missionary Friend in the Barbados. Hearing of the new
law prescribing banishment upon pain of death, he had come
to Boston deliberately to test whether the Bay Colony's
magistrates would execute visiting Quakers.[35] William
Robinson began his career as a travelling Friend in the
company of two notorious Quakers, Christopher Holder and
William Leddera. Only five days before his arrest in
Boston, Robinson and Leddera had been in a New Plymouth
jail for preaching at Sandwich.[36] The last Quaker arrested, Nicholas Davis, was a Barnstable, New Plymouth, merchant on his first missionary trip. While Robinson and
Stephenson represented the experienced subversive, Davis
proved their ability to lead residents of the weaker sort
into acts of public defiance.[37]

The presence of the three Quakers in Boston could not
have pleased a General Court already frustrated in its
attempts to close the colony to visiting Quakers. Furthermore, Robinson and Stephenson refused to conform to
any minimal expectations of penitent behavior once they
were imprisoned. In fact, they seemed even more determined to challenge civil authority. Quakers as a whole
were poor prisoners, and Robinson and Stephenson were
exceptional in their ability to exasperate the magistracy.
To avoid aggravating divisions within the General Court
over the actual application of the death penalty, Governor John Endecott and colony secretary Edward Rawson met
informally with Robinson to advise him of the fate that
awaited him if he continued to challenge the magistrates
to hang him. According to Robinson, Rawson was the more
extreme of the two, promising to tie the knot of the
halter if need be. Endecott, thought Robinson, seemed
more conciliatory and reasonable in his attempt to point
out the folly of defying Rawson and the Court and cited
examples of other Quakers who had left the colony and not
returned. Both magistrates, however, did not realize that
neither fear nor reason would move Robinson and Stephenson.
They were determined to resist the laws of the Bay Colony
and to deny the authority of the men that made them even
if it meant death. Robinson informed the two Bay magistrates that where others had drawn back from martyrdom,
he and Stephenson would not. "It being so that they are
fled, on the same Day that I heard of it, the Lord laid
on me my life to give up BOSTON'S BLOODY LAWES to try,...
and alsoe my Brother and Companion Marmaduke Stevenson our
testimonies to finish at this town of Boston."[38]

Soon after Robinson had made clear his defiance, Mary
Dyer returned a second time. Exiled for her Antinomian
sympathies in 1635, she had returned to Boston in 1657.
While there was some question regarding the moment of her

conversion to Quakerism, her previous support of Anne
Hutchinson should have been sufficient grounds to suspect
that she was unconcerned for the welfare of the Bay Colony. She was soon forced to leave with the wife of another visiting Quaker. Her return in 1659 removed any
doubt about her dangerous tendencies, especially when she
declared her support for Robinson and Stephenson. The
Suffolk County Court reported that "hir coming into these
partes was to visit the Prisoners now in Hold[g] and that
she was of the same religion that Humphrey Norton was
which shee affirmed was the truth." Faced with such can-
dor, the General Court had no other alternative but to
jail her with the others.[39]

The intrusions of these visiting Quakers demonstrated
the failure of the new legal procedure and their continued
contempt for civil authority. For their magistrates' efforts to secure the colony from the pernicious effects of
Quakerism, Puritans had only received further abuse. Not
only did the Quakers proclaim their supposedly superior
faith and moral virtue, they also claimed temporal law
sanctioned their activities. When he challenged the right
of Massachusetts magistrates to control his activities,
Robinson, in Puritan eyes, speciously claimed a superior
knowledge of English law. The actions of the General
Court, Robinson claimed, were illegal because they violated basic English liberties. "We that are Free-born
Englishmen, we demand our liberty for the Excercise of
our pure Consciences in this Country as well as other
Englishmen."[40]

However appropriate this argument might have been for
English conditions during the Interregnum--it was inappropriate in light of the precedents governing vagabonds
and the assumption of an established church--the citation
by the Quakers of the virtue of liberty of conscience
denoted the depth of their perfidy. The General Court
assumed that Quaker demands for liberty of conscience
were their means of subverting true religion and public
order. Quakers demanded liberty of conscience because it
gave them the chance to wean others from the rule of
Scripture and from obedience to Christian magistrates.
The spurious claims for religious freedom only showed that
the Quaker knowledge of law was shaped by the same evil,
disorderly intentions that had initially brought them to
Boston.[41]

Since the General Court was familiar with the precedents in English law that justified its actions and
since the colony in 1659 was virtually free of imperial
regulation, the Court could ignore the rantings of the
Quakers. It could not overlook, however, the threat to
order that the Quaker presence posed. William Dyer's
declaration that to be a Quaker was not an overt threat
to order did not make sense when the Court looked at the
activities of Dyer's wife. In Mary Dyer, like Robinson
and Stephenson, the Court had an example of a person who

refused to allow others to worship at orthodox services
and who defied the authorities trying to stop her interference with those services. Moreover, the Quakers went
even further by claiming that no one owed any allegiance
to secular authorities who acted as did the General Court
magistrates. By claiming that the Bay Colony's power was
ungodly and that it was man's duty to place God's power
above "Unrighteous Powers," Robinson and Stephenson seemingly gave everyone the right to disobey civil magistrates
as they pleased.[42]

Ironically, arguments justifying the overthrow of
civil government in defense of true religion were not
unique to Quakers; Puritans in Old England had struggled
with the same problem of reconciling a virtuous population with a godless magistracy. The reaction of Massachusetts Puritans was also similar to that of church and
civil authorities who had driven them from England. As
the guardians of order in church and state, the General
Court magistrates developed an argument that confirmed
the right of civil government to intervene in cases like
that of the Quakers. Romans 13 sanctioned the right of
the magistrates to demand obedience and deference to their
authority. Rulers were terrors to evildoers; and those
who resisted civil authority denied the ordinances of God
and "the powers that be [that] are ordained by God."[43]
Quakers, by denying magistrates the deference and obedience owed them, substantiated the charges of sedition.
As John Norton noted, all one had to do was "witness their
scripts and behaviors wherein they deny obedience to all
Christian magistrates," and he had all the evidence he
needed for justifying the punishment of Quakers.[44]

Seen in this context, the Bay magistrates felt they
had no choice but to hang the Quakers. From their perspective, they had provided Quakers with every reasonable
incentive to leave the colony. The incentives had failed.
Quakers seemed to be drawn perversely to the colony by
the very devices designed to encourage them to leave or
stay away. To the Puritans, the Quakers seemed to want
"to scatter their corrupt opinions to drawe others to
their way and so to make a disturbance."[45] There was no
other alternative: on 12 September 1659, the Court found
Stephenson, Robinson, Dyer, and Davis "by their own Con-
fessions, words and Actions to be Quakers" and ordered
them banished. If they were still found in the colony
after 14 September, they were "to be Committed and suffer
death according to the lawe."[46] Within two weeks of their
banishment, three of the four, Dyer, Robinson, and
Stephenson, were found in Boston, "boldly and presumptu-
ously resolving to outvie the authority of the country."
The interval between the Quakers' banishment and their
return had been an illusory moment of respite. During the
two-week interim, the Quakers seemed to have organized a
conspiracy against the peace of the colony. Joining the
three Quakers were eleven others who intended to support

the others' defiance of the General Court. Six of these
were nonresident Quakers attracted to Boston by the pros-
pect of seeing the martyrdom of the three or the surren-
der of the General Court. Present were Christopher
Holder; Robert Harper, a confessed New Plymouth Quaker;
and Daniel Gold, a Newport resident and son-in-law of a
former Bay Colony deputy and a supporter of Anne Hutchinson, John Coggeshall. Also, five inhabitants of Salem
were in Boston to witness the executions. All were members of the Salem meeting, and four were related to
residents banished the year before.[47]

The spread of support for the visitors by the inhabitants gave a new urgency to the crisis. It raised the
immediate spectre of a Quaker-inspired chaos. Earlier,
in Norton's justifications for the lesser punishments of
ear cropping and whipping, he had described the Quakers'
"bold contempt of these inferior restraints," and noted
that the Quakers returned "againe and againe to the
seducing of diverse, the disturbance and vexation and
hazzard of the whole colony."[48] The presence of the condemned Quakers in the company of their supporters convinced the magistrates of the futility of any policy
short of permanent elimination. The threat of hanging
had not deterred Quakers from sowing sedition among
residents. Indeed, local activity took an ominous turn
in the summer of 1659. A year earlier, the General Court
had had to banish a number of residents for providing the
visitors with shelter. Now the local supporters had become inspired to demonstrate publicly and to act like the
visitors.

If the General Court were to prevent the spread of
subversion and if it were to maintain the dignity of and
obedience to civil authority, it could not permit these
rebellions to go unchallenged. The Court could not allow
the sentence of banishment upon pain of death become an
empty threat by not enforcing the death penalty in this
instance. When Marmaduke Stephenson wrote to friends in
England, "they that will not bow to his God's government
must be destroyed and broken to pieces," Puritans could
not have agreed more.[49] Commenting on the decision to
use the death penalty, John Hull wrote in his diary,
"most of the Godly have cause to rejoice, and bless the
Lord that strengthened our magistrates and deputies to
bear witness against such blasphemers."[50]

On 18 October 1659, the General Court ordered what it
believed would be the final solution to free the colony
from the menace of Quakerism: it sentenced Dyer, Robinson, and Stephenson to hang. In passing the sentences of
execution, the Court submitted that it had no other alternative if it were to expel the evil that was Quakerism.
Since the prisoners were all familiar with the terms of
their banishment, they, not the Court, had brought about
the executions. In returning to the colony, the Quakers
had cast themselves upon the sword of state. "The

considerations of our graduall proceedings will vindicate us, calling upon us other means failing to offer the points which these persons have violently and wilfully rushed upon and thereby become _felons de se_."[51]

The Court argued that the thrust of its legislation had been directed toward keeping visiting Quakers out of its jurisdiction so that it might better preserve order within it. Although the colony was aware of the Quakers' potential for subversion and while it had endured such abuse at their hands, the Court had acted, by its own account, with great forebearance and had resorted to hanging only when no other alternative seemed effective. The motives behind their actions, the Court asserted, rested upon a natural desire for domestic peace. "The precedence of this Court was onely excersised in making provission to secure peace and order heere established against their [the Quakers'] attempts whose designs (wee were well assured by our own experience) as well as their predecessors in Muenster was to undermine and ruine the same."[52]

What the Quakers saw as a necessary attribute of their idealism, Puritans saw as the product of an uncontrollable fanaticism born of perversity and depravity. From the Puritan perspective, when the Quakers refused to abide by the laws prohibiting them from places where their only interest was the subversion of existing political and ecclesiastical institutions, they proved themselves to be habitual criminals of a most dangerous sort. The only solution to this kind of criminality was its permanent elimination. "Can any man doubt," recorded Edward Rawson in the General Court minutes, "that in such a case, the father of the family in defense of himself and his withstand the intrusion of such infected and dangerous persons and if he cann not keepe them out, may kill them?"[53]

Even as they made their brief for the executions, the magistrates seemed to respond to secular pressures to ameliorate the harshness of the punishments. Personal influence tempered even this reluctant use of capital punishment. Mary Dyer was not to be hanged. She was to stand on the gallows with the halter around her neck and witness the executions of her fellow Quakers Robinson and Stephenson. Dyer was to be spared because her judges may have feared alienating potential allies in Rhode Island and Providence who might have been subject to the influence of her husband. Also, sparing Dyer allowed the Court to present its anti-Quaker legislation as the product of obvious and understandable desires to maintain public peace and not the result of a dispute over narrow religious issues that might prove politically embarrassing during the Interregnum.[54] Sparing Dyer could also provide a dramatic moment that would impress upon other Quakers how very close to death even those with considerable influence might come. Presumably, the chafe of the rope would show radical and stubborn wills the length to which secular officials were prepared to go to preserve the peace.[55]

The Court also chose to be more merciful in its treatment of other nonresidents who attended the executions. Although he was liable to having his tongue bored with a hot iron, Christopher Holder was only banished upon pain of death. Mercy seemed to moderate his behavior. Six days after the executions, Holder asked the Court to release him from jail so he could arrange his passage to England. The Court seemed to believe that he would no longer attempt to disturb the tranquillity of the colony and granted him considerable latitude in preparing for his departure. It allowed him his freedom one day a week and released him three days before he was to leave the colony.[56]

The experience with Holder indicated to the Court that what lay at the heart of the Quakers' motives was individual evil. Some Quakers like Dyer were clearly incorrigible criminals who used the facade of religious language to disguise horrid natures. By granting Dyer a reprieve in 1659, the Puritan magistrates had only postponed her inevitable execution. She returned to Boston at noon, 21 May 1660. Her actions thus seemed to be the manifestation of a form of criminal madness uncontrollable by the strongest means of intimidation.[57] Asked by close friends to turn back and save herself, she replied that she only had the power to advance. Asked by Governor Endecott if she were the same Mary Dyer who had visited the colony previously, though he apparently knew full well she was, Dyer openly admitted her identity and gave him no ground for maneuver.[58] Actions like these revealed Dyer's determined and mad desire to subvert order in Massachusetts and suggested that such behavior ought to be suppressed sooner rather than later. Like Dyer, William Leddera seemed to be incorrigible. Arrested on 9 March 1661, Leddera was already under sentence of banishment.[59] Although the Court could have proceeded immediately with his execution, it informed him that should he promise to leave and not return, the sentence would be suspended again. Leddera rejected the offer of clemency. There was, he claimed, a higher law than the General Court and that it forbade his execution. Moreover, he owed "no Subjectio[n] to the wicked Laws of this Jurisdiction."[60] Here was still another example of an unrepentant, habitual criminal who would neither leave the colony alone nor cease his attacks upon its defenders of public peace. If the peace was to be preserved, it could be achieved only by the absolute neutralization of these madmen, and that could be achieved only by a rope's end.

For other Quakers, however, execution deterred further challenges to the magistracy. By offering Holder and the other Quakers the alternatives between life outside the colony or death within it, the Court impressed

upon them its determination to purge the evil that it saw
embodied in them. By responding to the obvious induce-
ment to stay away, Holder also demonstrated a form of
Quakerism controllable by civil authority. When Holder
accepted the terms of his banishment, he demonstrated the
utility of coupling more lenient alternatives with the
stark reality of the gallows.

From its actions, the Court seemed to prefer to have
the Quakers leave the colony rather than be obliged to
hang them. On the day before the execution of Dyer, the
General Court arrested Joseph and Jane Nicholson in Salem.
It had previously condemned them both and could have
hanged them with Dyer; however, the Court gave the Nichol-
sons an additional four days to leave the colony. It
thought that they had intended to depart on time but had
been delayed because of their child's birth. Furthermore,
the Court also had an implicit promise of control over
these Quakers. As Jane Nicholson was about to give birth,
John Southwick, a Salem resident, the son of two banished
local Quakers and a member of the local meeting, assumed
financial liability for the child and, in the process,
provided a surety for the future behavior of the parents
as well.[61] Finally, there was still considerable reluctance to hang these Quakers. "Boston people," Joseph
Nicholson wrote to Margaret Fell, "were glad at our
departure, for there were not many, I believe, who would
have had us to have been put to death."[62]

Although John Hull complained in his diary of the
"timidity of spirit to execute the sentence of God's holy
law upon such blasphemous persons," the General Court
seemed increasingly reluctant to hang other Quakers after
Leddera.[63] The last condemned Quaker, Wenlock Christison,
also used the Court's inclination for mercy. Arrested at
the same time as Leddera, Christison was also sentenced
to hang. Unlike Leddera, Christison petitioned the Court
for his release while making known his intention to leave
the colony permanently. The Court granted his request.
Indeed, as long as it had a sense that the visitors were
willing to leave for good, the Court allowed them the
liberty of the town while they awaited their ship's
departure.[64]

Despite the advocacy of Hull for the strict enforcement of the laws against Quakers, the use of capital
punishment coupled with liberal suspensions of sentence
broke the pattern of confrontation between the General
Court and the chronic offender. Allowing the Quakers to
leave not only substantiated the Court's statement's regarding its moderation, it also provided a key indicator
in the process of determining an individual Quaker's
threat to the ordering of the commonwealth. When a condemned Quaker left, he demonstrated a remnant of fear for
law and civil authority that subdued the perverted impulses of his depraved Quaker idealism. This fear,
furthermore, gave some assurances that one could establish

a degree of institutional control over the unruly heretic.
Condemned Quakers could even be allowed to return without
disavowing their faith as long as they recognized the need
for some regulation of their civil behavior. Nicholas
Davis, for example, was allowed to return to the colony to
collect some outstanding business debts. Asking the Court
for permission to return to the colony and providing Major
Simon Willard as surety for his behavior, Davis showed an
acceptable level of respect for the Court and its processes that justified a deviation from the strict letter of
the law.[65]

Observers like John Davenport in Connecticut noted
that the effectiveness of this moderation would not have
been possible without the deterrence of capital punishment. Too many foreign Quakers had not recognized in the
lesser corporal punishments and deportations the fervent
desire of the Bay Colony to protect public peace. Only
after four hangings did that determination become apparent
to the Quakers. Davenport approved of the executions because they seemed to be a "real cutting them off from all
opportunity and liberty of doing hurt in the colonies."[66]
Furthermore, to return in the face of certain execution
revealed a contempt for law and a depravity beyond redemption or control. Any returning Quaker who insisted
upon being hanged substantiated the Puritan case. No
community, the Bay magistrates claimed, could endure a
perpetual threat to its peace and expect to survive.
What community would choose anarchy over order merely
because its condemned criminals told them it should?

> The Quakers died not because theire other
> crimes, howsoever capitoll but upon their
> superadded presumptuous and incorrigible
> contempt of authority, breaking in upon us
> notwithstanding their sentence of banishment
> made knowne to them. Had they not been
> restrained, so farr as appeared, there was
> too much cause to feare wee ourselves must
> quickly have died.[67]

Seen in this context, the Puritan magistrates of the
General Court were not the calculating, legalistic, self-
righteous persecutors of Quakers that Kai Erikson suggests
they were.[68] In the attempt to formulate a solution to
the rise of seditious heterodoxy, the General Court never
intended that its dispensation of justice be inhumane or
irrational, and it tried, though admittedly from its own
perspective, to make clear that in the end the visitors
always had the liberty to stay away.[69] Frustrated by
their inability to control a phenomenon they associated
with anarchy, these frightened men turned to the ultimate
solution of capital punishment. Yet even here, the
magistrates were prepared to offer leniency if they could
be assured that the threat to order could be neutralized

in some other, less drastic fashion.[70]

After the 1661 Leddera execution, the Court seemed to sense that it could soften the rigor of its definition of habitual criminality with regard to Quakers. What made this possible were the secular imperatives that inhered in the justifications and institutions used for suppressing Quakerism. Because the institutions responsible for treating heterodoxy were secular in nature, the justifications for the policies that evolved were governed not by religious criteria of heterodoxy but secular ones of disorder. At no time did the General Court attempt to convert the visitors as a prerequisite to granting mercy; it only asked what was the capacity of the accused to threaten the public peace. The magistrates' responsibilities were limited to stopping secular disorder. All that could matter was the preservation of outwardly civil behavior. With the Quakers, the purpose of Court policies was not the elimination of heterodoxy but the suppression of the sedition seemingly embodied in the sect's heresy. The Court's delving into questions of conscience would have infringed upon the prerogatives of the clergy or attempted to make depraved men regenerate, a power beyond the reach of men. Because Quakers like Leddera, Dyer, Robinson, and Stephenson saw their prohibition from the colony as a stimulus to challenge and, perhaps, destroy the authority of the General Court, they were dangerous, incorrigible criminals. To have allowed such persons the right to disturb the peace simply because they claimed immunity from prosecution for their consciences was an absurdity that neither magistracy nor clergy would tolerate.

Having established that the judgment of Quakerism's threat to Massachusetts depended upon the extent to which individual Quakers disturbed the public peace, however, the General Court opened the process of enforcing its policies to a variety of factors that were to make consistent enforcement impossible. Crucial to the justifications for punishing Quakers was the expectation that they were prepared to destroy the kinds of virtue indispensible to the ordering of society. Yet this also meant that if Quakers could be seen to behave more traditionally, the General Court would have to reconcile apparently peaceful behavior with its presumption that Quakers were seditious. But because civil institutions could not use the Quakers' consciences as evidence of their sedition, the General Court and its inferior county courts had to depend upon secular evidence, evidence that increasingly came to depend upon a specific context of place, influence, and interest. Thus, as the 1660's and early 1670's progressed, the treatment of Bay Colony Quakerism had to be considered within a set of peculiar circumstances and had to reconcile a number of factors, only one of which was religious in nature.

NOTES

1. Nathaniel B. Shurtleff, ed., Records of the Governor and Company of the Massachusetts Bay in New England, 1628-1686, 5 vols. in 6 parts (Boston, 1853-54), 4, pt. 1:276 (hereafter referred to as Mass. Records).

2. Council Records as to the Disposition of Anne Austin and Mary Fisher, 11 July 1656, Massachusetts Archives, 10:234, State House, Boston.

3. Examination of the Quakers, 8 September 1656, Suffolk County Court Files, no. 256b, New Suffolk County Court House, Boston.

4. William Brend to the Governor and Magistrates, 7 September 1656, Chamberlain Manuscript Collection, Boston Public Library.

5. John Hull, "Diary," Archelogia Americana, 3 (1857):179.

6. George Bishop, New England Judged by the Spirit of the Lord (1661; rept. London, 1703), pp. 8-9.

7. Shurtleff, Mass. Records, 4, pt. 1:23, 63.

8. For the range of magisterial discretion, see Carol F. Lee, "Discretionary Justice in Early Massachusetts," Essex Institute Historical Collections, 112 (1976):120-39.

9. Response of the Council to the Petition of Robert Lord, n.d., Massachusetts Archives, 10:236. Robert Lord to the General Court, 16 August, 1656, ibid., p. 237. The endorsement of the deputies is noted on the Council's resolution.

10. Shurtleff, Mass. Records, 4, pt. 1:277.

11. Ibid., 4, pt. 2:387.

12. Hugh Barbour, The Quakers in Puritan England (New Haven, Conn., 1964), pp. 217-18.

13. Thomas Bond to the General Court, 15 May 1658, Massachusetts Archives, 10:240. Magistrate's Order Regarding Thomas Bond, 25 May 1658, ibid., p. 242a. Shurtleff, Mass. Records, 4, pt. 1:328-29.

14.   Joseph Besse, A Collection of the Suffering of the People Called Quakers, 1650-1689, 2 vols. (London, 1753), 1:182-83.   Edward T. Corwin, ed., Ecclesiastical Records of the State of New York, 7 vols. (Albany, N.Y., 1901-16), 1:400.

15.   Hull, "Diary," 3:182.

16.   Corwin, Ecclesiastical Records of New York, 1:400, 433.

17.   M. Louise Green, The Development of Religious Liberty in Connecticut (1905; rept. New York, 1970), pp. 164-67.

18.   Nathaniel B. Shurtleff, ed., Records of the Colony of New Plymouth in New England, 1620-1692, 12 vols. (Boston, 1855-61), 3:123-27.   Also see George F. Willison, Saints and Strangers: Being the Lives of the Pilgrim Fathers and Their Families with Their Friends and Foes (New York, 1945), pp. 378-82.
     The peace testimony was not an essential part of Quaker doctrine at this time.   Quakers, as it will be seen, served as militia officers.   See, for example, the case of Nicholas Shapleigh of Kittery in chapter 5. Prominent eighteenth-century Friends who subscribed to the peace testimony like Anthony Benezet still believed that observance of it was a matter for individual conscience.   Neither Peter Brock, Pacifism in the United States from the Colonial Era to the First World War (Princeton, N.J., 1968), pp. 22-24, 28-30; Sidney James, A People among Peoples: Quaker Benevolence in Eighteenth-Century America (Cambridge, Mass., 1963); nor Arthur Worrall, Quakers in the Colonial Northeast (Hanover, N.H., and London, 1980), pp. 128-40 discuss Quaker acceptance of the peace testimony at this early date.

19.   Shurtleff, Records of New Plymouth, 10:156, 181.

20.   John R. Bartlett, ed., Records of the Colony of Rhode Island and Providence Plantation in New England, 1636-1782, 10 vols. (Providence, R.I., 1856), 1:366-67, 379.   Carl Bridenbaugh suggests that there might be more concrete and material motives for defending the principle of religious toleration in Rhode Island.   According to Bridenbaugh, the travelling Quakers provided a network of trading relationships that used Rhode Island as its North American center.   While Bridenbaugh's thesis is supported by the work of Frederick Tolles, I believe that 1657 was too early for these benefits to be apparent to the Rhode Island General Assembly.   Furthermore, the establishment of a trade network would have been extremely difficult in light of the determination of the other New England colonies to prohibit the entry of nonresident Quakers.

Bridenbaugh, Fat Mutton and Liberty of Conscience:
Society in Rhode Island, 1636-1690 (Providence, R.I.,
1974), pp. 65-66. Tolles, The Atlantic Community of
Early Friends (London, 1952), pp. 25-26, 32.

21. Despite the apparently simple methodology and
the abundance of numerous manuscript lists, determining
the exact number of Quaker visitors to Massachusetts
during this period appears to be an extraordinarily difficult task. No one agrees on the correct figure. G. J.
Willauer, Jr., believes that there were twenty-one prior
to 1659 and Robert Pope, forty. Carla Pestana argues for
forty-three between 1656 and 1661. Pestana's figures are
taken from Quaker sources. One of the major flaws in
Willauer's compilation was his reliance upon manuscripts
compiled by Friends in the early nineteenth century.
Pope's figures were presented in a preliminary paper and
did not include either a list of the Quakers or references
to the sources from which the numbers were derived. I
compiled my list from Massachusetts Bay sources in order
to be consistent in deriving the analysis from the point
of view of the Bay Puritans. Standard Quaker commentaries
like Bishop and Besse were used only to substantiate the
identities of Quakers found in General Court, county
court, and local records. One should note that from the
perspective of Bay magistrates the number of Quakers was
of less significance than the fact of their presence.
Robert Pope, "Society, Security, and Persecution" (paper
presented at Thomas More College, Ft. Mitchell, Ky.,
April 1975), Appendix 1. G. J. Willauer, Jr., "First
Publishers of Truth: A Composite List, 1656-1775,"
Quaker History, 65 (1976):35-44. Carla Gardina Pestana,
"The City upon a Hill under Seige," New England Quarterly,
56 (1983):325, 325n, 347n.

22. Rous to Fell, 3 September 1658, quoted in James
Bowden, The History of the Society of Friends in America,
2 vols. (London, 1754), 1:120. Marmaduke Stephenson to
the General Court, October 1659, quoted in Bishop, New
England Judged, pp. 132-33.

23. In addition to rowdy Harvard students, whipping
was used to discipline persons over the age of fourteen
who were guilty of second offenses of pernicious lying.
Edwin Powers, Crime and Punishment in Early Massachusetts,
1620-1692: A Documentary History (Boston, 1966), pp.
170-71. Shurtleff, Mass. Records, 4, pt. 1:279. Bishop,
New England Judged, pp. 53, 59-60.

24. Shurtleff, Mass. Records, 4, pt. 1:308-9.

25.   The magistrates' motives are inferred from their
later justifications for the application of the death
penalty. Shurtleff, Mass. Records, 4, pt. 1:385. Also
see John Norton, The Heart of New England Rent (Cambridge,
Mass., 1659), p. 54, and Hull, "Diary" p. 188.

26.   The law decreed the loss of an ear for the
second and third visits of a male Quaker; fourth offenders
of either sex were to have their tongues bored with a hot
iron. Shurtleff, Mass. Records, 4, pt. 1:309. Even if
Brend received the 107 lashes Bishop claimed he did, the
Puritan magistrates never intended that whipping be a
form of judicial execution as it was in the eighteenth-
century British navy. When Endecott received word that
Brend's wounds were serious, he sent his son, a physician,
to attend them. Bishop, New England Judged, pp. 68-69.
Powers, Crime and Punishment in Early Massachusetts,
pp. 164-65. Thomas G. Barnes, ed., The Book of the
General Lawes and Libertyes Concerning the Inhabitants of
the Massachusetts (1648; rept. San Marino, Calif., 1975),
p. 50. Sidney Perley, The History of Salem, Massachusetts, 3 vols. (Salem, Mass., 1924-27), 2:246.

27.   "The penalty inflicted on themselves proving
insufficient to restraine their impudent and insolent
intrusions, was encreased by losse of eares of those that
offended the second time which being too weake a defence
against theire impetuous and fanaticke fury." Shurtleff,
Mass. Records, 4, pt. 1:385.

28.   Brend's example also distressed Quakers because
he joined a "spirite (in the Creature) which the Lord God
abhors." William Robinson to George Fox, 12 July 1659,
Chamberlain Manuscript Collection, Boston Public Library.
Bishop, New England Judged, pp. 92-93, and Perley, History
of Salem, 2:246.

29.   Petition for more Stringent Laws on Quakers,
October 1658, Massachusetts Archives, 10:246.

30.   Shurtleff, Mass. Records, 4, pt. 1:345-47.

31.   Hathorne's position on capital punishment can be
seen in William Sabine's deposition given in the fall of
1659. In his deposition, Sabine reported the circumstances of his meeting two Quakers somewhere between
Dedham and Reheboth. When Sabine asked the Quakers why
they had not acted to save their comrades from hanging,
the two replied that they had lacked a leader. Sabine
pressed the issue by asking why they had not sought the
help of Hathorne who was commonly thought to be for
"more liberty." The Quakers responded in a manner revealing the characteristic disillusion true believers
have for trimmers: "Hang him." they reportedly said

"Hee would runn with the streame for the great streame ran the other way." The deposition, dated 13 June 1660 is in Shurtleff, Records of New Plymouth, 3:189.

32. See chapter 6.

33. Shurtleff, Mass. Records, 4, pt. 1:371.

34. Suffolk County Court Files, no. 329.

35. Stephenson to the General Court, October 1659, quoted in Bishop, New England Judged, pp. 132-33.

36. Robinson to Fox, 12 July 1659.

37. Suffolk County Court Files, no. 329.

38. Robinson to Fox, 12 July 1659.

39. Davis apparently left the colony shortly after his arrest. Suffolk County Court Files, no. 329.

40. Worthington, Chauncy Ford, ed., "William Robinson and Marmaduke Stephenson to the General Court, August 1659," Proceedings of the Massachusetts Historical Society, 42, 3d ser. (1908-09):361-62.

41. Norton, The Heart of New England Rent, p. 50.

42. William Dyer to the General Court, 30 August 1659, Chamberlain Manuscript Collection. Ford, "Robinson and Stephenson to the General Court, August, 1659," pp. 359-61.

43. Shurtleff, Mass. Records, 4, pt. 2:357.

44. Norton, The Heart of New England Rent, p. 31.

45. Shurtleff, Mass. Records, 4, pt. 1:386.

46. Suffolk County Court Files, no. 329.

47. Shurtleff, Mass. Records, 4, pt. 1:391, 410-11.

48. Norton, The Heart of New England Rent, pp. 50-51.

49. Stephenson to Neighbors in Shipton, Old England, September 1659, quoted in Bishop, New England Judged, p. 209.

50. Hull, "Diary," p. 188.

51. Shurtleff, Mass. Records, 4, pt. 1:383, 385.

52. Ibid., p. 385.

53. Ibid., p. 390.

54. Ibid., p. 385.

55. Quaker commentators argued that Dyer did not know that she would be spared on this occasion. The stay of execution, however, was a matter of public record and was intended to be widely known. Ibid., p. 384.

56. Ibid., p. 391. Suffolk County Court Files, no. 162034b. Holder left Massachusetts and retired from missionary activity temporarily. He tended some fifty acres of land in Rhode Island. Fox's 1672 visit to New England revived Holder's sense of mission and he left Rhode Island to preach in England. He did not return to Massachusetts. Charles F. Holder, The Holders of Holderness: A History and Genealogy of the Holder Family with Special Reference to Christopher Holder (Pasadena, Calif., 1902), pp. 70-84.

57. Hull, "Diary," p. 193.

58. Besse, A Collection of the Sufferings of Quakers, 1:206-7.

59. Court Order Regarding Quakers, 11 June 1658, Massachusetts Archives, 10:244.

60. John Noble, ed., Records of the Courts of Assistants of the Colony of the Massachusetts Bay, 1630-1692, 3 vols. (Boston, 1901-28), 3:93-94.

61. Bowden, History of the Society of Friends in America, 1:206. Shurtleff, Mass. Records, 4, pt. 1:419. William P. Upham et al., eds., Town Records of Salem, Massachusetts, 1634-1691, 3 vols. (Salem, Mass. 1868-1934) 2:6.

62. Nicholson to Margaret Fell, 10 July 1660, quoted in Bowden, History of the Society of Friends in America, 1:206.

63. Hull, "Diary," p. 197.

64. Shurtleff, Mass. Records, 4, pt. 2:23. Petition of Wenlock Christison, 6 June 1661, Massachusetts Archives, 10:272. Agreement of Christison to Leave the Colony, 7 June 1661, ibid., p. 273. Order to Discharge Christison, 7 June 1661, ibid., p. 274.

65. Petition of Nicholas Davis, 10 August 1661, Massachusetts Archives, 10:275.

66. John Davenport to John Winthrop, Jr., 6 December 1659, Winthrop Papers, Collections of the Massachusetts Historical Society, 4th ser. (Boston, 1863-65), 7:507-9.

67. Shurtleff, Mass. Records, 4, pt. 1:451.

68. Kai T. Erikson, Wayward Puritans: A Study in the Sociology of Deviance (New York, 1966), p. 190.

69. Nathaniel Ward, The Simple Cobbler of Aggawam, ed. P. M. Zall (Lincoln, Neb., 1969), p. 6.

70. Shurtleff, Mass. Records, 4, pt. 1:450-51.

4
Local Quakers and the General Court, 1656-61

> "Diverse of our inhabitants have been infected and seduced."

The decision to resist the invasion of the visiting Quakers rested upon the General Court's fear that local religious dissidents would also become agents of sedition.[1] Deterring residents from becoming Quakers would also prevent them from giving the kind of assistance that encouraged the visitors to come to Massachusetts. Deterrence seemed appropriate since Quakerism initially had little appeal for Massachusetts residents. In the eighteen months that followed the first Quaker visit, the General Court only punished two residents for Quaker-related crimes: Nicholas Upshall of Boston and William Marston of Hampton. Of the two, Marston was less dangerous; his crime was the possession of two Quaker pamphlets. His immediate reaction to the charges cleared him of any suspicion of being involved with the Quakers: fined for having the pamphlets, he turned them over to the General Court, expressed his regret for his offense, and asked for a reduction of his sentence. Recognizing his apparent contrition, the Court remitted a third of the fine.[2]

Upshall showed, however, that Quakers had a potential for subverting the weak and disaffected. When the Court ordered visiting Quakers Anne Austin and Mary Fisher jailed and isolated from the public, Upshall, the owner of a wharf and tavern in Boston, bribed the jailer to allow him to provide the women with food and drink. Upshall was precisely the kind of person who might be susceptible to the blandishments of the Quakers. He had been a member of Boston's First Church but, for reasons unknown to anyone, had stopped attending services in 1651. As a result, the church excommunicated him. The expulsion from church membership did not subject Upshall to further

civil discipline. Deficient in religious matters, he was
still obviously capable of living a civil life. Moreover,
his wife Dorothy remained a full member of the church.[3]
     Upshall's association with the two visiting Quakers,
however, raised questions about his future willingness to
conform to nominally civil behavior. His support of the
second group of visiting Quakers revealed a commitment to
what appeared to be vicious forms of blasphemy and sedition. His sustained support of the Quakers resulted in
his being fined twenty pounds and ordered to appear before
the next session of a county court to acknowledge his
crime and give assurances for his future behavior. In
view of his ability to pay the fine and the Puritan fear
of the seditious implications of his activities, the
punishment seemed to have been intended as a measured
deterrent. Also, the expectation of some evidence of
contrition was not unusual. As ship captains who had
carried Quakers into the colony and William Marston had
discovered, repentance brought about the reduction of
one's fine. Upshall, however, chose to leave for Sandwich in New Plymouth, where he spent the winter with
other early supporters of the visiting Quakers.[4]
     Upshall's seduction by the Quakers and his stubborn
defense of them to the detriment of estate, family, and
community demonstrated to the General Court the first
conversion by an inhabitant. Unfortunately for him, Upshall became associated with the Quakers before the
General Court developed procedures that differentiated
between visiting and local varieties of Quakerism. Because these procedures defined a graduated system of
offenses, Upshall might have had a number of instances
where the state might have been able to intervene and
check his descent into heterodoxy and sedition. Once
the church had withdrawn its supervision of Upshall's
religious life, however, the state could not act without
specific secular guidelines until Upshall's actions became seen as being unequivocally seditious; and then it
could only act because the gravity of his offenses warranted the application of discretionary powers.[5]
     After the summer of 1656, it became apparent that local
Quakerism would continue to be a chronic problem. To
counter this, the General Court enacted legislation designed specifically to prevent conversions. The legislation intended to deter the weak of mind from committing
open acts of defiance like Upshall's and from contributing
to the seditious disorder caused by the visitors. Barring
the entry of visiting Quakers, the Court established a
series of increasingly severe punishments for those who
might be tempted to help them. The first two offenses of
defending heretical Quaker opinions were punishable by
fines of forty shillings and four pounds, respectively.
After a third offense, the Court considered the malefactor
a habitual criminal beyond redemption and subject to
banishment. Also seeing an apparent connection between

Quakerism and disrespect for authority, the Court ordered
a severe whipping or a five-pound fine for "those persons
soever shall revile the office or person of magistrates
or ministers as is usuall with Quakers."[6]

The specific form of the new anti-Quaker legislation
embodied assumptions about Quakerism's impact upon the
local populace. These assumptions recast the definitions
of the criminal nature of the sect's adherents that in
turn provided the logical determinants for shaping the
treatment of local converts. Gradations in punishment
implied that there was a spectrum of disorderly behavior
associated with the sect's activities; that the visiting
Quakers seduced residents into committing progressively
more serious acts of disorder or sedition; that the descent into sedition, because of its gradual, insidious
nature, could be checked at a number of points; and that
not all cases of conversion required the immediate application of the harshest of penalties. Fines, for example, illustrated the broader range of controls available to magistrates and suggested that local Quakers
might be amenable to milder, more reasonable, and more
conventional forms of social control. Fines also implied
that resident Quakers were less dangerous to public peace.
The migratory nature of the visiting Quakers made it
senseless to fine them. Because the visitors had no real
property subject to attachment in the event of nonpayment,
fines would be ineffective. The encumbrance of a fine
would have required that the visitors remain in the colony
until the debt was satisfied and, therefore, would have
frustrated the General Court's wish to be free of the
noxious visitors. In contrast, fines against inhabitants
with real property were easily enforceable and provided a
measurable test of an offender's threat to public peace.
If the malefactor continued to defy authority after a
series of extensive fines, he indicated a degree of criminal behavior or intent that justified corporal punishment
and banishment. On the other hand, as long as the individual seemed concerned about his material losses and the
disposition of his property, he demonstrated that there
were effective forms of social control over him besides
physical restraint or coercion.

Despite the new laws, local Quaker activity increased
after 1656. The General Court had to face more insistent
and outspoken visitors and larger numbers of more active
local converts. Where in 1656 and 1657 the Court had had
to contend with only Marston and Upshall, in 1658 it had
six incidents; and in 1659, twenty-one.[7]

The connection between the more demonstrative strains
of visiting Quakerism and increased numbers of local converts was more coincidental than casual. Before December
1656, a number of Salem residents had begun to meet on the
western edge of town. In light of the early focus of the
first Quaker missionaries on Boston and the General
Court's prompt jailing of them, it is unlikely that the

twenty or so Salem residents became Quakers because of direct contact with the visitors. Probably they were already dissatisfied with Salem's church. The town's minister, Edward Norris, had been hostile to more evangelical, Antinomian sentiments. When he fell prey to illness and age and the pulpit was transferred to John Higginson, the disaffected had found in Quakerism a convenient mechanism to express their displeasure with the orthodox church.[8] Similarly, in Kittery in York County, while contact between the missionaries and local Quakers before 1659 was unlikely or incidental, those people who became Quakers had had prior histories of discontent with Massachusetts Bay. As early as 31 October 1655, Richard Nason, a future convert, committed blasphemy of sufficient proportions to warrant being placed on probation and barred from holding public office for a year. Nason and others later found the Quaker meeting to be a convenient forum for expressing support for the claims of the heirs of Sir Ferdinando Gorges to the proprietary of Maine.[9]

In Salem, however, the visitors brought increased attention to the activities of the resident dissidents and provided the catalyst that prompted the General and Essex County Courts to act. When Christopher Holder and John Copeland, two visiting Quakers, arrived in Salem in late September 1657, it was not to preach to the embryonic Quaker meeting but to disturb the services of the orthodox Salem congregation. After Constable Edmund Batter arrested Holder for disrupting the worship of the Salem church, authorities discovered that the visitors had spent the previous night at the home of Lawrence and Cassandra Southwick.[10] For the next eighteen months, this kind of connection made it difficult for either the General Court or the Essex County Court to distinguish between the Southwicks' dissent and the visitors' Quakerism.

Like Upshall, the Southwicks had become suspect. While both were members of the orthodox church, they had ceased to attend services during 1656. The judges of the Essex County Court seemed sufficiently concerned to invoke the colony's mandatory church attendance law against Cassandra in July 1657, but they only admonished her and required her to pay minimal court costs of two shillings, sixpence. Since the law was rarely enforced, Southwick's conviction was an indicator of the county court's concern that the communal loyalties of the family were ebbing. With the citation the court did three things: it moved itself to act in the absence of ecclesiastical authority, it singled out an individual for correction, and it warned others that such behavior was unacceptable. Yet the minimal fine also revealed the failure to enforce the new General Court laws and a reluctance at confronting Lawrence Southwick, his family, and the rest of the dissidents.[11]

Two months after Cassandra Southwick was cited, Copeland and Holder arrived in Salem and forced the county court to reconsider the widespread absenteeism, this time, in the context of the growth of Quaker activity. The visit of the two seemed to have been made possible by the support of the dissidents and seemed to suggest future danger. Shortly after the two men were sent to Boston to be deported, William Hathorne, the resident county court magistrate in Salem, assessed fines on Lawrence Southwick, his son Josiah, and Edward Harnet for failing to attend the services of the church. Unlike the nominal fine first levied on Cassandra Southwick, Hathorne demanded heavier penalties: the two Southwicks were to pay thirty shillings each for missing six sabbaths, while Harnet was to pay thirty-five shillings for his absence from seven services.[12] Exacted in March 1658, the fines did not bring the Southwicks back to orthodox services or deter the absence of others. When Lawrence, Cassandra, and Josiah continued to absent themselves, Hathorne fined them each an additional two pounds, five shillings. Hathorne also levied fines on four other Salem residents, including Samuel Shattock, a member of the orthodox church who had tried to stop Constable Batter from silencing Holder with a gag during the disturbance of the previous September. But even these fines proved ineffective, and Hathorne had to order the three Southwicks to be jailed at Ipswich.[13]

Despite his prominence in these first attempts to suppress the growth of Quakerism in Salem, Hathorne was not among the sect's most vigorous opponents. The punishments he ordered were far milder than those prescribed under the strict letter of the law. For example, after 1656, Hathorne could have cited Josiah and Lawrence Southwick for violating the 1657 General Court legislation and assessed them fines of forty shillings each. Subsequent offenses then would have subjected them to fines of four pounds and possibly banishment. Yet Hathorne chose to cite the Southwicks on the far less serious charges of absence which carried only a five-shilling fine for each offense. Even on the lesser charges, it does not appear that Hathorne cited each member of the family for every possible offense. It is unlikely that either Lawrence or Josiah missed only fifteen of the some twenty-six meetings of the church that occurred between the visits of Holder and Copeland's visits in September 1657 and Hathorne's citation on 8 March 1658. Moreover, Cassandra Southwick, having already established a pattern of habitual absence as early as July 1657, would probably not have attended church services more frequently than her husband or son; yet she was cited for six fewer absences during the same period.

Hathorne also failed to cite other members of the meeting before the June 1658 session of the Essex County Court despite evidence of previous activity. The failure to include Nicholas Phelps among those fined before June was a curious omission since his home became the site of the Quaker meetings after the Southwicks had been jailed.

The citation of Samuel Shattock at the June session for
missing nine sabbaths expressed a minimal reaction to his
support of visiting Quakers. For defending the actions of
a seditious Quaker (Christopher Holder), for helping him
to resist arrest, and for contributing to the disruption
of the Salem orthodox congregation, Shattock received a
total fine of forty-five shillings.[14]
A member of the General Court as well as the Essex
bench, Hathorne could not have been ignorant of its intentions regarding the Quakers. The attempt to insulate
the colony from visiting Quakerism would have had little
hope for success without active cooperation from local
authority, the county courts. Indeed, the presence of
local converts seemed to spur Quaker missionary activity.[15]
Yet the Southwicks and Phelps were clearly guilty of
serious crimes for which they had not been punished.
After October 1657, the Essex County Court could have
fined the Southwicks and Phelps forty shillings for each
hour the visiting Quakers were in their homes. They also
could have been banished under the law that decreed "any
Quakers arising from amongst ourselves shall be dealt
with and suffer the like punishment as the law provides
against foreign Quakers."[16] By early 1658, the General
Court was aware of the existence of local meetings like
the one at Salem, and it had tried to suppress them by
authorizing fines of ten shillings for attending a meeting and five pounds for speaking at it. Second violations
for addressing a Quaker meeting were punishable by whipping and imprisonment until two persons provided sureties
for the future behavior of the offender or until he or she
left the colony.[17]
The ambivalence of local authorities like Hathorne
toward local Quakers explains the lapses in carrying out
the will of the General Court. In Salem, Hathorne's
citation of the Quakers reflected neither the fear of
sedition nor the belated discovery of a threat to public
peace. Rather, it revealed the evolution of patterns of
political power in town and country that forced him to
abandon old friends.[18] In Kittery, local officials were
also negligent. No Quakers were cited for any Quaker-
related crimes until 1663. In view of the activities of
Richard Nason and the likely conversion of Nicholas
Shapleigh and others around 1659, this was not for a lack
of local Quakers. Indeed, John Hull observed that magistrates seemed reluctant to prosecute Quakers in the
northern parts. The omission is not surprising: both
Nason and Shapleigh were men of prominence in the county--
Shapleigh was a member of the York County Court bench--and
local circumstances and not the discovery of heterodoxy
dictated the timing of the punishment of resident Quakers
in Kittery.[19]
By allowing the Quakers to meet even under ostensibly
onerous financial penalties, the General Court tacitly
acknowledged that a form of local Quakerism could exist

if the community were willing to be responsible for its
members. In the provision allowing two individuals to
post bonds for the behavior of convicted Quakers, the
Court confirmed the role local institutions played in the
evaluation of the seditious or disorderly tendencies of
the accused. Everyone in the town and county would have
to agree that individual Quakers were uncontrollable before colonial institutions could strip them of their pro-
tected status as residents and expel them.

Although the procedure seemed cumbersome, it could
still deny an individual crucial support when he seemed
to threaten the well-being of the colony. Toward the end
of June 1658, an apparent acceleration of those kinds of
seditious activities resulted in the erosion of Salem's
tolerance for its resident Quakers. On 5 June, constables
discovered a Quaker meeting under way at the home of the
Southwicks. Despite the Southwicks' previous records,
the constable did nothing except to record the names of
those in attendance and forward the list to the county
court for its consideration at its regular session on the
twenty-ninth. On the twenty-seventh, however, the Salem
constables learned of another Quaker meeting, this time
at the home of Phelps. Upon investigation the constables
discovered the presence of two visiting Quakers, William
Brend and William Leddera. Apparently aware of Brend's
notoriety, the constables arrested him and Leddera and
sent them to Boston for further punishment, broke up the
meeting, and ordered all the local participants to appear
before the county court when it convened in two days. At
the session of 29 June, the men appeared and refused to
remove their hats, symbolically declaring their affiliation with Brend and Leddera and denying their obedience
to the authority of the court. Lest there be any doubt
about their actions, three men, Shattock, Joshua Buffum,
and Samuel Gaskin, openly admitted that they were "such
as are called Quakers."[20]

The presence of the two foreign Quakers together with
the frank admissions of conversion forced the county to
act. It cited Shattock, Buffum, Gaskin, Phelps, the three
Southwicks, and twenty-two other town residents for absence from regular church services.[21] Attacking what
appeared to be the center of the meeting, the courts also
ordered that Shattock, Buffum, Phelps, and the three
Southwicks be sent to Boston with Brend and Leddera. By
doing so, the county court, in effect, had admitted that
it faced threats to order that exceeded its control and
that obviously and unavoidably needed the intervention of
higher authority. Furthermore, by abdicating its responsibility for these residents, the county court also
initiated the legal process by which they would be trans-
formed into aliens.[22]

On the other hand, the county court still refrained
from applying the anti-Quaker legislation against residents who, while heterodox in belief, still seemed amenable to relatively traditional and comparatively mild

forms of social regulation. Other participants of the
local meeting had had larger fines than the six sent to
Boston but had not faced punishment outside the county.
In effect, the county court had refrained from initiating
the process of separating all local Quakers from community
and colony. By using the crime of absence rather than
Quakerism against the remaining members of the meeting,
the county court either deliberately shielded them from
harsher punishments and allowed them time for redemption
or indicated that it did not consider them a sufficient
threat to public peace to warrant more severe treatment.[23]

Despite its earlier decree, the General Court appeared
to be reluctant to treat its resident Quakers like the
visitors. While Brend and Leddera were immediately banished from the colony, the General Court could not expel
the residents without violating the legal rights that
inhered in residence. There were probably no compunctions
against the lash once financial penalties had failed to
deter continued support for the visiting Quakers. The
difficulty of the situation lay in banishment. The
justification for banishing the visitors rested upon the
right of English communities to regulate the entrance of
nonresidents into their respective jurisdictions. When
the General Court prohibited the entry of the visiting
Quakers or when it ordered their deportation, it only
acted as any other English community might when faced
with unwanted or disorderly immigrants. Presumably, as
each succeeding jurisdiction deported the unwanted vaga-
bond, the pariah would eventually have to return to his
original residence, where he would become, most properly,
the ward of his home community.[24] This practice posed a
problem for the General Court because it required the
drastic step of making the Salem Quakers homeless vagabonds. Yet there would still be a degree of legal
ambiguity that might force Massachusetts to continue to
accept responsibility for the six. On the other hand,
the Court could not simply release the six and send them
home until it had some reasonable assurance that they
would cease their increasingly seditious activities.
There was a further complication: the General Court
could do nothing to reduce the one indicator of the
Quakers' sedition, their heterodoxy. A secular institution, the Court could not demand changes in the consciences of individual Quakers without violating the
boundary between church and state in the Bay Colony.
Finally, the Court could not legally keep the six Quakers
imprisoned since each would most assuredly be able to
obtain bonds of good behavior from other members of the
Salem meeting.

Lawrence Southwick realized that he had considerable
resources preventing the Court from detaining him indef-
inately or moving to deport him.[25] His strength lay in
the secular ties that he and his fellow prisoners had to
the town and that tended to deny the charges they were

dangers to public peace needing deportation. The early
release of Samuel Gaskin probably reinforced Southwick's
perception. A youth of eighteen, Gaskin was apparently
released into the custody of his parents, both of whom
were members of the regular church.[26] While the elder
Southwicks had strayed from orthodoxy of late, they too
were still full church members and had been long-time
residents of the town. Shortly after their arrival in
1639, they had become church members. A glazier, Lawrence
had come to Salem to participate in an early attempt by
the town to establish a glassworks. When it became apparent that the enterprise, even with town subsidies,
could not support its three partners, Southwick abandoned
his trade and began life anew as a farmer. With diligence
and in the face of the fines exacted by the county court,
he still accumulated an estate worth 196 pounds at his
death in 1660, a personal history hardly indicative of a
threat to property and order.[27]

Like the Southwicks, Samuel Shattock was also a member of the town's middling classes. A feltmaker and
hatter, Shattock's year as a Quaker contrasted with the
fifteen he had spent as a full member of the church. Unlike most of the Quakers who lived on the southwestern
edge of town, Shattock lived near the town center and had
a number of influential family connections. His step-
father Thomas Gardner was one of Salem's most prominent
citizens. An Old Planter, that is, one who had settled
in the town before the arrival of John Endecott and the
Massachusetts Bay Company, Gardner had been a deputy to
the General Court and, in 1658, had been a member of the
jury that had indicted the Quakers for absence from the
orthodox church. Gardner at that court session had par-
ticipated in the indictments of his natural son and
daughter-in-law as well as that of Shattock. Obviously,
if Quakerism was a problem in Salem, it ran in the best
of families.[28]

Unlike his fellow cellmates, Joshua Buffum was not a
church member, but his ties to the community were no less
extensive and influential. Both a former deputy and town
constable had thought enough of Buffum and his mother
Tamosin, also a Quaker, to leave them small bequests in
1655 and 1657. Buffum's father Robert never became a
Quaker, and he probably maintained regular attendance at
the orthodox church. More important, Robert was fairly
wealthy, having assets that placed him along the richest
twenty-five percent of the town's population. In addition, Joshua was a carpenter and shipbuilder and thus
possessed skills that made him invaluable to the town's
emerging commercial interests.[29]

While family ties, church membership, and economic
standing in the town had not fully shielded the Quakers
from punishment, they separated the inhabitant from the
visitor. The desire to deport these particular inhabitants from the colony because they were Quakers and supposed to be seditious contrasted with their records of

reasonably acceptable personal behavior. Moreover, even
if one linked their recent disorderly behavior to their
conversions, deportation required the consideration of
whether the degree of disorder practiced constituted the
radical rejection of the existing structure of society
that denoted sedition. Conversely, deportation might
threaten orderly processes in the community. The public
good might be better served by the restoration of the
local Quakers to their customary places in the community,
an argument advanced by Lawrence Southwick in his petition
for the release of himself and his family. If all three
Southwicks remained in the Boston jail, Southwick declared
to the Essex County Court judges, they, as well as the two
youngest members of the family, would be unable to tend to
the family crops and would become the wards of the town.[30]
    Although imprisoned under the authority of the General
Court, Southwick directed his appeal to the county court
and touched upon a crucial loophole within the institutional mechanisms intended to control Quakerism. By asking the local court to reconsider its abdication of responsibility for him and the other jailed inhabitants,
Southwick seemed to expect that the inferior court would
be more responsive to local patterns of influence and that
it would have the power to intervene. Southwick was correct in both his assessments because the issues involved
dealt with matters of civil disorder. For if the county
court no longer considered the imprisoned Quakers harmful
to the ordering of the locality or if it deemed that its
or the locality's best interest lay in their release, the
General Court would find itself in the position of over-
ruling the judgment of a lower court. While this was not
impossible, to do so under these circumstances placed the
Court in the logically untenable position of insisting
that the crimes of the resident Quakers were serious
enough to warrant banishment while an inferior jurisdiction accustomed to dealing with more trivial cases of
disorder saw little threat to public peace.
    The release of the local Quakers later that summer
indicated that neither the county court nor the General
Court were sufficiently disturbed to continue their incarceration. Despite the release of the Quakers, the
General Court still had reason to be concerned. The
colony was unable to stop the continued presence of
visiting Quakers, and it could not suppress the local
conversions that encouraged them to return to the colony.
Furthermore, disaffection for orthodox religion, law, and
government seemed to be increasing. The conflict over
the criteria for church membership resulting in the Half-
Way Covenant, the open defiance of the Anabaptists in
Charlestown, and the emergence of an independent congregation in Salisbury with vague connections to the Quakers
offered other sources of potential converts.[31]
    In spite of the release of the remaining five Salem
residents, there was little relief from judicial harassment. During its September session in Ipswich, the Essex

County Court continued to pressure the Quaker meeting.
Finding that Phelps, Shattock, and Joshua Buffum were
"persisting still in their course and opinions of Quakers," the court ordered the three remanded to the Ipswich
jail until they either renounced their opinions or left
the colony.[32]
    This act of imprisonment demonstrated a crucial denial
of local support for the Quakers. Because the order for
imprisonment originated at an Ipswich court session, its
judgment upon the Salem residents represented a significant change of venue. Usually the court's jurisdiction
was divided into two relatively autonomous regions, one
with Ipswich at its center and the other with Salem. Although the composition of the bench remained the same for
both sessions, indicting and trial juries would be drawn
from residents of the different geographical areas.[33] At
sessions held at Ipswich, magistrates Daniel Dennison and
Simon Bradstreet would be more influential than Hathorne
because the juries would reflect patterns of deference
and interest tending to favor the former while working to
the disadvantage of the latter and the Salem Quakers.
Once the county court changed the venue for the Quakers,
they became dependent solely upon Hathorne for their
defense.
    Yet, this was the moment at which Hathorne's ambiva-
lence toward Quakerism was turning toward opposition and
at which his political influence in town and county was
ebbing. Already pressured in the General Court to vote
in favor of the death penalty for visiting Quakers,
Hathorne was beginning to see political liabilities in
continuing to support the Quakers in Salem. Hathorne's
primary constituency was the town's agrarian interests,
which generally resided outside its geographic center.
In the years 1657-58, this political base included the
support of selectman and Quaker Joseph Boyce. When the
Ipswich Court convened, it was becoming apparent that what
had been an asset--the large numbers of Quakers who supported both Boyce and Hathorne--was fast becoming a
liability. In fact, Quakerism provided Hathorne's opponents with a useful focus for their animosities. Allied
with Simon Bradstreet and Daniel Dennison was Edmund
Batter, Hathorne's rival for political primacy in Salem.
Like Bradstreet, Batter was fiercely anti-Quaker, and,
like Bradstreet and Dennison, he opposed Hathorne on the
issue of colonial autonomy. By attacking local Quakerism
in Salem, by acquiescing in its suppression by Ipswich
juries and judges, and by cooperating with the General
Court's threats to expel certain Quaker freemen, the anti-
Hathorne elements in the town and colony could galvanize
support for their position; imply the future disenfranchisement of Quakers, thereby neutralizing their long-term
political influence; and ultimately weaken Hathorne's
influence in town, county, and colony. In 1659, the
settlement of the ardently anti-Quaker and anti-Hathorne

minister John Higginson, the defeat of Boyce for reelection, and the domination of the town's board of selectmen by commercial interests were severe blows to the political fortunes of both the Quakers and Hathorne.[34]

The loss of the Quakers' political connections and their imprisonment had wider ramifications. These actions helped remove part of the dilemma in which the General Court found itself. Once the inferior jurisdiction considered the local Quakers to be a sufficient problem to warrant jailing them, the logical and jurisdictional barriers to harsher treatment by the General Court were reduced. Thereafter, the Court could begin to treat local Quakers like visitors. At its next session, the General Court confirmed the actions taken at Ipswich and added Lawrence, Cassandra, and Josiah Southwick to the list of Quakers to be imprisoned.[35]

Simultaneously, the Court defined the circumstances that justified the stripping away of the protections afforded by residence, allowed for the treatment of residents like the visitors, and resolved the problem posed by inhabitants acting like the seditious nonresidents. The residents were to be treated like the visitors and to be liable to banishment when they revealed their heinous natures

> either by taking up, publishing, and defending
> the horrid opinions of the Quakers, or by stirring
> up mutiny, sedition, or rebellion against the
> government, or by taking up theire absurd and
> destructive practice,...and endeavoring to dis-
> affect others to civil government and church
> order...manifesting thereby their compliance
> with those whose designe it is to overthrow the
> order established in church and commonwealth.[36]

The justification for regulating this variant of Quakerism was not because its adherents were heterodox but because allegiance to it indicated a desire for destroying the institutions upon which civil order depended. Salem Quakers like the Southwicks could be banished because their activities resembled those of the visitors. Their previously reasonable behavior was unable to compensate for the larger threat they seemed to pose to order in Massachusetts.

Despite the threat of banishment that the new policy presented to the six inhabitants, the General Court was still reluctant to eliminate the last distinctions that kept them from being seen as visitors. While the Court had, after 1658, the policy of immediately banishing all visiting Quakers upon pain of death, it continued to allow inhabitants an intermediate step. The resident offender had to be deported first. Only after he returned to the colony, could he then be sentenced to banishment upon pain of death.[37]

There were other loopholes that differentiated the resident from the visitor and revealed the General Court's continued concern for its own. Before banishing the resident habitual offender, the Court allowed him the opportunity to recant and apologize for his actions. Because repentance expressed a loyalty and obedience to the state for which it was not ungrateful, it was a way to avoid punishment. Fined in June 1658 for his participation in two Salem meetings, Thomas Brackett, with perhaps hat in hand, appeared before the General Court to ask for a remission of his fines. A full member of the regular church, Brackett acknowledged that he had been "drawn away by Quakers to the dishonor of God, Commonwealth, wife, family, and conscience." In return for his apology, the Court ordered half of his fine remitted and referred Brackett back to the Essex County Court for the cancellation of the remainder.[38]

While the General Court offered Brackett as an example of its mercy, it also served notice to the six jailed Quakers that it intended to enforce the law strictly if they failed to conform outwardly and, presumably, refrain from Quaker activities. In its endorsement of the county court's imprisonment of them, the General Court ordered the six to recant or leave the colony by the Court's May 1659 session, which was to be held seven months later. Failure to do either would cost the Quakers their last defense before the gallows--the fact of their residence; if they were in the colony after May 1659, they would be considered visitors and subject to banishment upon pain of death. At its May session, the Court ordered the six to leave the colony by 8 June. Being in the colony after the eighth would constitute a breach of their sentence of banishment and make any of the six liable to immediate execution.[39]

Whereas the visiting Quaker had little to lose save his own life, Salem Quakers who were, by this time, legal aliens were more vulnerable to General Court coercion. The manifestations of years of sober and industrious lives in family, farms, and property made the material and emotional risks of martyrdom all the greater. A rejection of these material realities would have confirmed the profound and insidious dangers that these converts allegedly posed to public peace; it would have confirmed their intentions to turn the world upside down. Ironically, the achievements of lifetimes of reasonable behavior provided the General Court with more effective weapons to control local Quakerism. One could use the temporary indebtedness caused by the fines for absence to compel the cooperation of other family members. Revealing the range of its discretionary powers, the Court empowered the colonial treasurer to sell the two youngest Southwick children, Daniel and Provided, into indentured servitude in Virginia or the Barbados to satisfy their outstanding fines.[40]

Even as it exhibited these extortionate tactics, the General Court still hoped for the return of its wayward flock. Having also banished Samuel Shattock on pain of death, the Court granted the petition of his sister Mary Hamor. Hamor proposed that, in one last effort to obtain his conformity, Shattock be placed in the home of Boston minister John Norton. There Shattock would be subject to Norton's arguments against the sect, arguments based less upon the heretical nature of the sect and more upon the threat its adherents posed to public peace. If Shattock could be made to recant, he would have repudiated the seditious tendencies implied in his conversion and mani-fested in his behavior. Hamor conceded that there was little hope of Shattock changing his mind, but, in a plea all too reminiscent of those who care for the terminally ill, the effort still seemed worthwhile. "Methinks," Hamor pleaded, "I am not quite out of hope so long as there is life."[41]

Ultimately, Shattock, Buffum, Phelps, and the South-wicks refused to conform. The care of family, the argu-ments of Norton, and the threats of the General Court failed to bring about any minimal conformity by the six Quakers. Martyrdom, however, was avoided. In an apparent exchange for dropping the threat to sell Daniel and Provided Southwick into servitude, the older Southwicks agreed to leave the colony and presumably precipitated the departure of the other three Salem Quakers.[42]

By refusing to conform during the spring of 1659, the domestic strain of Quakerism had brought the legal system of the colony full circle. Where previously the visit of a foreign Quaker had brought down the wrath of the General Court upon resident converts, the spread of a more odious form of domestic Quakerism demonstrated the capacity of the visitors to spread disorder within the colony. Fur-thermore, local Quakers gave added justification to the decision to execute the most obnoxious of the visitors. Executions were a means of preventing the spread of a virulent disease, sedition, to the local population, and the magistrates, as fathers to their communities, were obligated to take whatever steps were necessary to isolate the colony from such horrors. "Who can make question but that a man that hath children and family both justly may, and in duty ought to preserve them of his chardge (as far as he is able) from the daingerous company of the persons infected with the plague of pestilence of some other con-tageious, noysom, and mortall diseases?"[43]

Although the General Court had established a machinery for expelling local Quakers, it still could not seem to curb enthusiasm for the sect. Quakers continued to meet in Salem, and other incidents throughout the colony in-dicated future support for the sect. Missionaries seemed to be making inroads in the town of Kittery. The General Court had had to disfranchise three Kittery residents, two of whom were former deputies, and a Hampton resident for entertaining travelling Quakers. Some cases were incon-sequential. James Rawlings had been gulled into giving a

Quaker missionary shelter. But the Court recognized
Rawling's lack of malevolence and only admonished him
observing that he had been "more innocent and ingenious
[ingenuous]." Other cases were more serious. The Court
was more troubled by Thomas Macy, a member of an orthodox
but separatist faction in Salisbury, who allowed, inadvertently he claimed, Salem Quaker Edward Wharton to stay
in his barn during a driving rainstorm. While the Court
believed Macy had forced Wharton to leave the moment he
learned the latter's identity, it still fined Macy thirteen shillings.[44]

The need to resort to more systematic and harsher
penalties was an admission of the Court's inability to
prevent the spread of local Quakerism. In fact, Salem
Quakers seemed to grow more obnoxious. After William
King received fifteen lashes from the General Court for
his persistence in defending Quakerism, he informed the
Court that if it were displeased with him, God and Christ
were not. Edward Wharton was given twenty lashes for
guiding visiting Quakers through the colony, but punishment did not deter his other demonstrations of contempt
for authority.[45]

Even worse, local Quakers began to support openly the
most obnoxious of the visiting Quakers. In the fall of
1659 a number of Salem women gathered in Boston to witness
the impending martyrdom of visitors William Robinson and
Marmaduke Stephenson. The presence of Margaret Smith and
Mary Trask among the women must have troubled the magistrates. Smith seemed especially dangerous since her husband had initially had little to do with the meeting. To
the contrary, in June 1658 he had helped the constables
break up the first Quaker meetings. The possibilities of
Smith's visitor-like behavior seemed all too obvious: at
the very least, her activities threatened to upset the
patterns of authority within her family; at their worst,
they defied the will of the Court and threatened to cause
the conversion of her husband, a threat that was to be
realized within a year.[46]

These manifestations of defiance raised new dilemmas
as the General Court attempted to suppress the growing
disorder. For all the trouble they caused, Smith and
Trask could not be punished by jail or deportation without
adding to the dislocation of their households and punishing their husbands and families. For their first demonstration of support for Robinson and Stephenson, the
women were whipped and released.[47] Both women, however,
immediately returned to demonstrate their support for the
two visitors. Had the Court followed its own precedents,
the two should have been banished; however, the Court
procrastinated and ordered that the women be jailed until
they promised to stop their disorderly conduct or until
their husbands took them out of the colony.[48]

The reasons for the delay, the Court claimed, rested
upon sympathy for the women's husbands who were "innocent

persons in that respect [Quakerism] so farre as we know and are inhabitants of this jurisdiction."[49] The Court was wrong about the husbands, and at least five members of the General Court should have been aware of the error. Former Salem resident and Governor John Endecott might be excused for not knowing the recent sympathies of John Smith and Henry Trask since he had moved to Boston before the Quaker problem had developed. Had he known about Smith, there might have been good cause for his ignoring the recent past and treating Smith leniently since both had been neighbors. But the assertion of the innocence of the two Quakers showed a curious lapse of memory and awareness on the part of the other four Essex men in the General Court. All of them, Samuel Symonds, Simon Bradstreet, Daniel Dennison, and William Hathorne, had been on the county court bench during the trials of the local Quakers and were the judges who ordered Trask fined for absence from church services in 1658. Trask had received his first indictment for Quakerism the same time his wife was first cited. Smith's conversion took place after June 1658 and before September 1660, when he was jailed for supporting visiting Quakers in Boston.[50]

When the Court jailed the Smiths and Trask, it ordered indeterminate sentences based upon its perception of its ability to rehabilitate or, more accurately, to neutralize them. Thus, while Mary Trask was released for two months between March and November, Margaret Smith remained in jail during the entire period. The reason for Smith's continued incarceration may have been because her husband had been jailed as well. In commenting on Trask's release, John Smith complained bitterly that he and Margaret expected to be confined through the winter. In contrast, the General Court released other visiting Quakers like William Leddera and Joseph and Jane Nicholson once they had given the Court some assurance that they would leave the colony as soon as possible.[51] While the application of an indeterminate jail sentence seemed arbitrary from the perspective of the Smiths, its use provided the General Court with some degree of discretion in a confusing and ambiguous situation. It would not have to release the unrepentant individuals, and it could try to minimize the dislocation that might be inflicted upon innocent third parties. Trask could be released into the custody of her husband who, despite his Quakerism, seemed less dangerous and more likely to provide some assurance that he could control his wife.

The Court's treatment of Nicholas Upshall demonstrated another way in which discretionary justice curbed the disorderly behavior of a resident Quaker. Although the Court might have banished him upon pain of death after he returned from his self-imposed exile, it only jailed him.[52] Sometime between November 1660 and May 1661, the Court allowed him to leave for England; however, by June 1661, he was again in Boston, in jail, with his opinions

unchanged. To prevent his attraction of "many Quakers
and others affected to that sect" to the Boston jail, the
Court ordered Upshall removed to the isolation of Castle
Island and prohibited from having any visitors except his
family. Upshall's wife Dorothy, however, interceded in
his behalf and prevented the transfer.[53] Earlier, Dorothy
had petitioned the Court to cancel a portion of the fines
levied against Nicholas, and it was upon her appeal in
June 1661 that the Court placed him under house arrest in
the Dorchester home of town deputy John Capen. In Capen's
home, Upshall was virtually at liberty as long as he kept
his behavior within reasonable bounds. In fact, the
Court once chided Capen for failing to keep a close enough
watch over Upshall.[54] By its actions, however, the Court
demonstrated that its supervision of Upshall was designed
to prevent his Quakerism from growing into a more general-
ized threat to the peace of the colony. Once Upshall's
Quakerism seemed to pose no larger threat, there was
little need to keep him under close arrest.

The treatment of Upshall was the product of his particular strain of Quakerism and the standing of his wife
in the community. While he had been an early and ardent
supporter of the visiting Quakers, his actions were more
individualistic and less serious than those of the Salem
Quakers. While he might have encouraged the activities
of John Chamberlain, another, though more disorderly,
Boston Quaker, Upshall was not the instigator of a large,
overtly offensive meeting in Boston. Moreover, throughout
all his years of contentiousness, his family never wavered
in its support of him or in its loyalties to the existing
legal, political, and religious institutions of town and
colony. When the General Court cancelled his 1656 fine,
it did so because it wanted to be sure that "the innocent
may not suffer with the nocent."[55] In the intervening
years, Upshall's family suffered no obvious economic
penalty because of his activities. His wife assumed the
management of the family enterprises and seems to have
been reasonably competent. At Nicholas's death in 1666,
Dorothy had been running the family wharf and tavern in
Boston and had been licensed to serve beer and strong
drink for over eight years, activities that she continued
to carry out until her death nine years later. Considering that Nicholas's assets at his death were over 543
pounds and his wharf remained in family hands until 1691,
the estate did not appear to have suffered greatly under
Dorothy's supervision.[56]

Although the intervention of royal authority after
1661 made the execution of Quakers by the Bay Colony more
difficult if not impossible, the application of the
penalties of banishment and imprisonment seemed to have
stemmed the tide of the more seditious forms of Quakerism.
The Court apparently had stopped the conversion of dissident religious groups in Salisbury and Hampton, it had
effectively quarantined Nicholas Upshall, and it had

curtailed the excesses of the Salem meeting. All the Bay
Colony's secular mechanisms seemed to be controlling the
disorderly activities of the Quakers. Having cut off the
visitors, the Court presumed the future decline in Quaker
activity. With the cooperation of the Essex County Court
in the prosecution of the Salem meeting, the largest group
of local Quakers, small disorders seemed less likely to
blossom into the seditious activities reminiscent of the
most hateful of the visitors.

Yet having using sedition to justify the punishment of
Quakers, the General Court still left unresolved the degree to which personal reputation might influence the
operations of justice. The Court, by its reliance upon a
secular definition of criminality, had to predict the oc-
currence of extraordinary disorder from an individual's
character and past behavior. Indeed, the process of
mitigating penalties because of familiarity with the
personal background of the accused had been demonstrated
within the General Court. The Court's treatment of Upshall contrasted with that of the Smiths and Trask because of the different social and legal contexts of the
cases. By coming to Boston, the Salem Quakers had changed
the venue of their crimes. In Boston, they faced a judicial system more concerned with curtailing sedition, while
less familiar, less caring, and thus less likely to allow
the personal backgrounds of the accused to compensate for
the implications of their disorderly behavior.[57]

As the General Court tried to become more systematic
in its attempts to suppress domestic Quakerism, it required the use of county court mechanisms that obstructed
the superior court's intent. Trying to suppress Quaker
heterodoxy through the use of civil institutions was one
means of preserving the separation of church and state;
yet it also meant choosing between civil and ecclesiastical criteria for determining patterns of continued
communal association. By choosing the civil criteria,
the General Court and Massachusetts Bay allowed the rise
of a rudimentary form of religious toleration, especially
as circumstances placed greater responsibility for the
suppression of local Quakerism upon the county courts.
Within the counties, the use of inferior judicial jurisdictions would reinforce the importance of secular criteria of personal behavior, influence, and connection.
A county court composed of friends, business associates,
and relatives of Quakers would be even less likely to see
those Quakers as subversive and seditious merely because
they preferred to absent themselves from orthodox services. Furthermore, the persistence of local meetings in
Kittery and Salem in the face of prosecution undermined
the accusations that anarchy would emerge out of Quaker
actions. Every month and year that passed without the
creation of a Muenster belied the original justification
for continued prosecution and suppression. Invariably,
the disturbances connected with the practices of local

Quakerism proved to be neither unexpected nor extraordinary. Once the local courts demonstrated their minimal fear of sedition by their increasingly haphazard and diffident enforcement of anti-Quaker legislation, the justifications for continuing the suppression of the sect by higher judicial levels became virtually impossible. To have attempted to sustain charges of sedition against Quakers without specific evidence of disorder would have placed the civil magistracy in the position of punishing men for their consciences. Yet with the exception of Jesuits, other Catholics, and atheists, where the threat of subversion was patently obvious, civil authorities did not have the power to punish men solely for their heterodoxy without breaching the barriers erected between church and state and violating another fundamental axion of life in Puritan Massachusetts.

Finally, the Restoration of Charles II encouraged the General Court to delegate responsibility for the prosecution of all Quakers to the lower courts. Royal challenges to the Bay Colony's autonomy were impressed upon it in many ways, not the least of which was its freedom to punish all Quakers with impunity. Just as questions of economic regulation and political sovereignty came to involve decisions made at Charles's court, so too were those regarding Quakers, who, by the fact of their treatment by Bay Puritans, had common cause with Stuart office holders and courtiers. But as the General Court was to discover, Quakers might be a useful example to show the colony's continued need for freedom from imperial interference. Moreover, the county courts could continue to punish Quakers while avoiding criticism for those actions by Quakers in England.

NOTES

1. John Norton, The Heart of New England Rent (Cambridge, Mass., 1659), pp. 52-53.

2. Nathaniel B. Shurtleff, ed. Records of the Governor and Company of the Massachusetts Bay in New England, 1628-1686, 5 vols. in 6 parts (Boston, 1853-54), 4, pt. 1:314 (hereafter referred to as Mass. Records).

3. Richard D. Pierce, ed., Records of the First Church of Boston, 1630-1868, Colonial Society of Massachusetts Publications, vols. 39-41 (Boston, 1961), 39:52-53.

4. Shurtleff, Mass. Records, 4, pt. 1:279. General Court Order Regarding Nicholas Upshall, 28 October 1656, Massachusetts Archives, 10:238, State House, Boston. Nathaniel B. Shurtleff, ed., Records of the Colony of New Plymouth in New England, 1620-1692, 12 vols. (Boston, 1855-61), 3:111. For an evaluation of Upshall's assets, see Suffolk County, Massachusetts Registry of Deeds, Suffolk Deeds, 14 vols. (Boston, 1880-1906), 3:200, and a copy of his will, 9 August 1666, Suffolk County Court Files, no. 2650, New Suffolk County Court House, Boston.

5. That the Court later allowed Upshall to return in 1659 and remain, albeit under house arrest, may have reflected its feeling that it had acted precipitously in banishing him and that it sensed that there was a distinction between his actions and those of the visiting Quakers. Shurtleff, Mass. Records, 4, pt. 2:120.

6. Ibid., 4, pt. 1:277-78.

7. Ibid., pp. 349, 388-89.

8. Henry Fell to Margaret Fell, 19 December 1656, quoted in James Bowden, The History of the Society of Friends in America, 2 vols. (London, 1854), 1:55, Rufus M. Jones, The Quakers in the American Colonies (1911; rept. New York, 1962), p. 65. The figures are extrapolated from the first indictments of 30 June 1658, Essex County Court Files, 4:67-69, Essex Institute, Salem, Mass. See Appendix 1. On Norris's hostility to Antinomian and Anabaptist tendencies, see Stephen Foster, "New England and the Challenge of Heresy, 1630-1660: The Puritan Crisis in Transatlantic Perspective," William and Mary Quarterly, 3d ser., 38 (1981):637-39, and Philip F. Gura, A Glimpse of Sion's Glory: Puritan Radicalism in New England, 1620-1660 (Middletown, Conn. 1984), pp. 145-47.

9. See the complaint of Richard Waldron to the General Court, 13 December 1662, Massachusetts Archives, 3:262. Also see Result of an Agitation by the Commissioners of Ferdinando Gorges Esq., att. Wells in Charles Thornton Libbey et al., eds., Province and Court Records of Maine, 6 vols. (Portland, Me., 1928-75), 1:196-98. Shurtleff, Mass. Records, 4, pt. 1:245, 263.

10. George Bishop, New England Judged by the Spirit of the Lord (1661; rept. London, 1703), pp. 50-53. Sidney Perley, The History of Salem, Massachusetts, 3 vols. (Salem, Mass., 1924-27), 2:246.

11. Prior to 1657, magistrates in the county courts rarely used the 1656 statute unless the individual cited was implicated in other minor offenses. Often, an indictment for absence would be withdrawn when it was discovered

that the accused was unable to attend services because of
illness. Fines collected were also a means of compounding
the penalty or providing one when no single infraction
seemed justified on other grounds. The citation of
Cassandra Southwick here indicated more than a problem of
a chronic absence despite the court's charge of her
"usual absenting herself." The citation was unusual by
its failure to specify other charges. Thomas G. Barnes,
ed., The Book of the General Lawes and Libertyes Concerning the Inhabitants of the Massachusetts (1648; rept. San
Marino, Calif., 1975), p. 20; Salem Court Records,
1655-66, June Term, 1657, no. 44, Essex Institute, Salem,
Mass. For a further discussion on the regulation of
church absence, see Emil Cberholzer, Jr., Delinquent
Saints: Disciplinary Action in the Early Congregational
Churches of Massachusetts (New York, 1956), pp. 45-56.

    12. Salem Court Records, 1655-66, June Term, 1658,
no. 49. Although Harnet was cited for absence with two
known Quakers, I do not believe that Harnet was a Quaker
and driven out of town by the fines, as Perley claims in
The History of Salem, 2:246. Harnett left town in August
1658 under, from the town's perspective, honorable circumstances. Entrusted with the care of a town ward and
her son, Harnett relieved the town of any further financial responsibility when he left town. William P.
Upham et al., eds., Town Records of Salem, Massachusetts,
1634-1691, 3 vols. (Salem, Mass., 1868-1934), 1:128-19.
Also see Bishop, New England Judged, p. 44.

    13. Salem Court Records, 1655-66, June Term, 1658,
nos. 48, 50-51.

    14. Richard D. Pierce, ed., Records of the First
Church in Salem, Massachusetts, 1629-1736 (Salem, Mass.,
1974), p. 11 (hereafter referred to as Salem Church
Records). Perley, The History of Salem, 2:244-45.
Bishop, New England Judged, p. 51. Bishop believed that
Shattock had been fined twenty pounds. While he had been
indicted for absence in November 1657, Shattock has no
record of such a large fine in either the county or
General Court records. The possibility exists that the
fines may have been levied and not recorded, but this is
unlikely in view of the completeness of both county court
and General Court records, the redundancy in the Essex
County Court files, and the smaller fine, compared to the
Southwicks, he received on 8 March 1658. Salem Court
Records, 1655-66, June Term, 1658, no. 51; Essex County
Court Files, 3:145.

    15. Shurtleff, Mass. Records, 4, pt. 1:308-9; also
see H. Fell to M. Fell, 19 December 1656 in Bowden,
History of the Friends in America, 1:55.

16.   Shurtleff, Mass. Records, 4, pt. 1:321.

17.   Ibid., pp. 124-25.

18.   Richard P. Gildrie, Salem, Massachusetts, 1626-1683: A Covenant Community (Charlottesville, Va., 1975), pp. 149-52.   Also see chapter 6.

19.   Libbey, Maine Court Records, 2:113, and Waldron to the General Court, 13 December 1662, Massachusetts Archives, 3:262.   John Hull, "Diary," Archelogia Americana, 3 (1857):206.   Also see chapter 5.

20.   Essex County Court Files, 4:67-70.   Salem Court Records, 1655-66, June Term, 1658, nos. 19, 51.

21.   Salem Court Records, 1655-66, June Term, 1658, nos. 55-78.

22.   Ipswich Court Records, 1646-66, September Term, 1658, no. 31, Essex Institute, Salem, Mass.

23.   Two of those cited, Anne Needham and Sarah Southwick, received the largest fines of fifty and fifty-five shillings, respectively, indicating the lack of correlation between the size of the fines and the court's perception of the depth of seditious intent.   Salem Court Records, 1655-66, June Term, 1658, nos. 55-78.

24.   A. L. Beier, "Vagrants and the Social Crder in Elizabethan England," Past and Present, 64 (1974):23. For an important discussion of the role of the locality, law, and order in seventeenth-century England, see Keith Wrightson, "Two Concepts of Order: Justices, Constables, and Jurymen in Seventeenth-Century England," in An Ungovernable People: The English and Their Law in the Seventeenth and Eighteenth Centuries, ed. John Brewer and John Styles (New Brunswick, N.J., 1980), p. 25.

25.   Lawrence Southwick maintained that he was detained illegally and should have been released.   To the Essex County Court, 16 July 1658, Essex County Court Files, 4:75.

26.   Southwick listed himself, his wife Cassandra, his son Josiah, Shattock, and Buffum as the only prisoners from Salem.   Essex County Court Files, 4:75.   Pierce, Salem Church Records, pp. 12, 17.

27.   The town subsidy for the glassworks may be found
in Upham et al., Salem Town Records, 1:89.   Only twenty-
five percent (49 of 199) of the estates probated in Salem
before 1660 exceeded the Southwicks' in value, and the
Southwick assets were greater by about a third than the
average estate of town residents (174 pounds, 6 shillings,
7 pence).   Donald Koch, "Income Distribution and Political
Structure in Seventeenth-Century Salem," Essex Institute
Historical Collections, 105 (1969):54.   George F. Dow,
ed., Probate Records of Essex County, Massachusetts,
3 vols. (Salem, Mass., 1916-20), 1:318-19.   Pierce, Salem
Church Records, p. 8.

28.   Salem Court Records, 1655-66, June Term, 1658.
Perley, The History of Salem, 1:10n.; 2:268n.   James D.
Phillips, Salem in the Seventeenth Century (Boston, 1933),
pp. 139, 143, 197.

29.   Joshua Buffum prospered in Salem during the
1660's and after.   His account book reveals the patronage
of a broad spectrum of Salem's commercial community, including William Trask, Henry Bartholomew, and Bartholomew
Gedney, all of whom were alleged to be opposed to the
Quakers.   The patronage of Gedney is a particularly ironic
note for it was commonly held that the trials of the Quakers took place in his tavern.   At his death in 1705,
Buffum had assets of 604 pounds, 10 shillings.   His father
had had assets of about 270 pounds.   J. Buffum, Account
Book, 1655-1702, Buffum Family Papers, Essex Institute,
Salem, Mass.   Dow, Essex Probate Records, 1:174-76, 210,
257.   On the antipathy of Trask et al. toward the Quakers,
see Gildrie, Salem, pp. 134, 137.   Also see Walter N.
Buffum, "Notes Relating to Robert Buffum and His Children"
(unpublished manuscript, n.d.), Caleb Buffum, "An Account
of the Buffum Family" (unpublished manuscript, 1875), and
a notarized copy of Joshua Buffum's will, all of which are
also in the Buffum Family Papers.

30.   Southwick to Essex County Court, 16 July 1658,
Essex County Court Files, 4:75.

31.   Robert Pope, The Half-Way Covenant: Church Membership in Puritan New England (Princeton, N.J., 1969),
especially chapter 1.   William McLoughlin, New England
Dissent, 1630-1833: The Baptists and the Separation of
Church and State, 2 vols. (Cambridge, Mass., 1971),
1:49-56.   Despite an early, tenuous connection to the
Quakers through Thomas Macy, dissidents in Salisbury remained orthodox.   Caleb A. Wall, The Puritans vs. the
Quakers: A Review of the Persecutions of the Early Quakers and Baptists in Massachusetts (Worcester, Mass., 1888),
pp. 41-42, incorrectly, though understandably, identified
the Salisbury group as Quakers.   While Macy subsequently
migrated to Nantucket and became a Quaker, he also established clearly his distance from the Quakers in November

1659 when he was admonished for entertaining Quaker
Edward Wharton. At the time he was part of a group of
dissidents trying to establish a separate but orthodox
congregation in Salisbury. Shurtleff, Mass. Records, 4,
pt. 1:341, 351-52, 378, 390-91, 393-94, 407, and D.
Hamilton Hurd, The History of Essex County, Massachusetts
with Biographical Sketches of Many of Its Prominent Men,
2 vols. (Philadelphia, 1888), 2:1496, 1498. Arthur
Worrall sees Nantucket's conversion coming much later and
as a result of islanders attempting to resist an established Puritan church. Quakers in the Colonial Northeast
(Hanover, N.H. and London, 1980), pp. 72-73.

    32. Ipswich Court Records, 1646-66, September Term,
1658, no. 31.

    33. David T. Konig, Law and Society in Puritan
Massachusetts: Essex County, 1629-92 (Chapel Hill, N.C.,
1979), pp. 26-27. George Lee Haskins, Law and Authority
in Early Massachusetts: A Study in Tradition and Design
(New York, 1960), pp. 72-73, 76, 212-13. See also
Wrightson, "Two Concepts of Order," pp. 25-32 for the
English experience.

    34. Both Richard Gildrie and Christine Young believe
that Hathorne was an opponent and thus a persecutor of
Quakers; however, they differ on his place in Salem
politics. Young sees strong connections between Hathorne
and Batter that made the former a representative of the
town's emerging commercial interests and an opponent of
Joseph Boyce, a Quaker selectman and a defender of the
town's agrarian interests. Gildrie sees Hathorne as a
supporter of the agrarian faction but not of Boyce.
Gildrie, Salem, pp. 133-36, 149-50, and Young, From Good
Order to Glorious Revolution: Salem, Massachusetts 1628-
1689 (Ann Arbor, Mich., 1980), pp. 50-51. For my position
on Hathorne and Salem town politics during this period,
see chapters 2 and 5.

    35. Shurtleff, Mass. Records, 4, pt. 1:346, 349.

    36. Ibid., p. 349.

    37. Ibid., pp. 346, 349.

    38. The Essex County Court remitted Brackett's fine
in 1660. Ibid., p. 347, and Essex County Court Files,
5:108.

    39. Shurtleff, Mass. Records, 4, pt. 1:345-57, 367.

    40. Ibid., p. 366.

    41. Mary Hamor to the General Court 17 May 1659,
Massachusetts Archives, 10:250.

42. Bishop claimed that dropping the attempt to sell the Southwick children into servitude was an assertion of the humanity of Massachusetts's shipmasters who, he supposed, refused to transport them. Gildrie ascribes the failure to a general revulsion against the growing severity of the Quaker punishments. While both explanations are plausible, they need to consider the broader context in which the sentence was passed. Punishments like these were common solutions to the problems of indebtedness. More important, it seems unlikely that in view of shipmasters' cooperation with the Bay Colony's prohibition of visiting Quakers no one could be found who was willing to profit from the Quakers' plight. Also, if Bishop's contention is correct, he would substantiate my assertion that local concerns superseded the belief that Quakers were seen as threats to order solely because of their religious beliefs. While Gildrie's view is in less direct conflict with mine, I believe that he underestimates the extent to which residence and local influence reduced the severity of the punishments. Bishop, New England Judged, p. 46; Gildrie, Salem, p. 135; Perley, The History of Salem, 2:257; and Jones, Quakers in the American Colonies, p. 77.

43. Shurtleff, Mass. Records, 4, pt. 1:389.

44. Ibid., pp. 406-7.

45. Ibid., pp. 407, 410.

46. Ibid., p. 411.

47. Ibid., pp. 410-11.

48. Ibid., p. 433.

49. Ibid.

50. Phillips, Salem in the Seventeenth Century, p. 175. Smith reported being jailed on 6 September 1660, to Joshua Buffum on 4 November 1660 in Perley, The History of Salem, 2:262. Salem Court Records, 1655-66, June Term, no. 62.

51. Smith to Buffum, 4 November 1660, in Perley, The History of Salem, 2:262. Shurtleff, Mass. Records, 4, pt. 1:419.

52. Upshall was in London on 17 May 1661. W. Noel Sainsbury, ed., Calendar of State Papers: Colonial, 1661-1668 (London, 1880), no. 89. Shurtleff, Mass. Records, 4, pt. 1:419.

53. Dorothy Upshall to the General Court, 20 August 1666, Massachusetts Archives, 10:282. Shurtleff, _Mass. Records_, 4, pt. 2:50.

54. Shurtleff, _Mass. Records_, 4, pt. 1:337; pt. 2:50.

55. Ibid., 4, pt. 1:337. Chamberlain may have been part of the more enthusiastic Perrotonian wing that was sub-sequently purged by George Fox. Worrall, _Quakers in the Colonial Northeast_, pp. 29-31. In his will, Upshall left his greatcoat to Chamberlain's children, who had moved to Newport. Chamberlain died eight months before Upshall. Suffolk County Court Files, no. 2650, and Rhode Island Monthly Meeting Records: Deaths, 1647-75, p. 2, the New England Yearly Meeting of Friends Manuscript Collection, Rhode Island Historical Society Library, Providence.

56. City of Boston, _Second Report of the Record Commissioners of the City of Boston Containing the Boston Records, 1634-1660/61_ (Boston, 1877), pp. 80, 120-21. _Seventh Report...Boston Records, 1660-1694_ (Boston, 1877), pp. 2, 6, 15, 21, 25, 97.

57. The punishment of the Smiths, Trask, and Upshall by the General Court may be seen as the superior court's assumption of the jurisdiction of a lower court. Darrett Rutman believes that the Suffolk County Court functions were superseded by the General Court. _Winthrop's Boston: Portrait of a Puritan Town, 1630-1649_ (New York, 1965), p. 235n. In the absence of Suffolk County Court records for the early seventeenth century, it would appear that Rutman is correct. Also, because one could appeal decisions of the county court to the Court of Assistants (the General Court acting in its judicial capacity), there would have been great temptation to avoid a superfluous intermediate step in resolving legal difficulties and to file one's case before the equally accessible, especially for Boston and its nearby environs, but superior legal body. There is, however, some evidence in the file papers that indicate that the Suffolk County Court may have been more active than Rutman supposes. Regardless of whether the Suffolk or General Court assumed jurisdiction over the Quakers, because they were from Salem, these particular Quakers had placed themselves at the mercy of courts removed from their residence. Examination of the Quakers, 12 November 1659, Massachusetts Archives, 10:262-63.

5
The Restoration, Quakers, and the General Court

For the Bay Colony Puritan, the contrasting developments
of the release of Quakers from their English prisons and
the display of the head of Hugh Peter, regicide and former
Salem minister, atop Tower Bridge were clear reminders of
the shift political fortune took in the aftermath of the
Restoration. Many saw in the Restoration the opportunity
to use the colony's lack of favor at court to redress old
grievances and secure new political and personal interests.
The execution of the four Quakers and the exclusion of
Anglicans from the franchise were tangible manifestations
of Puritan hostility that suggested a common focus of
action. Prominent Friends like Edward Burroughs and
George Fox also saw an opportunity to use the antipathy of
Anglicans and royalists for things Puritan to argue for
the establishment of religious toleration on both sides of
the Atlantic. Exploiting the temporary weakness of Massachusetts, Burroughs and Fox arranged an audience for two
victims of Puritan persecution, Samuel Shattock and
Nicholas Upshall, to petition for royal nullification of
the colony's capital punishment law for Quakers and thereby commit the Crown to a rudimentary form of religious
toleration.[1]
   The access of their Quaker opponents to sources of
royal influence spurred the Puritans to counter with representations of their own to defend their treatment of
the Quakers and to reassert their claims to continued
autonomy in the handling of their local affairs. Among
the flurry of its first communications to the Crown after
its restoration was the General Court's strongly worded
defense of its charter privileges. The General Court
further instructed its colonial agents in England to make
clear the sanctity of the charter and the practical need
for preserving the local autonomy that it guaranteed. To
allow individuals to weaken the charter by circumventing
it with appeals to the Crown was most dangerous. It would

lead, the General Court claimed, to a fatal questioning
of all authority in Massachusetts Bay. "No appeale," the
General Court argued, "may be permitted from hence in any
case civil or criminal which would be such an intolerable
and unsupportable burthen as this poore place (at this
distance) are not able to indulge but would render authorities and government vain and ineffectual."[2]

The Bay Colony presented the obviously seditious
nature of Quakers as an example of the kind of phenomena
that threatened disorder and that could be avoided if the
charter's privileges were preserved. "Such was their
dangerous and impetuous and desperate turbulence both
to religion and state, civil and ecclesiasticall," that
Quakers had compelled the General Court to harry them out
of the colony or to hang them. If the Crown listened to
the Quakers and allowed them to return to Massachusetts
under royal protection, it would violate the charter and
the colony's local authority and, more significantly,
imperil its ability to preserve the public peace.[3]

Yet the use of Quakerism as an issue in support of its
case against royal interference in colonial affairs proved
to be a mistake once the colony discovered that the king's
distaste for Quakerism did not dampen his efforts to curb
Bay autonomy. Also, the General Court soon learned that
it could regulate Quakerism by foisting responsibility for
their punishment upon inferior local courts. As royal
intrusions into colonial affairs increased in other
spheres between 1661 and 1665, the General Court's concern
for the sanctity of the charter superseded its fear of
Quakerism's potential for seditious activity, confirming
the utility of using the local courts to regulate what was
coming to be seen as a less serious threat to public
peace.

Despite the early activities of Burroughs and Fox in
London, the Crown seemed hesitant to support Quakers at
the expense of Massachusetts. Showing little sense of
urgency in stopping the executions of Quakers, Charles
shuttled the Shattock-Upshall petition to the Council for
Foreign Plantations, where it languished for five months.
In September 1661, a year after Burroughs began his attempt to obtain the suspension of capital punishment for
Quakers in Massachusetts, the Council ordered that the
Crown review all Massachusetts cases in which Quakers were
condemned. The order had no impact on any pending executions. Three months previously, the General Court had
suspended the sentence of death for a Quaker in exchange
for his agreement to leave the colony.[4]

Although it had issued the order, the Crown made no
great effort to notify Massachusetts of the fact. When
the Crown did make its will known, it exhibited to the
Puritans a corrupted view of its intentions. Seeing the
procrastination of the Crown, Burroughs suggested that
Salem Quaker Samuel Shattock, at his own expense, carry
the writ suspending the capital punishment law to Boston.[5]

The order to review the sentences of condemned Quakers
alone would have been seen as part of the Crown's attack
upon the charter, but the debate would have been over a
moot issue. With the departure of Wenlock Christison, the
last Quaker to receive a sentence of hanging, there were
no candidates immediately liable to the death penalty,
nor, in light of the apparent success of the colony's
anti-Quaker programs, were there likely to be any in the
near future. Furthermore, the royal order neither re-
futed the claims of Massachusetts to its autonomy nor
precluded a confirmation of the right of the General Court
to hang Quakers for sedition. By sending Shattock ostensibly as a royal servant, the Crown presented the General
Court with a case that called for the immediate application of capital punishment, while simultaneously seeming
to limit its authority to do so. In Shattock, the Crown
impressed upon Massachusetts an image of an active and
unwelcome royal presence in colonial affairs.

When Shattock returned to Boston in September 1661,
he seemed intent upon causing a public disturbance. After
his arrival, Shattock, apparently expecting to be arrested, waited on board ship. When no one came, he walked to
the home of Governor John Endecott through a crowd that
had gathered in anticipation of the confrontation. At
Endecott's, Shattock interrupted a meeting called to
decide the General Court's reaction to him and challenged
the governor and assembled magistrates with his hat firmly
upon his head. In the face of this open disrespect for
his office and authority, Endecott ordered the offending
hat stripped from Shattock's head. Shattock responded by
presenting Endecott with the royal writ. After reading
the writ, Endecott, in a gesture that Shattock interpreted
as submission, returned the hat.[6]

The brief confrontation between Shattock and the representatives of the General Court triggered a debate over
the extent to which the colony would accept royal limitations upon its authority. Clearly, earlier strongly
worded statements defending colonial autonomy only had
provoked the Crown to support one of the Bay Colony's most
obstreperous enemies. For Endecott, the presentation of
the writ by Shattock and his apparent immunity from further punishment was not only a personal affront to his
gubernatorial dignity, it was a repudiation of his political tactics in defense of the charter. Endecott was the
leader of the faction that historian Paul Lucas labelled
the commonwealth and that had been responsible for the
strong statements defending colonial autonomy the previous
December. Shattock's return precipitated a shift of political sentiment in the Court toward the moderate position.
While the moderates agreed with the commonwealthmen on
the sanctity of the charter, they feared that strong
statements would only stimulate further royal intrusions
into colonial affairs and thus argued for more moderate
language in the colony's defense of its autonomy.[7]

Compared to the moderates, the commonwealth's more outspoken defense of colonial privileges did not correspond to an insistence for harsher treatment of Quakers. While Quaker historians have accused Endecott of being the instigator of many Friends' punishments, those who suffered in Massachusetts noted Endecott's more temperate behavior.[8] Also, William Hathorne, an Endecott supporter in the General Court and his successor as the dominant political figure in Salem, had a reputation for being more tolerant of Quakers.[9] Commonwealthmen would have had less reason to be preoccupied with the threat that Quakers allegedly posed to order. From the commonwealth perspective, the issue of Quakerism was of less consequence than the need to defend colonial autonomy. An autonomous colony would be as free to resolve the problems Quakers caused as it had been during the Interregnum.

The moderates were far more obvious in their hatred of the Quakers. Most of the colony's ministers, including John Norton of Boston and John Higginson of Salem, supported the moderates and were quite vocal in their condemnation of Quakers. Boston selectman John Hull, an advocate of hanging the Quakers, supported General Court moderates Simon Bradstreet and Thomas Clark, both of whom were anti-Quaker. Both Clark and Hull had signed the Boston petition urging the General Court to pass the death penalty for Quakers, and Bradstreet had been active in the attempt to have Rhode Island prohibit the entry of visiting Quakers from England.[10]

Quakerism, it would appear, provided moderates with an issue that allowed them to defend colonial autonomy while remaining ostensibly subordinate to royal authority. When, for example, the king interfered with colonial courts by demanding the review of all cases involving condemned Quakers, he unwittingly encouraged their seditious activities. If he were made aware of this, argued moderates, he "would be farr from giving them such favor" and see the necessity of allowing the colony great latitude in the handling of its affairs.[11] At the same time, the moderates could attack the commonwealthmen for failing to stop royal interference in colonial affairs and for pursuing policies that freed Quakers.

Because, however, the moderates could not both demonstrate the compatability of royal control and colonial autonomy and defy the writ staying the Quaker executions, their supremacy in the General Court could not be translated immediately into action against the Quakers. As a gesture of compliance with what seemed to be the implications of the Shattock mission, the moderates suspended capital and corporal punishment laws. The suspensions were expected to be temporary; the Court also delegated John Norton and Simon Bradstreet to go to England and inform the Crown fully of the Bay Colony's situation. The two men were to make clear the colony's continued need to be free to punish Quakers.[12]

Although the king had endorsed more restrictive policies for the Quakers, the General Court still did not restore the death penalty.   After Shattock's return in 1661,
the colony confronted a number of individuals who might
have been exiled or hanged under the old legislation.
Shattock, who returned to live in Salem and continued to
attend the Quaker meeting, was one candidate for hanging,
as was Nicholas Upshall, under house arrest in Dorchester.
Executing Shattock and Upshall might have been unpalatable
because of their status as inhabitants, but there were
also a number of visiting Quakers who courted the hangman.
Elizabeth Hooten was in the colony four times between 1661
and 1665.   Ann Coleman was arrested twice in 1662 and 1663.
On her second visit, Coleman accompanied Joseph Nicholson,
a Quaker already under sentence of hanging if he were
found in the colony.   In none of these cases were Quakers
threatened with hanging or banishment upon pain of death.[15]

During their stay in London, Norton and Bradstreet had
had difficulty justifying the executions of the Quakers.
The reasons that had seemed so pressing in Boston lacked
compulsion in Restoration London.   While Fox believed that
Norton and Bradstreet were afraid that they would be held
legally liable for the colony's persecution of Quakers,
the absence of any real Quaker influence upon the Crown
made that a slight possibility.[16]   Rather, Norton and
Bradstreet must have sensed the awkwardness of their
position.   While they justified Bay policy as a product
of their desire to preserve order, they could not be seen
as being opposed to religious toleration, a cause then
being championed by Quakers and the colony's natural political allies, the Nonconformists.   Moreover, to oppose
toleration might well lead to demands that Bay Puritans
conform to Anglicanism.   Also, others, for more particular
narrow interests, used Bay intolerance to justify royal
interference with the ecclesiastical and civil polity of
Massachusetts.[17]

To continue to hang Quakers would have kept the image
of religious intolerance alive as the Crown contemplated
its policies on colonial autonomy.   Thus, to be able to
continue the regulation of Quakers, the General Court
shifted primary responsibility for their punishment to
local and county institutions.   To close the colony again
to visiting Quakers, the Court restored corporal punishment by lifting the suspension of the Cart's Tail Ordinance.   Passed in early 1661 as a means for expelling
visiting Quakers, the law relied upon local constables for
its enforcement.   Town constables were to arrest any
visiting Quakers found within their jurisdiction, tie them
to the tail of a cart, whip them, and deliver them to the
constables of the neighboring town where the process was
to be repeated until the offender was outside the boundaries of the colony.   When the Court restored the law, it
did not revive the use of capital punishment for repeat
offenders, and it limited the number of towns through

which the Quakers could be whipped to three.[18]   The assign-
ment of the responsibility for the Quakers to local authorities and the absence of the capital punishment provision reduced the visibility of the Court's enforcement
machinery.   The Court made seditious Quakerism, in effect,
a misdemeanor to be enforced by the colony's smallest
legal unit.   The issue was thus placed beneath the attention of a distant royal government.   It was one thing for
the Crown to be concerned with cases of juridical murder
and another to meddle in the petty disturbances of the
nation's smallest legal jurisdiction.
    Furthermore, the application of a largely dispersed
and relatively autonomous means of regulation permitted
the abuse of visiting Quakers outside the letter of the
law.   When Alice Ambrose, Mary Tompkins, and Ann Coleman
arrived in Dover in 1662 after having been whipped out of
the jurisdiction once before, their subsequent suffering
illustrated the considerable latitude for discretionary
punishment local magistrates had.   Tompkins was beaten a
second time; Ambrose, dragged through the snow and placed
in stocks; and Coleman, denied shelter by the constables'
order after she had fallen into a river during freezing
winter weather.   The varied and severe punishments convinced Tompkins and Ambrose not to return again, but not
Coleman.   Returning in 1663, she was stripped to the
waist, tied to a post, and flogged on her back and chest.
According to Quaker sources, her wounds became infected
and she nearly died.[19]   Only this last scourging apparently convinced Coleman not to return to Massachusetts.
    The vigorous harassment of these women demonstrated
another facet of local justice.   Under the law, the General Court had created a pervasive mechanism of enforcement.   Each local unit could inflict the maximum punishment.   By entrusting the initiation of the Cart's Tail
Ordinance to the local constable or court, the General
Court empowered its smallest unit to banish visitors
despite the supposed restriction of that jurisdiction to
the Court of Assistants.   When a constable ordered the
removal of an individual, succeeding jurisdictions were
bound by a spirit of cooperation to remove the malefactor.
When the Suffolk County Court ordered Sarah Mills to be
whipped in succeeding towns until she was returned to her
home in Scarborough, the constables of Wenham and Rowly
complied since Suffolk's cooperation had been instrumental
in helping them expel Coleman and her companions.[20]
    The punishment of Mills, "a knowne Vagabond Quaker,"
further illustrated the continuing problem the sect posed.
Although a resident of the colony, Mills revealed the
ability of Quakerism to sway the minds of the weak and
disaffected.   Her obnoxious behavior in 1668 followed the
patterns established by other Quakers when she "in an
Audatious manner came into the meeting of Boston and there
publiquely affronted the Reverend minister."[21]   Mills was
the center of a particularly disorderly group of converts

in Scarborough who substantiated the belief that Quakerism
encouraged disorder among the eccentric.[22]
    The proliferation of local Quakers like Mills, as well
as the growth of the meetings in Kittery and Salem, troubled moderates like Hull who noted an increasing reluctance on the part of local communities to suppress the
rise of Quaker activity. In 1662, the General Court attempted to encourage the county courts to be more active
in the suppression of religious heterodoxy. In March, it
ordered the town of Boston to be more vigilant and con-
scientious in reporting the meetings of dissidents. There
was a twofold irony in the Court order. First, while a
Quaker meeting had arisen in Boston, both Kittery and
Salem meetings which, in terms of absolute numbers and
in proportion to town populations, were far more significant than Boston's; and second, the object of the order
was not the Quakers but the emergent Baptists.[23]
    General Court pressure upon Kittery took other forms.
In response to his pleas, the Court granted Richard Waldron powers to prosecute all the Quakers guilty of disorder in Dover. In all likelihood, Dover had no resident
Quakers at the time; however, immediately across the
Piscataqua River, a number of Kittery residents had converted. By granting these powers to Waldron, the Court
not only demonstrated its distaste for the Kittery meeting
but, more significantly, showed its ability to favor a
political faction at its expense. Unlike the other Bay
counties that owed their origins to Massachusetts, York
was the result of a series of annexations of different
settlements that had taken place during the 1650's. In
the early sixties, two factions--one supporting Bay government, the other opposing it--vied for political supremacy in the county. Waldron represented the faction that
consistently supported the interests of the General Court.
Waldron's opponents not only had the misfortune of having
leaders who were Quaker but who, with the Restoration,
championed the claims of the heirs of Sir Ferdinando
Gorges to the proprietorship of the county. By favoring
Waldron and giving him free rein to punish his political
enemies, the Court struck at both challenges to its
authority in York.[24]
    The following year, the General Court took another step
to ensure the continuation of local control by factions
hostile to the Quakers and other religious dissidents.
Declaring that inhabitants who failed to yield to authority and who made it their religion to deny obedience to
magistrates were enemies to civil and ecclesiastical
government, the Court ordered the disenfranchisement of
"all persons, Quaker and others, which réfuse to attend
the public worship of God established here."[25] The disenfranchisement of Quaker dissidents further helped Waldron to expel his opponents from political office in
Kittery while undermining the political influence of
Quakers in Salem. In Salem, the disenfranchisement of

the Quakers, affecting as it did some ten percent of the
electorate, deprived commonwealthman William Hathorne of
a significant part of his constituency and strengthened
his political rivals in town and country.[26]

This last restriction upon Quakers hardly differed
from those placed upon Nonconformists in England. The
opprobrium that English Quakers heaped upon Massachusetts
for its persecution of the sect was intended to apply,
although more obliquely, to a wider audience. For if the
General Court were guilty of persecution, it did no more
than Parliament. By encouraging the harassment of Quakers and disenfranchising religious dissidents, the General
Court did only that enjoined by the Act of Uniformity.[27]
As such, the moderate position was relatively immune to
criticism except when royal authorities sought to bring
the specific, narrow religious qualifications for the
franchise under review. At issue in these instances was
not the Crown's sympathy for the Quakers but concern over
the political exclusion of Anglicans. But in its attempts
to support the few Anglicans concerned, the Crown again
raised fears that it would attack the colony's charter
privileges.[28]

The appointment of the Commission of 1664-65 to the
New Netherlands with the secondary task of reviewing the
activities of Massachusetts upset the political equilib-
rium within the General Court and gave rise to renewed
suspicion of royal intentions. The commission's visit,
however, had two somewhat contradictory effects upon
Quakers. First, it lessened the influence of the one
magistrate, Hathorne, who had acted in the Quaker interest.
Initially, the commission's presence caused a resurgence
of commonwealth influence, but the extreme statements
made by Hathorne and Endecott in defense of the charter
and a number of tactical errors convinced the bulk of the
General Court that such a posture would only provoke
further royal interference.[29] After Endecott's death in
1665, Hathorne found himself isolated and under attack by
moderates in the General Court and Salem and by royal
officials in England. Indeed, the Crown ordered the Bay
Colony to send a delegation, one of whose members had to
be Hathorne, to London to account for the colony's intem-
perate remarks. Fortunately for Hathorne, the General
Court did not comply with the request and diverted the
Crown's attention elsewhere, but he must have had little
comfort in the petition of Edmund Batter and thirty-three
other Salem townsmen urging that he be sent to England to
explain his actions to Charles II.[30]

Despite Hathorne's waning influence, the commission's
activities still did not cause a corresponding rise in
anti-Quaker activities by the General Court. The activities of the royal commission in 1665 indicated far more
troublesome threats to the well-being of the colony than
those posed by the Quakers. After the commission visited
New Amsterdam, it returned to Massachusetts and began to

demonstrate the ways in which royal intervention in
colonial affairs could disturb the peace of the colony.
To the dismay of the residents of York, the commission
recommended the separation of the county from Massachusetts and its establishment as the royal province of
Maine. Nowhere, however, were the actions of the commissioners so blatantly an attack upon the ability of the
colony to preserve order locally than in their willingness
to review the arson conviction of John Porter. By arro-
gating the right of judicial review in this case, the
commissioners directly challenged the claims of the colony
to the independence of its courts in a way calculated, it
seemed, to give men license to commit violent crimes
without fear of retribution.[31] Fortunately, from the
point of view of the colony, the General Court managed to
frustrate the commission's efforts in the Porter case and
sent it from the colony with only the temporary success
of having made York a royal colony. Because of Charles's
subsequent preoccupation with the Anglo-Dutch wars, there
was little time or inclination for further encroachments
upon the colony's charter, and fear of an active royal
influence in colonial affairs subsided after the commission's visit.[32]

The decline of the fear of royal interference did not
lead to renewed punishment of the Quakers. By the late
sixties, the General Court seemed to have sensed that it
had fashioned an adequate instrument of social control.
The numbers of visiting Quakers had declined, and the
county courts seemed to be able to control the local Quakers. Moreover, once reduced to the concern of the local
courts and magistrates, the Quakers no longer seemed as
dangerous. The seditious behavior once seen as governed
by uncontrollable passions came to be seen as more familiar forms of madness or hysteria and thus were more com-
prehensible. When Deborah Wilson first walked through
Salem nude in 1662 to demonstrate the spiritual barrenness
of the orthodox church, the county court treated her like
a visiting Quaker and ordered her to be whipped. When she
disturbed the town in a similar manner in 1668, the court
dismissed the charges because "she being distempered in
her head." Samuel Sewall, no great friend of Quakers,
described the appearance of Margaret Brewster in his
Boston church as an occasion of the "greatest and most
amazing uproar that I ever saw." That was his reaction.
Nowhere in his diary did Sewall rail against the timidity
of magistrates, urge stronger punishment, or condemn the
arrogance and false pride of the Quakers as his father-
in-law John Hull had done.[33]

In 1675 and 1677, the General Court attempted to renew
its assault upon local Quakers, but these last efforts
paled in comparison to its earlier efforts. In 1675, the
Court outlawed the Quaker meeting for the first time,
ordering all persons apprehended at one either to be disciplined at the House of Correction, kept at work, and fed

bread and water for three days or to pay a fine of five
pounds. In 1677, the Court further empowered constables
to break down doors if necessary to enforce the prohibitions against Quakers meeting.[34] The apparent harshness
of the prohibitions only masked the diminished fear of
Quakerism. While Quakers were prevented from meeting
legally, the penalties were relatively mild and, it would
appear, not enforced. Even the traditionally anti-Quaker
moderates did not see the laws as ends in themselves but
as preludes to larger reform efforts aimed at arresting
the more serious decline of church and commonwealth. By
enacting these measures first against the Quakers, the
moderates vainly hoped that the General Court would begin
and sustain a more general purge of all offensive social
and religious behavior. Yet, by combining anti-Quakerism
with prohibitions against long hair, periwigs, and the
wearing of garments inappropriate to one's social station,
the General Court only revealed the trivial nature of the
case made against the Quakers in the seventies. What was
at issue was not seditious behavior but a definition of
social dislocation about whose dangers not all men
agreed.[35]

   While the passage of the laws in the seventies indicated the continuation of anti-Quaker sentiment within
the General Court, there were no guarantees that the will
of the Court could be translated into actual enforcement
at the local or county level. Provisions attempting to
deal with the failure of constables to enforce the laws
proved ineffectual. Although the Court provided inform-
ants with a third of the fines assessed delinquent constables, there were no takers. After 1677, when the Court
reduced the fines upon delinquent constables, there were
still no indictments of constables for failing to suppress
Quaker meetings and no Quaker meetings suppressed. The
failure of the constables to enforce the new laws followed
the lead of magistrates who, according to Hull, "did not
permit any punishments to be inflicted on heretics as
such."[36] The colony had become so inured to the presence
of resident Quakers that Manassas Marston, the orthodox
son of a Quaker, was appointed a tithingman for Salem in
1679 despite his refusal to swear to the portion of the
oath that applied to Quakers.[37]

   During the seventies, other circumstances contributed
to the decline of Quakerism's seditious image. In 1672,
visiting Quakers Nicholas Alexander and Solomon Eccles
were banished from the colony. Superficially, the men
fit the model of Quaker disorder. They were agents sent
by George Fox to the local meetings and were supposed to
bring Massachusetts's Quaker meetings into the institutional network of the New England Yearly Meeting. What
was surprising about the expulsion was that neither man
was whipped and that there seemed to have been considerable protest against the Court's action. According to
William Coddington, the Quaker governor of Rhode Island,

a group of Boston merchants objected to the expulsions
because of the adverse effects they might have upon trade
between Rhode Island and Massachusetts.[38]

The reactions of the Boston merchants confirmed the
existence of fissures within the town's mercantile community that had begun with the Restoration. New merchants
arriving in the sixties seemed more concerned with profit
and trade than the criteria of religious virtue that seemed to mark the older generation of Hull. While Coddington's observation of the protest of the merchants may have
overstated the relative influence of the newer merchants,
men like Thomas Deane and Thomas Breedon added to the
confusion over the dangers the Quakers posed when they too
defied the civil and ecclesiastical institutions of Massachusetts Bay. Breedon by refusing to remove his hat before the General Court mocked the Court's preoccupation
with hat honor and obscured what had been, heretofore, an
obvious indicator of the Quakers' anti-social behavior.
The contempt was clear enough. But Breedon's sentiments
were common knowledge: he was no Quaker leveller protesting hierarchy, status, and deference. Rather, he saw
himself as a loyal subject of the Crown, and because he
had supported the activities of the royal commissioners in
1665 he was a royal agent and presumed that he did not
need to show obedience to a government that seemed to
oppose his king's wishes.[39]

Deane also obscured the criteria that seemed to
separate the Quakers from the rest of the colony. His
social and trade connections revealed the way in which
materialism weakened the thrust of the anti-Quaker moderate position. From his earliest experiences in Massachusetts, Deane found himself competing with moderate merchants like Joshua Scottow. Yet in his marriage to the
daughter of Salem's leading merchant William Browne,
Deane indicated the strange bedfellows the quest for
profit made. While moderates, Browne and Scottow had a
common point of opposition to Quakers and commonwealthmen,
Browne, Deane, and Quaker merchants like Joshua Buffum had
highly profitable business connections.[40]

Trade also played an important role in changing the
collective mind of the General Court with regard to Quakers. In 1674, two years before the General Court outlawed
the Quaker meeting, Boston allowed a visiting Quaker merchant to assume residence in the town. Nicholas Moulder
and his wife Christian could not be expelled from the
colony without giving offense to William Coddington.
Moulder was Coddington's commercial agent. Although
Moulder conducted a meeting that drew local residents,
the regulation of his activities never extended beyond
minor fines for his failure to attend the orthodox services. Neither the county nor the General Court made any
effort to halt what was an illegal Quaker meeting.[41]

The toleration of Moulder by Bay authorities contrasted with their intolerance of another Quaker, Alexander
Calman. But then there were significant differences

between the two men. Moulder was a merchant and well
connected; Calman, a shoemaker with no connections. Where
Moulder was content to meet with others of like mind in
the privacy of his home, Calman insisted upon interrupting
the services of a Boston church while wearing a bloody
coat. Between 2 September 1678 and 3 March 1679, the
county court fined Calman a total of six pounds and gave
him fifteen lashes for disturbing public services and for
opening a shop without the consent of the town selectmen.
Calman's refusal to abide by the external forms of orderly
behavior and his propensity to cause disorder were sufficient reasons for ordering his deportation from the
colony.[42]

The utility of attacking Quakerism as a threat to the
ordering of Massachusetts, while an important issue for
the moderates, was lost when the king agreed that Quakers
were a baleful lot fully deserving of punishment and still
tried to interfere in colonial affairs. In the years that
followed the Restoration, Quaker meetings in Boston, Salem,
Hampton, and Kittery never produced any disorder remotely
approaching anarchy. In contrast, the slightest hint of
royal interference offered far more destructive possibilities. Not only was there the threat of violence posed
by the granting of asylum to convicted felons like John
Porter, but even innocuous suggestions like making land
law consistent with common law precedents threatened the
colony with social and economic chaos. At the very moment that such suggestions were broached, older towns
like Salem were reaching their geographical limits and,
not coincidentally, becoming embroiled in bitter disputes
over titles. Any change in the rules of land tenure for
the sake of imperial consistency would have thrown all
ownership into question. With suggestions like these,
royal agents perpetuated the fear that royal encroachment
upon the charter would cause profound changes in colonial
institutions at immense cost.[43] These threats contrasted
with the activities of Quakers during the same period.
For even if they were disorderly, they never seemed to be
beyond the control of colonial institutions.

Furthermore, the emergence of forms of religious
diversity that were more acceptable and still threatened
the capacity of the General Court to maintain ecclesiastical orthodoxy and civil order militated against the fear
of Quakers who were, in theory, far more unacceptable and,
in actuality, far less dangerous to Massachusetts. Toleration of Baptists and Anglicans threatened to divide the
established order. Anglicans could not be barred from the
county without raising the specter of royal interference
in colonial affairs. More critically, Baptists emerged
out of Puritan congregations and often had the sympathies
of orthodox laymen. The support of a prominent merchant
like Simon Lynde and of fellow townsmen in Charlestown
provided Baptists with friends that limited the ability
of ministers and the orthodox to call upon the state for

the suppression of all religious dissidence. The growth
of open support for the Baptists graphically illustrated
the fissures among the orthodox that weakened further the
ability of ministers and others to insist upon conformity.
When William Turner and Edward Drinker were arrested in
1670, the magistrates had to veto a resolution by the
deputies calling for the release of the two Baptists.
Drinker noted that the Baptists' best advocates had been
the ministers of the Boston First Church who "laboured
abundantly...as if it had been their best friends in the
whole world." If regular ministers disagreed over the
proper response to heterodoxy, there could hardly be a
single, consistent plan recommended to the General
Court.[44] For, while Quakers had fewer friends and less
influence than Baptists or Anglicans, any degree of toleration or relaxation in the persecution of heterodoxy
worked in favor of those resident Quakers whose lives as
peaceful and contributing members of their communities
hardly differed from their neighbors.

Under these circumstances, orthodoxy in the middle of
the seventeenth century became increasingly difficult to
maintain. While Bay Puritans may have been sure of the
existence of an absolute religious truth, they were unsure of its forms in an imperfect world. In addition to
the growth of Quakerism and Baptists, the Puritan magistrates had to be concerned with the controversies issuing
out of the Half-Way Covenant. To the lay Puritans,
clerics, and magistrates, the division of congregations
over the criteria of membership must have been far more
troubling than the affairs of the few unregenerate Quakers who quietly absented themselves from regular services.[45] The unregenerate the world would always have;
but how could a model of Christian charity survive if its
saints were unsure of themselves?

If after all this, men could still regard Quakers with
suspicion, King Philip's War made impractical their continued harassment. Some societies are able to single out
dissidents and aliens as agents of subversion in times of
crisis; however, the Bay Colony had significant reasons
not to do so with Quakers. The racial and cultural similarities of Quakers and Puritans were far too obvious to
allow the slightest hint of a dangerous Quaker-Indian
alliance. "Is this a time," asked Baptist Peter Folger,
a former resident of both Massachusetts and New Plymouth,
"For you to press/ To draw the blood of those that are
your Neighbors and Your Friends/ As if you had not
Ties?"[46] The answer to Folger was to end the harassment
of Baptists and Quakers in the interest of pursuing the
war effort. When in October 1676, the Suffolk County
Court indicted Thomas Matson, the Boston jailer, for
failing to keep in custody a group of Boston Quakers,
he produced an order from Deputy Governor Samuel Symonds
authorizing their release. Despite the presence of
significant sentiment for sustaining the punishment of

the Quakers, other factors intervened. Symonds and the
General Court could not permit the punishment of Moulder
and the Boston Quakers without antagonizing William
Coddington and imperiling the inter-colonial cooperation
the Bay Colony needed to fight the Indians.[47]
     This recognition of the importance of matters of state
over the compulsion to suppress Quaker heterodoxy was
consistent with the Court's previous behavior. The General Court had thought that to be a Quaker, especially a
visiting one, was convincing evidence of sedition. But
its experiences with local Quakers and royal authority
had taught that there were greater threats to the peace
of the colony than those posed by the sect. Although the
General Court had granted increased responsibility to the
county courts partly to shield its treatment of Quakerism
from royal supervision, it had also done so in the belief
that they were adequate to meet the threat Quakers posed
to public peace. Moreover, the allocation of responsibility for the Quakers to the counties did not ensure that
anti-Quaker legislation would be enforced precisely as the
General Court wished, and their reactions to Quakers were
products of local circumstances as well as the will of the
General Court majority and the assumptions made about
Quakers. Once given the responsibility to treat Quakerism
on home ground, each county was free to make adjustments
to the sect within the context of the balance of its own
political, social, and economic interests and thereby
underscored the practical accommodations to the heterodox
person.

NOTES

     1. George Fox, Journal of George Fox, Being an
Historical Account of the Life, Travels, Sufferings,
Christian Experiences and Labours of Love in Christ,
2 vols. (London, 1891), 1:507-10. Representations to the
King, 17 May 1661, in W. Noel Sainsbury, ed., Calendar of
State Papers: Colonial, 1661-1668 (London, 1880), no. 89.

     2. General Court to John Leverett et al., 10
December 1660, Thomas Hutchinson, ed., Collection of
Original Papers Relative to the History of Massachusetts
Bay (Boston, 1769), pp. 328-31. Nathaniel B. Shurtleff
ed., Records of the Governor and Company of the Massachu-
setts Bay in New England, 1628-1686, 5 vols. in 6 parts
(Boston, 1853-54), 4, pt. 1:451 (hereafter referred to
as Mass. Records).

     3. Massachusetts General Court to King Charles II,
Hutchinson, Original Papers of Massachusetts, p. 328.

     4. King to Governor Endecott, 9 September 1661, in
Sainsbury, Calendar of State Papers: 1661-68, no. 168.
Shurtleff, Mass. Records, 4, pt. 2:24.

5. Fox, Journal, 1:510.

6. Shattock to Friends in London, 10 December 1661,
Chamberlain Manuscript Collection, Boston Public Library.

7. Paul Lucas, "Colony or Commonwealth, Massachusetts Bay, 1661-1666," William and Mary Quaterly, 3d
ser., 24 (1967):88-107.

8. See George Bishop's description of Endecott's
concern for the welfare of William Brend in New England
Judged by the Spirit of the Lord (1661; rept. London,
1703), pp. 68-69, and William Robinson to George Fox,
12 July 1659, Chamberlain Manuscript Collection.

9. William Sabine, Deposition, 13 June 1660 in
Nathaniel B. Shurtleff, ed., Records of the Colony of
New Plymouth in New England, 1620-1692, 12 vols. (Boston,
1855-61), 3:189.

10. Lucas, "Colony or Commonwealth," p. 94. John
Hull, "Diary," Archelogia Americana, 3 (1857):213.
Petition for More Stringent Laws on Quakers, October 1658,
Massachusetts Archives, 10:46, State House, Boston.
Bradstreet remained an opponent of Quakers throughout his
life. In 1683, two years after Massachusetts suspended
all of its laws regulating Quaker behavior, Bradstreet,
then governor of the colony, reacted to a Quaker request
for permission to preach in the colony thusly: "I have
read the books of some of your leaders and found them
most pernicious and heretical, and I should think it as
reasonable to let a Jesuit or Popish priest preach as
you." To James Martin, 27 March 1683, in J. W. Fortescue,
ed., Calendar of State Papers: Colonial 1681-1685
(London, 1898), no. 1022. Also see John Higginson to the
General Court, 6 June 1663, typewritten copy of the original manuscript owned by Lawrence Jenkins, Essex Institute,
Salem, Mass.

11. Instructions to the Delegates to the King, 4
January 1661, Massachusetts Archives, 106:46a.

12. Shurtleff, Mass. Records, 4, pt. 2:34.

13. John Hull, "Diary," pp. 153, 206.

14. King to Governor of Massachusetts Bay, 28 June
1662, in Salisbury, Calendar of State Papers: 1661-68,
no. 314.

15. Essex County Court Files, 8:42, Essex Institute, Salem, Mass. Shurtleff, Mass. Records, 4, pt. 2:50. On Hooten, see her journal in Henry J. Cadbury, "Early Quakers at Cambridge," Cambridge Historical Society Publications, 24 (1936-37):70-73. James Bowden, The History of the Society of Friends in America, 2 vols. (London, 1854), 1:253-55.

16. Fox, Journal, 1:511-12.

17. There was good cause for this. Twenty years later, the colony still had to respond to charges that it had executed loyal subjects, the Quakers, for their religious beliefs, charges born less of any sympathy for Quakers and more for justifying royal intervention in colonial affairs. Michael G. Hall, Edward Randolph and the American Colonies, 1676-1703 (New York, 1969), p. 34. Perry Miller, The New England Mind: From Colony to Province (Boston, 1961), pp. 127-28.

18. Shurtleff, Mass. Records, 4, pt. 2:59.

19. Bishop, New England Judged, p. 130.

20. Suffolk County Court Files, no. 871, New Suffolk County Court House, Boston. Joseph Besse, A Collection of the Suffering of the People Called Quakers, 1650-1689, 2 vols. (London, 1753), 2:232-33.

21. Suffolk County Court Files, no. 871.

22. Charles T. Libbey et al., Province and Court Records of Maine, 6 vols. (Portland, Me., 1928-75), 2:236-38.

23. The General Court had ordered the banishment of Boston resident Anne Gilliam in 1662 but had allowed her to remain after the return of Shattock and the petition of her husband. By 1666, Boston had a Quaker meeting to which Nicholas Upshall left a bequest. Proceedings of the Magistrates to Suppress Illegal Meetings, 27 March 1662, Massachusetts Archives, 10:277-78; General Court Order Relating to Anne Gilliam, May 1662, ibid., p. 278a; Benjamin Gilliam to the General Court 9 May 1662, ibid., pp. 278a, 279; and the Will of Nicholas Upshall, 9 August 1666, Suffolk County Court Files, no. 2650. For a further discussion on the Kittery and Salem meetings see chapters 5 and 6, respectively. On the problems of early Baptists, see William G. McLoughlin, New England Dissent, 1630-1833: The Baptists and the Separation of Church and State, 2 vols. (Cambridge, Mass., 1971), 1:49-72.

24. Shurtleff, Mass. Records, 4, pt. 2:69.

25. Ibid., p. 88.

26. Richard Gildrie, Salem, Massachusetts, 1626-1683: A Covenant Community (Charlottesville, Va., 1975), pp. 133-37, and below, chapter 6. Also see Christine Young, From Good Order to Glorious Revolution: Salem, Massachusetts, 1628-1689 (Ann Arbor, Mich., 1980), pp. 50-52.

27. Richard T. Vann, The Social Origins of English Quakerism, 1650-1750 (Cambridge, Mass., 1969), pp. 90-93.

28. David S. Lovejoy, The Glorious Revolution in America (New York, 1972), pp. 128-29. Lucas, "Colony or Commonwealth," pp. 99-102.

29. Lucas, "Colony or Commonwealth, pp. 103-5.

30. Hathorne made a public apology before the General Court. Shurtleff, Mass. Records, 4, pt. 2:149; Gildrie, Salem, p. 151; and James D. Phillips, Salem in the Seventeenth Century (Boston and New York, 1933), p. 208.

31. Lucas, "Colony or Commonwealth," pp. 105-6.

32. Ibid., p. 107.

33. Salem Court Records, 1655-66, June Term, 1662, no. 35, Essex Institute, Salem, Mass. Ibid., 1667-79, November Term, 1668, no. 58. Samuel Sewall, Diary, 1674-1729, 2 vols. ed. M. Halsey Thomas (New York, 1973), 1:44.

34. Shurtleff, Mass. Records, 5:60, 134.

35. For the ministers' sentiments see Sewall, Diary, 1:29-30. For the specific legislation, see Shurtleff, Mass. Records, 5:59-60.

36. Shurtleff, Mass. Records, 5:134, and Hull, "Diary," p. 236.

37. Essex County Court Files, 32:12, Essex Institute, Salem, Mass.

38. William Coddington to John Winthrop, Jr., 23 September 1672, Winthrop Papers, Collections of the Massachusetts Historical Society, 4th ser., vols. 6-7 (Boston, 1863-65), 7:291-92.

39. Bernard Bailyn, New England Merchants in the Seventeenth Century (New York, 1964), pp. 115-17. Suffolk County Court Files, no. 516.

40. Bailyn, New England Merchants, pp. 121-23. Gildrie, Salem, pp. 113, 134, 151.

41.   William Coddington, A Demonstration of True Love unto You the Rulers of the Colony of Massachusetts in New England (London, 1674), p. 3.   Samuel Eliot Morison and Zacheriah Chaffee, eds., Records of the Suffolk County Court, 1671-1680, Publications of the Colonial Society of Massachusetts, vols. 29-30 (Boston, 1933), 29:238, 274, 438-39.   John Noble, ed., Records of the Courts of Assistants of the Colony of the Massachusetts Bay, 1630-1692, 3 vols. (Boston, 1901-28), 1:12.   Testimony on Quakers by Moses Paine, 16 March 1674, Miscellaneous Bound Manuscripts, Massachusetts Historical Society, Boston.

42.   Morison and Chaffee, Records of the Suffolk County Court, 29:997.   City of Boston, Seventh Report of the Record Commissioners of the City of Boston Containing the Boston Records, 1660/1661-1694 (Boston, 1881), p. 125.

43.   Hall, Edward Randolph, pp. 21-41.   David T. Konig, "Community, Custom, and the Common Law: Social Change and the Development of Land Law in Seventeenth-Century Massachusetts," American Journal of Legal History, 18 (1974):137-77.

44.   This kind of division was further reflected in the degrees of toleration found by E. Brooks Holifield in Boston churches.   Holifield found that newer churches which were more flexible on admission standards were often less tolerant of heterodoxy.   Drinker to John Clarke and the Church at Newport, 30 November 1670, quoted in Nathan E. Wood, The History of the First Baptist Church of Boston (Philadelphia, 1899), p. 94.   Holifield, "On Toleration in Massachusetts," Church History, 38 (1969):197-98.   Richard Frothingham, The History of Charlestown (Charlestown, Mass., 1845), pp. 171-72.   Petition for the Release of the Baptists, 14 October 1668, Massachusetts Archives, 10:227.

45.   See, for example, Robert G. Pope, The Half-Way Covenant: Church Membership in Puritan New England (Princeton, N.J., 1969), pp. 150-60.

46.   Peter Folger, A Looking Glass for Our Times (1676; rept. Newport, R.I., 1763), p. 6.

47.   Douglas Edward Leach, Flintlock and Tomahawk: New England in King Philip's War (New York, 1958), pp. 119-20.   For a different perspective on the treatment of Quakers during King Philip's war, see Arthur J. Worrall, "Persecution, Politics, and War: Roger Williams, Quakers, and King Philip's War," Quaker History, 66 (1977):82-85. The sources of our differences rest in our focus upon different regions.   Neither the Salem nor the Kittery meetings were punished after 1670, and most of the adult male Quakers in Salem (fourteen of twenty-three) took the

oath of allegiance. Of the remaining nine, only Robert
Gray was noted to have refused. Essex County Court Files,
30:51, 54-56.

6
Quakers in Kittery

> "In some of our eastern plantations many
> have become Quakers and [are] no little
> trouble thereby." - John Hull -

As circumstances forced greater responsibility for anti-
Quaker legislation upon the county courts, they punished
local Quakers in markedly different ways. Hostile Puritan
magistrates like Simon Bradstreet occasionally complained
that variations in the degrees of severity seemed to produce no discernible effect in reducing the presence of
local Quakerism.[1] Bradstreet should not have been sur-
prised since the local courts only followed the lead of
the General Court when differentiating between activities
that separated local from visiting Quakers. Giving local
courts the discretion to regulate heterodoxy allowed the
exercise of Puritan localism that superficially seemed to
reflect the general persecution of religious dissidence
but actually were for more particular, local reasons.
Even in the sixties when significant punishments were
meted out in the two counties with the largest concentra-
tions of Quakers, Essex and York, the circumstances of the
punishments indicated local concerns that did not wholly
reflect patterns of intolerance or the General Court's
fear of heterodox disorder. In Essex, in the town of
Salem, as we shall see later, the systematic indictment
of Quakers for over a decade did not reflect extensive
animosity toward the sect but other economic, political,
and social tensions. In York, in the town of Kittery, the
treatment of Quakerism depended upon the diverse and cos-
mopolitan nature of the county; the influence of the
General Court; the peculiar balance of political forces in
county, colony, and empire; and the nature of the Quakers
themselves.[2] By tracing the counties' adjustment to local
Quakerism, an adjustment made within the context of events
and Bay Colony institutions, we can see the responses that

shaped the treatment of heterodoxy as well as the emergence of religious toleration in seventeenth-century
Massachusetts.

In late 1662 and through the summer of 1663, the York
County Court launched a concerted attack against Quakers
in its part of Massachusetts.   York County magistrate
Richard Waldron arrested three visiting Quaker women and
had them beaten out of the jurisdiction; then apparently
in response to his recommendations, the court proceeded
to cite local Quakers living in Kittery for their failure
to attend orthodox church services.[3] Although Waldron's
actions did not occur until five years after the General
Court had begun its program of suppressing Quakerism, they
seemed consistent with a pattern of persecution in seventeenth-century Massachusetts Bay: the discovery of heterodoxy followed by an immediate attempt to produce local
conformity.[4] Yet the considerable delay in Kittery first
in confronting Quakerism and then in failing to carry out
a systematic program of suppression raises questions about
the extent to which prejudice against religious differences was the sole motive for punishing the sect in Massachusetts.   Between 1663 and 1675, the York County Court
attacked Quakerism only on a limited number of occasions.
Each of the incidents suggests that Kittery Quakers were
punished not because their religious beliefs offended the
court but because those beliefs denoted certain positions
on secular issues, and men like Waldron could employ ecclesiastical sanctions to enlist sources of power from
outside the locality to undermine those positions supported by Quakers.

The need for external help to challenge the power of
the Quakers in Kittery should hardly be surprising in
light of their extended web of influence and connection.
Although numbering only fourteen of the town's approximately one hundred adults, the Quakers were a significant
political force.[5] During the period 1648-63, Quakers were
a large proportion of the town's leadership. Six of the
twelve men who served as town selectmen during the fif-
teen-year period were Quakers. One of the six, Richard
Nason, had been a deputy to the General Court; another,
Nicholas Shapleigh, was the most frequently elected
selectman, a member of the county court bench, and a major
in the militia.[6]

Quakers dominated the political life of Kittery because they were individuals of economic consequence.
Shapleigh, for example, had important connections to
Robert Mason and the younger Ferdinando Gorges, the grand-
sons of the original proprietors of the Laconia Company,
the concern responsible for settling Kittery, and claimants, respectively, to New Hampshire and Maine. Because
of these connections, Shapleigh had considerable influence
over the distribution of property and timber rights on
both sides of the Piscataqua River. In comparison to his
fellow townsmen, Shapleigh had considerable wealth in saw-
mills, lumber, and commerce. While no inventory of

Shapleigh's assets seems to have survived, the 4,000 pounds in bonds required of his executors for only the portion of the estate in litigation provides some indication of his wealth.[7]

The personal holdings of other Quakers were more modest but extensive. At his death, John Hurd left his granddaughters Mary and Elizabeth a total of sixty acres of land. To each of three younger grandchildren, he left cash bequests of twenty pounds and then gave the major assets of his estate, his farm lying in both Sturgeon Creek and Kittery and its stock, to his grandson. Quaker Thomas Spencer arrived in the New World an indentured servant and died owning property and goods worth almost 250 pounds, more than twice the average estate probated during the last half of the seventeenth century in the larger and more prosperous town of Salem. When Richard Nason distributed his land and stock to eight children, he expected that his legacies would generate sufficient surpluses to provide his widow with eight pounds of silver and an annual maintenance of twelve pounds.[8]

There had been considerable evidence of Quaker activity in Kittery as early as 1659, but the York County Court had not acted.[9] What triggered Waldron's attacks upon Quakerism in 1662 was the instability caused by the Restoration of Charles II. The Restoration troubled York more than other Massachusetts counties because it had been established when the Bay Colony annexed towns originally organized under the proprietary of the elder Ferdinando Gorges. A number of factors, including Georges's royalist sympathies, his death in 1647, and the outbreak of civil war in England, led to lapses of government in Maine corrected only when, as early as 1651, towns submitted to the authority of Massachusetts. Maine towns had been forced to rely upon the Bay Colony for institutions guaranteeing security, order, and, in a number of instances, protection of property rights.[10] After the Restoration, the younger Ferdinando petitioned the Crown to return the family holdings in the New World and thus made his proprietary a reasonable alternative to Bay government.[11]

So sure were Gorges and others about the eventual restoration of his proprietary that he was able to form a new local government.[12] Kittery Quakers were sympathetic to Gorges (in addition to Shapleigh's connections, Thomas Spencer and John Hurd were original Laconia Company settlers), and, because they dominated local government in 1663, they kept the county's largest town in the Gorges camp. In 1662 and 1663, three Quakers, Shapleigh, James Hurd, and Miles Thompson, were Kittery selectmen. In addition, Shapleigh was the proprietary militia commander, while Hurd and Thompson were ranking members of the town militia. Another Kittery Quaker, Richard Nason, was named the town representative to the conference of towns called by the Gorges commissioners to ratify the new proprietary government. Despite the pressure exerted by the proprietary forces, the conference overwhelmingly endorsed a

pro-Massachusetts position and resolved to remain under
the colony's jurisdiction until the Crown decided otherwise.   Only Nason opposed the resolution; he called for
the immediate support of the new Gorges government.[13]
     Why Kittery supporters of the proprietary were Quakers
is not readily apparent.   The conversion of the Kittery
Quakers probably took place after the first visits of the
missionaries in 1659.   While northern settlements are not
noted for their religiosity, Quaker converts like Richard
Nason seemed to have had a history of religious behavior
that offended the General Court.   Nason was cited for
blasphemy in 1652 and had been one of the first Kittery
residents (the other was Thomas Spencer) to be cited in
1659 for helping the visiting Quakers.   Nason was probably
a pivotal figure in the process of conversion and might
well have been the "little crooked Quaker" who Waldron
reported in December 1662 as having an abnormal and perverse influence upon Shapleigh.[14]   In any case, there are
two possible explanations for the connection of Kittery
Quakerism with the events of the sixties: the practice
of meeting without an ordained cleric present was the
product of patterns of religious belief already at odds
with Puritan communitarianism, antedated the political
crisis, was given religious justification by Quakerism,
and tended to confirm political differences; or to disassociate themselves from Bay authority, some Kittery
residents deliberately embraced a religious affiliation
known to be opposed to prevailing standards of Puritan
orthodoxy.
     Ultimately, Gorges's claims and the continued influ-
ence of the Quakers depended upon Charles II; but until
he decided, both factions had to compromise on the administration of local justice.   If the two claimants for
sovereignty allowed the creation of competing judicial
institutions, litigants would be encouraged to seek out
the particular body most sympathetic to their cause, and
one set of legal judgments would have no binding effect
after the king made up his mind.   The solution to this
dilemma came in July 1662 when both parties agreed to hold
the regularly scheduled county court with a bench composed
of an equal number of representatives from both factions.
The compromise also had the element of continuity: it
maintained the customary membership of the bench.[15]
     Despite the compromise, the Bay loyalists used the
Quakerism of the Kittery supporters of the proprietary to
alter the balance of political interest and power in town
and county without having to await the king's decision.
The strength of Gorges's claims rested upon the likelihood
that the Crown would favor him over Massachusetts Puritans.
While the Crown undoubtedly preferred Gorges to the Puritans, its actions in 1662 undermined a crucial element of
his support in Maine.   In his October 1662 message to the
General Court, Charles noted that some Quakers in England
needed strong restraint and that Massachusetts might find

need for similar kinds of controls upon the Quakers. Thus
encouraged by the king, the General Court not only revived
its use of corporal punishment for visiting Quakers, it
deputized Waldron to deal with the sect in his hometown
of Dover, a town just to the east and across the Piscataqua River from Kittery. At the same time, the Court appointed Waldron to administer the York County Court oaths
of office for the ensuing year. These two seemingly unrelated developments made Waldron de facto lord lieutenant
for York and together provided him with the means for
weakening the proprietary faction.[16]

Waldron used his new powers to destroy the compromise
court arrangement. At an extraordinary session of the
court held in November, Waldron tried to get Shapleigh
to take the oath of office from him; when Shapleigh refused, he was replaced on the bench by another Kittery
resident. Waldron justified his actions to the General
Court and argued that Shapleigh, according to Waldron,
had fomented civil disorder by giving shelter to the
visiting Quakers who disturbed Dover. "The people,"
Waldron reported,

> are much troubled and doe expect some speedy
> Coorse to be taken by your selfe and the Counsell
> that such proud Insolent sperits may be Crushed
> or elce the good pepell of the Contry and those
> that have stood Close to your government will be
> utterly undone and likewise a harbor for all the
> Rogs in the Country and our towne will be soe
> disturbed with the quackers [sic] and others that
> we shall hardly be at peace.[17]

The purge of Shapleigh and the other Gorges commis-
sioner, a non-Quaker, from the bench enabled the Bay
loyalists to pack the county court. Two local loyalists
replaced the proprietary representatives, and the General
Court sent two additional magistrates to attend the next
county court session. In full command of the local judi-
ciary, the loyalists turned upon the Gorges supporters and
charged them with rejecting the authority of the county
and General Court and for failing to attend to their
duties as freemen. In Kittery, Shapleigh, his nephew
John Shapleigh, John and James Hurd, and four other residents were cited for these offenses. The treatment of the
Kittery dissidents had a slight variation from other proprietary supporters in the county: Nicholas Shapleigh,
the Hurds, and their wives were also cited for being absent from orthodox church services.[18]

An analysis of the politics of 1663 suggests that the
citations served to compound the liabilities of being a
member of the political opposition and to demonstrate the
General Court's ability to use the county to punish its
enemies. The citation of the leaders of the proprietary
and their wives through hitherto rarely applied mandatory

church attendance laws multiplied the penalties for being
disloyal. When Kittery resisted by ordering the remission
of the church fines--the proceeds were normally allocated
to the town--the General Court ordered that all fines for
heterodoxy be retained by the county. The county court
also used the mandatory attendance law to punish Nason,
who, because he had been disenfranchised by the General
Court earlier in 1659, could not be punished for failing
to do his duties as a freeman.[19] By redistributing the
fines, the General Court increased the cost of resistence
to its will and illustrated graphically the way in which
it could use the county court to exploit divisions inside
the town. The loss of access to the funds did not seriously disturb the non-Quakers in the town. They had given
up the money when they allowed the remission of the fines.
But the intervention of the General Court was a blatant
exhibition of its ability to pressure town government
through the reallocation of county revenues.

The General Court used the Quakerism of the Kittery
supporters of the proprietary to influence local decision-
making. In October 1663, three months after the Kittery
citations, the General Court ordered the disenfranchisement of religious dissidents like the Quakers who had
failed to attend orthodox services.[20] The expulsion of
the Quakers from political participation in Bay government
required the rearrangement of the traditional structure of
town leadership if Kittery were to follow its general inclination to stay under the authority of Massachusetts Bay.
While there were only four identifiable adult male Quakers
in Kittery affected, they were crucial to maintaining the
balance of power in favor of the proprietary. All four
had been selectmen, and three of the four were serving at
the time. By excluding Quakers from its political institutions, the General Court in effect demanded that the
town's traditional leaders be purged if it wished to remain part of the Bay Colony.[21]

The strength of the loyalists contrasted with the instability and weakness of the proprietary opposition. In
1664, the Crown established a commission to visit New
England and review its affairs. Ostensibly, the commission was to supervise the transfer of New Netherland to
the proprietorship of the Duke of York, but it was also
supposed to report on Massachusetts and, more specifically,
upon the extent of its territorial jurisdiction. When the
commission turned its attention to the problem of York, it
sensed the mutual hostility of both factions and recommended the creation of a royal government as a compromise.
The recommendation, however, weakened the anti-Massachusetts faction by splitting it into Gorges and royalist
camps. In Kittery, the commissioners overlooked Shapleigh,
Nason, and the other Quakers in their recommendations for
royal colonial officers and subtly altered the balance of
political power in the town.[22] A majority of the town
favored the continuation of Bay jurisdiction, and all that

seemed to have prevented the town from openly aligning
with the loyalists was its tendency to follow its Quaker-
dominated leadership.[23] By ignoring the Kittery Quakers,
the royal commissioners played into the hands of the pro-
Massachusetts faction by suggesting that the traditional
leaders, the Quakers, would be unable to control or shape
events outside the town in a government not under Bay
Colony jurisdiction.

Neither the proprietary supporters nor the emerging
royalists in Maine were able to resist the obvious pre-
ference of the region to remain part of Massachusetts.
Despite Shapleigh's claims that Waldron and his friends
had been bribed with large land grants to mislead others
and encourage them "to stick to the government of Massachusetts," the dissidents were unable to create a popular
alternative. Shapleigh's recommendation to Robert Mason
that he encourage the King to form a single colony combining Mason's proprietary claim to New Hampshire with
Gorges's to Maine probably would have generated little
support. Certainly Shapleigh would have been unable to
obtain any help from Quakers living in New Hampshire.
In Hampton, a town that later became part of New Hampshire,
Quakers generally supported Waldron in his support of
Massachusetts and opposition to an independent New Hampshire. Even after the Crown recognized Mason's claims and
established the 1671 provisional government, the Council,
composed of men like Waldron and Hampton Quaker Christopher Hussy, remained hostile to Mason's interests.[24]

Although Maine remained a separate colony from 1663
to 1668, it was obviously ill suited to independence.
Neither the proprietary supporters nor the royalists were
able to resist the obvious conclusions that most preferred
to be part of the Bay Colony and that an independent Maine
was highly unstable. The justices of the peace soon discovered that dependence upon royal good will left York
subject to caprice, "tossing and tottering to and fro as
shaken reeds or shipps unballasted ready to overturn with
the least breath of Clayme or Pretended Authority."[25] For
John Wincoll, a Kittery resident and a royal justice of
the peace, the answer to the colony's problems was to
revert to Massachusetts control. Wincoll's solution was
probably consistent with his own interests as well as a
reflection of Kittery's sentiments since he had lived in
Watertown and had been a business partner of Quakerphobe
John Hull, the Boston merchant, mintmaster, selectman, and
diarist.[26] Wincoll's ability to combine royal patronage
and popular opinion thus effectively nullified Quaker
political power in the town and, by extension, in the
county.

The deterioration of support for royal government and
the Crown's apathy permitted the restoration of Bay authority in Maine in 1668. The General Court simply ordered
the York County Court to convene and sent a military force
to effect its will.[27] With the resumption of Bay authority, the Quakers were completely isolated from political

influence outside Kittery. In the town, the board of
selectmen was expanded from six to seven members and,
while the Quakers were retained, they became a distinct
and impotent minority. Clearly, the balance of power had
shifted; two of the new selectmen were Roger Plaistead and
John Wincoll, both of whom held significant offices outside the town. Wincoll was a judge on the county bench;
Plaistead, the man who had negotiated Kittery's return to
Bay jurisdiction, was the town deputy to the General
Court. In addition, non-Quaker Charles Frost was made the
town clerk, and other loyalists assumed militia offices
formerly held by the Quakers.[28]

The retention of the Quakers after 1668 on the board
of selectmen was more a reflection of habitual patterns
of deference than of an enduring base of political support. In 1669, all three Quakers were reelected to the
board after the county returned to Massachusetts, but the
county court, citing the prohibitions of the General Court
against Quakers being freemen, disqualified the candidates
and ordered their replacement. If the town did not elect
new selectmen, Wincoll and another loyalist were empowered
to appoint new men to office. With no choice in the
matter, the town replaced the Quakers.[29]

Kittery's attempt to retain its traditional leaders,
albeit in a diminished capacity recognizing the new distribution of power, demonstrated the ambivalent status of
Quakers after the restoration of Bay Colony authority.
The punishment of the Quakers in 1663 and their exclusion
from politics after 1669 had been made possible by laws
enacted by a distant central authority intent upon rooting
out a form of heterodoxy that appeared to have been a
threat to public peace. At the local level where the
specific threat to order appeared in the form of political
conflict, the law had been used to suppress a minority
faction. Had the local courts shared the General Court's
concern for the connection of heterodoxy and sedition, one
might have expected the loyalists to have been more systematic in their enforcement of anti-Quaker legislation
once their political control was assured. There had been
considerable tension within the town during the political
crisis, and vengeance would not have been unexpected.
Open violence, for example, had been threatened after the
Gorges marshal literally threw the loyalist town constable
into jail.[30] Still, the prohibitions against Quakers
holding political office had had to be initiated from
outside the town.

Although the county court continued to cite Quakers
for failing to attend orthodox church services after
1669--the citations occurred in 1670, 1671, and 1675--the
court's actions need to be considered within the context
of specific moments in the life of the town. The 1670
and 1671 citations seem to confirm the Quakers' inability
to comply with the religious prerequisites for the franchise. For the most part, the citations were prefunctory.

John and James Hurd, Nicholas Shapleigh, and their wives
were either admonished and paid court fees or did not appear to answer the charges made against them. Only two
Quaker couples, the Nasons and the Thompsons, received
significant fines, but the amounts of the fines were
relatively slight in view of what should have been assessed given the period of their offenses.[31] The pattern of
the citations of 1670 and 1671 suggests that the primary
concern of the county court was to affirm the Quakers'
heterodoxy and dash any immediate hopes they might have
of returning to political life.

     The remaining 1675 citation reflects not a persecuting
impulse but a local conflict unrelated to the earlier
political controversies. Some townspeople wanted to force
the Quakers and others to assume their fair share of supporting the town's minister. Kittery had never been con-
scientious in its support of a religious establishment.
In 1659 it had divided itself into two parishes to encourage, ostensibly, wider church attendance among a
small but dispersed population.[32] The attempt foundered
because of the continued apathy of the parishes, their
relatively small population, and the rise of Quakerism.
In July 1669, the northern parish, that in which most of
the Quakers lived, was cited for failing to have a minister for five or six years. The southern parish was also
negligent in its support of the ministry. In 1673, Jere-
miah Hubbard asked the county court to help him collect
the arrears on his salary; owed thirty-five pounds,
Hubbard was only able to recover twenty-three.[33] By 1675,
the reluctance to support an orthodox ministry seemed to
be spreading to education as well. The local instigators
of the indictments against the Quakers, John Wincoll and
James Emery also accused thirteen other residents of absence from church and chastised the town for not taking
proper care to see its children were "taught their
chaticismes and aeducation according to Law."[34] By link-
ing other reluctant taxpayers to the Quakers, Wincoll and
Emery made it more likely that the fines for absence would
be collected, town revenues increased, and reluctant taxpayers encouraged to pay.

     Even if the indictments of the Quakers during the
seventies had rested upon religious prejudice, what still
remained clear about the general experience of the Kittery
Friends was the lack of systematic action on part of the
county court that cannot be attributed to the political
chaos of the preceding decade. If this was persecution,
it was a form no more serious or disabling than that
suffered by contemporary Nonconformists and Catholics in
England and probably less so. The persecution was
troubling and indicated the potential vulnerability of
the meeting, but it did not make demands that were particularly onerous nor was it part of a pattern of confrontation between Quakers and the rest of the town or
county.

     The limited nature of the attacks upon Quakers in
Kittery should not be suprising since they were influential political and economic figures and integral parts
of the town's social life. People in Kittery had settled
along the tributaries of the Piscataqua River, and Quakers were geographically dispersed among them. The determinants of residence and land tenure were not religious
affinities but access to rivers providing power and transport for exploiting timber. While Quakers tended to live
in the northeastern section of the town about three miles
from the coast, they did not constitute a single, isolated
group. Quakers often lived near non-Quakers; in fact,
many of the tracts held by Quakers bordered ones owned by
their political opponents.[35]
     After the events of the sixties, Quakers still retain-
ed the respect of many non-Quakers. Edward Randolph,
that archetypal, late seventeenth-century imperial civil
servant, reported that Shapleigh was among the most popular and well-principled men in Massachusetts. While one
should be somewhat skeptical of Randolph's estimations of
popularity--he was Robert Mason's cousin and thus had an
indirect political connection to Shapleigh--he seemed to
voice an opinion held by others. Humphrey Chadbourn had
considerable personal affection for Shapleigh, his uncle
by marriage and former employer, despite their political
differences. In his will Chadbourn made Nicholas and John
Shapleigh the overseers of his estate and left Nicholas
his good beaver hat as a token of his regard. Richard
Nason helped James Emery inventory the estate of Daniel
Ferguson, a non-Quaker. Emery and Chadbourn had opposed
Nason and Shapleigh on the proprietary and had signed a
1667 petition by the town that asked for the return of
Massachusetts authority. Emery, although the son of a
Quaker, was one of the men chosen to replace the Quaker
selectmen in 1669, and Chadbourn replaced Shapleigh on the
county bench after the purge of November 1662.[36]
     Furthermore, political conflict and the potential for
friction among neighbors did not seem to prohibit intermarriage between Quakers and non-Quakers. Chadbourn
married Nicholas Shapleigh's niece, his sister married
Quaker Thomas Spencer, and his son married Elizabeth Hurd,
daughter of James and granddaughter of John. Daniel
Goodwin, another supporter of Bay government, married a
daughter of Spencer's. In fact, Goodwin's children illustrated again the amicable relationships that trans-
cended momentary political controversies: two sons
married daughters of Quaker Miles Thompson and another
married the daughter of Roger Plaistead.[37]
     The patterns of intermarriage also indicate that
Kittery Quakerism was probably not very intense. Whatever the original motives for conversion, Quakerism was
not a faith readily transmitted to subsequent generations
in seventeenth-century Kittery. Nicholas Shapleigh and
his wife died childless, and their nephew and principal

heir, John, remained outside the meeting. Moreover, none
of the children of the Hurds, Spencers, or Thompsons
seemed to have remained in the meeting either. The only
family that retained any connection to Quakerism in subsequent generations was the Nasons, but even here the
connections were tenuous. The only indication of a second
generation Quaker Nason was Jonathan, Richard's second
son, who married Sarah Jenkins, the sister of a member
of the Salem Monthly Meeting. Richard's grandson,
although not listed as a Quaker, also married the daughter
of a Friend.[38]
    The spatial and social connections within the town
indicate that the Quakers were likely to have more in
common with other members of the town than with other
Quakers in the county. Of the more than one hundred fifty
persons cited for church absence between 1652 and 1683 in
York, only twenty-one can be identified as Quakers. Fourteen were from Kittery and the remaining seven were gathered in the town of Scarborough around the person of Sarah
Mills. During the sixties, there was no apparent connection between the two groups other than their avowal of a
common religious belief. The Scarborough Quakers seemed
to be more like other disorderly individuals than the
conventionally behaved Friends living in Kittery. That.
is, Scarborough Quakers were presented for their disorderly and unsettled personal lives. Mills managed to
achieve the dubious distinction of being one of the few
individuals to be cited by both Bay loyalists and proprietary supporters. During the compromise court session
of July 1662, Quaker James Hurd, the foreman of the grand
jury, introduced Mills's indictment for living illegally
with George Garland. The remaining members of the Scarborough group included Garland, Mills's three adult children, Bridget Phillips, and Moses Collins, none of whom
were involved with the larger political controversies of
the sixties and all of whom demonstrated forms of disorderly behavior to the county court. While cited in 1670
and 1671 for church absence like the Kittery Friends, the
Scarborough Quakers were indicted by a separate local jury
and were more openly contemptuous of authority. According to the testimony of Ambrose Boaden, Collins "disownes
our worship as false and Idolitrous" and Sarah Mills said
Puritans "worship devills Ministers." The court was obviously more concerned over the disorderly nature of these
particular Quakers than over Nason and Thompson. Instead
of fiscal punishments, Collins and Mills received twenty
lashes. In its citation of Garland, the court's fears
were seemingly confirmed. The court later had to order
Garland to stop living with Lucretia Hitchcock until he
resolved the status of his alleged marriage to Mills.
Indeed, these particular Friends seemed to have more in
common with the visitors who bedeviled Bay authorities.
One of Mills's daughters accompanied Margaret Brewster, a
visiting Quaker, who, dressed in sack cloth and smeared
with ashes, disturbed Samuell Sewall's congregation.[39]

Both groups of Quakers demonstrated that the punishment of Quakers did not depend solely upon the fact of
religion. The Scarborough and Kittery Quakers were seen
to be different, and the latter, with their relatively
less intense manifestations of belief, seemed to reflect
patterns of behavior more like the rest of the conventionally behaved population of the county. Founded as
plantations of trade rather than as, in the case of the
Bay model, communities of religion, York towns were more
likely to have lukewarm Anglicans than rigorous Puritans;
moreover, persons with Anglican sympathies had split over
the political issues of the sixties. Some like Robert
Jordan had connections to the proprietary and had made
common cause with the Kittery Quakers, while other Anglicans had remained loyal to Massachusetts. Insistence
upon a rigorous test of Puritan orthodoxy for the franchise would have irritated loyal Anglicans and enabled
the dissidents to complain about religious discrimination
to royal officials in England. Finally, to have demanded
conformity to a vaguely defined orthodoxy was impractical.
In a town like Scarborough, where Anglicans were dominant,
any demand for conformity might have compelled Puritans
to attend services held according to the Book of Common
Prayer.[40]
     The demise of the proprietary faction and with it,
the influence of the Quakers, vested political supremacy
in the county in the hands of those who had kept it loyal.
None had been more loyal than Waldron, and through him
power and influence flowed. Within Kittery, loyalists
like Wincoll and Plaistead could retain local supremacy
by using the mechanisms of the county court to exclude
their still influential rivals.[41] But once the supporters
of Massachusetts Bay had secured their political victory,
they went no further, and the mechanisms regulating religious dissent were virtually unused. The general failure to act after the Kittery Quakers had been expelled
from the body politic suggests that had religious bigotry
been an element in the contest for political control in
Kittery it did not transcend the subsequent lassitude and
apathy of town and country once the loyalists' immediate
political objectives had been secured.
     Furthermore, by not acting in place of the town or
country, the General Court implicitly recognized Kittery's
right to determine its own patterns of community association and thereby, in a curious and ironic way, accepted
the secular ramifications of the colony's congregational
polity. Kittery could allow Quaker heterodoxy to exist,
and, in a circuitous fashion, this was consistent with
Bay Puritanism. If the local authorities proved wanting
in matters of local religious dissidence, the General
Court, in the absence of an ecclesiastical structure,
would have to act. But if the General Court interfered
in Kittery's religious affairs once the secular dangers
of the town's dalliance with Quakerism passed, it would

have violated its own prohibitions against involving civil magistrates in matters of conscience.[42]

Unable to act on religious grounds, the Court was also circumscribed by the structure of its local legal system. As long as county magistrates did not see sufficient evidence of secular disorder to warrant indictment, the General Court could not intervene. It simply could not invent felonious crimes of disorder and sedition when its inferior jurisdiction did not see misdemeanors.

Traditionally, the movement in Massachusetts from religious intolerance to toleration has been attributed to the courage of the early religious martyrs, the decline of Puritan fervor, the intervention of royal authority, or various combinations of these factors. Yet in Kittery, the religious idealism of Friends did not include martyrdom or even the defense of coreligionists in Scarborough; the townspeople never demonstrated any significant Puritan fervor; and the intervention of royal authority in Maine strengthened the supporters of the General Court and weakened the Quakers. Rather than emerging out of prejudice, forms of toleration seemed endemic to life in Kittery, and the Puritan General Court's encouragement of harsher, more hostile views of Quakerism seemed to have had little effect upon actual levels of toleration within the local community. What at first glance appeared to have been manifestations of religious intolerance of Quakerism were adjustments to a new political reality in one specific location where religion played an important but decidely secondary role.

Quakers in Kittery were vulnerable to harassment because of the laws of the central authority, the General Court, but the Court did not press the issue when the town seemed content to accept its resident Quakers. They were, after all, a special kind of Quaker. They were not given to the kind of demonstration of faith that had caused widespread opprobrium in seventeenth-century Anglo-American society; instead, they possessed considerable influence because of their social integration, economic value, and history of public service. Also, while Kittery and Maine may not have been Bay Puritan communities in the fullest sense, their treatment of Quakers illustrated the distinctions between visitor and resident already made by the General Court. To have harassed or persecuted resident Quakers might have denied other attributes of community association; disrupted to a far greater degree the social and economic patterns of life in town; dismantled the congregational, civil, and ecclesiastical polity of the colony; and violated the right of one Bay town to establish a consensual community on its own terms. In much the same manner, local Quakerism would force other more traditionally Puritan towns like Salem to weigh the costs of suppressing heterodoxy against the benefits of communal peace and social utility.

NOTES

1. John Hull, "Diary," Archelogia Americana, 3 (1857):206. Bradstreet to Richard Baxter, 5 February 1672, quoted in "Correspondence of John Woodridge, Jr. and Richard Baxter," ed. Raymond P. Stearns, New England Quarterly, 10 (1937):583.

2. York had twenty-one resident Quakers, fourteen in Kittery and seven in Scarborough; Essex had fifty-seven in Salem. See chapter 7 and Appendix 1.

3. Rufus M. Jones, The Quakers in the American Colonies (1911; rept. New York, 1962), pp. 103-4.

4. Kai T. Erikson illustrated this point in his study of Quakerism in Salem, Massachusetts, in Wayward Puritans: A Study in the Sociology of Deviance (New York, 1966), pp. 107-36.

5. The estimation of population is derived from two lists of adult males: the census taken at annexation in 1652 and a 1667 petition asking for the restoration of Bay authority. Together they provide sixty-three different names of adult males, a figure that accounts for neither death nor emigration. Robert Moody estimated the town's population to have been about 900, but this seems extremely high. The royal commissioners in 1665 noted there were only about thirty "very mean" houses in each of the Maine towns, an observation that tends to support my lower estimates of population. James P. Baxter, ed., Documentary History of the State of Maine Containing the Baxter Manuscripts, Collections of the Maine Historical Society, 2d ser., vols. 1-9 (Portland, Me., 1869-1916), 4:25, 141, 390 (hereafter referred to as Doc. History of Maine). Charles Thornton Libbey et al., eds., Province and Court Records of Maine, 6 vols. (Portland, Me., 1928-75), 1:199. Petition of the Inhabitants of Yorkshire, 14 May 1667, Massachusetts Archives, 3:269, State House, Boston. Robert Moody, "The Maine Frontier, 1607-1763" (Ph.D. dissertation, Yale University, 1933), pp. 260-61. Commissioners to Sir Henry Bennett, Boston, 26 July 1665, Documentary History of the State of New York, 4 vols., Edmund B. O'Callaghan, (Albany, N.Y., 1850-51), 1:101.

6. Kittery Town Records, 1648-1709, pp. 1-5, 96, Town Hall, Kittery, Me. James Savage, A Genealogical Dictionary of the First Settlers of New England, 4 vols., (Boston, 1860-62), 4:60, 390. Nathaniel B. Shurtleff, ed., Records of the Governor and Company of the Massachusetts Bay in New England, 1628-1686, 5 vols. in 6 parts (Boston, 1853-54), 4, pt. 1:263 (hereafter referred to as Mass. Records). Shapleigh's militia service would seem

to contradict his identification as a Quaker; however,
given the fluid nature of Quaker organization and doctrine
during this period, militia service would not preclude
membership in the meeting.

7. Libbey, Maine Court Records, 3:38, 41, 167. For
details of Shapleigh's connections to Robert Mason, see
Moody, "The Maine Frontier," pp. 156-57. John G. Reid,
Maine, Charles II, and Massachusetts: Government Relations in Northern New England (Portland, Me., 1977), pp.
39, 43.

8. The mean value of estates probated in Essex from
1661 to 1681 was between 100 and 149 pounds. Donald W.
Koch, "Income Distribution and Political Structure in
Seventeenth-Century Salem, Massachusetts," Essex Institute Historical Collections, 105 (1969):59. William M.
Sargent, ed., Maine Wills, 1640-1760 (Portland, Me., 1887),
pp. 67-68, 77, 113-14.

9. Three Kittery residents were fined and disenfranchised by the General Court on 12 November 1659 for
entertaining Quakers. Two other residents were also admonished for the same offense the following May. Shurtleff, Mass. Records, 4, pt. 1:406-7, 427.

10. Supporters of the proprietary, like Anglican
Robert Jordan, encouraged the extension of Bay jurisdiction into Maine to use its courts to resolve civil disputes. Libbey, Maine Court Records, 2:xxxii-xxxiii, and
Moody, "The Maine Frontier," pp. 77-80.

11. Gorges to the Crown, 4 April 1661, Calendar of
State Papers: Colonial, 1661-1668, ed. W. Noel Sainsbury
(London, 1880), no. 255. Reid, Maine, Charles II, and
Massachusetts, pp. 39, 43. Also see David E. VanDeventer,
The Rise of Provincial New Hampshire (Baltimore, 1973),
pp. 14, 17.

12. The Result of an Agitation by the Commissioners
of Ferdinando Gorges, Esq. att Wells, in Libbey, Maine
Court Records, 1:196-98.

13. John Hurd was one of the Kittery residents ad-
monished by the General Court for entertaining Quakers in
May 1660 (see note 9). Kittery Town Records, p. 96, Re-
solution of the Wells Conference, 27 May 1662, Baxter,
Doc. History of Maine, 4:244, and Libbey, Maine Court
Records, 2:75.

14. Waldron to the General Court, 13 December 1662,
Massachusetts Archives, 3:262.

15. The composition of the bench during this session of the county court was unusual for it omitted a representative from the General Court. Usually, the Court sent a magistrate or justice from one of the other county courts to attend the York sessions. To have had such a representative at this particular session would have imperiled the compromise by suggesting that the county was subject to the authority of the General Court alone. Without a General Court magistrate in attendance, the Gorges commissioners could participate in the court and still maintain their autonomy. Affidavits of Daniel Dennison, William Hathorne, and Richard Waldron, 28 May 1662, in Baxter, Doc. History of Maine, 2:242, 248; Moody, "The Maine Frontier," pp. 120-33. For the membership of the previous sessions of the county court, see Libbey, Maine Court of Records, 2:55, 61, 72, 88, 97, 113.

16. Shurtleff, Mass. Records, 4, pt. 2:55, 69, 165-69.

17. Waldron to the General Court, 13 December 1662, Massachusetts Archives, 3:262.

18. Libbey, Maine Court Records, 2:138-43. Quakers also had difficulties with Dover-Portsmouth courts in 1663 and 1664. In the light of the singular nature of the citations and the apparent neglect of constables, the punishment of Quakers at that time may have been intended to demonstrate the power of Bay courts over dissidents. See Nathaniel Bouton et al., eds., Documents and Records Relating to New Hampshire, 1623-1800, 40 vols. (Concord and Manchester, N.H., 1867-1953), 40:181-82, 185-86, 189, 193.

19. Shurtleff, Mass. Records, 4, pt. 1:263, 406-7, 427; Libbey, Maine Court Records, 2:137-39; Kittery Town Records, p. 20.

20. Shurtleff, Mass. Records, 4, pt. 2:87-88.

21. Kittery Town Records, pp. 1-3, 5, 96. Libbey, Maine Court Records, 2:140.

22. See the negative recommendation of Shapleigh given by Joseph Mason to Robert Mason on 28 September 1667, in Sainsbury, Calendar of State Papers, 1661-1668, no. 1588. Order of the King's Commissioners, 23 June 1665, in Baxter, Doc. History of Maine, 4:202-3. Reid, Maine, Charles II, and Massachusetts, pp. 61-66, 89-90.

23. Thirty-one men signed the 1667 petition of submission to the authority of Massachusetts. Comparing that
list with those granted the franchise in 1652, one can
account for twenty-nine others who did not sign it. This
last figure includes all the Quakers except Anthony Emery,
who emigrated before 1663. Since the submission occurred
fifteen years after annexation, the possibility does exist
that the petition does not represent the majority of the
town in 1667; however, in light of the much smaller number
of people who signed other anti-Massachusetts petitions,
it is far more likely that the loyalists commanded a considerable majority. Shurtleff, Mass. Records, 4, pt.
1:124. Petition of the Inhabitants of Yorkshire, 14 May
1667, Massachusetts Archives, 3:269.

24. Shapleigh to Mason, 20 May 1667, Piscataway, in
Bouton, Documents and Records Relating to New Hampshire,
17:513-14. VanDeventer, Rise of Provincial New Hampshire,
p. 17.

25. Inhabitants of Maine to the King, 1665, in Baxter, Doc. History of Maine, 4:204.

26. Petition of the Inhabitants of Yorkshire, 14 May
1667, Massachusetts Archives, 3:269; Everett F. Stackpole,
Old Kittery and Her Families, (Lewiston, Me., 1903), p.
134; G. Frederick Robinson and Ruth Robinson Wheeler,
Great Little Watertown: A Tercentenary History (Cambridge,
Mass., 1930), p. 136.

27. Shurtleff, Mass. Records, 4, pt. 2:371-72. Ultimately, Gorges settled the legal issue by selling his
proprietary rights to the Bay Colony. See Reid, Maine,
Charles II, and Massachusetts, pp. 172-73.

28. Kittery Town Records, p. 100. Libbey, Maine
Court Records, 2:44n.

29. Libbey, Maine Court Records, 2:177.

30. Petition of Daniel Goodwine, Constable of Kittery,
10 December 1662, in Baxter, Doc. History of Maine,
4:184-85. Also see Waldron to General Court, 13 December
1662, Massachusetts Archives, 3:262.

31. The fines were fifty and twenty shillings, respectively, for the Nasons and the Thompsons. In view of
the admitted Quakerism of Nason, his fines should have
been twice as large to be consistent with the laws governing attendance at Quaker meetings. Libbey, Maine Court
Records, 2:197-98, 221-22. For the fines governing absence from orthodox services, see Thomas G. Barnes, ed.,
The Book of the General Lawes and Libertyes Concerning the
Inhabitants of the Massachusetts, (1648; rept. San Marino,

Calif., 1975), p. 20. For an expanded discussion of this process, see chapter 3.

32. Kittery seemed to prefer smaller congregations that were more conveniently located. In 1660, the town established three parishes in place of the two mentioned here. The evidence of the seventies suggests a reversion to two parishes. Kittery Town Records, p. 12.

33. Of the twenty-two persons cited for absence from regular church services that year, nine had been identified previously as being Quakers, three had some vague connections with the Quakers, and the remaining ten had not been associated with the Quakers previously or at the time of the indictment. The three with tenuous connections were Reynold Jenkins, Nicholas Hodesden, and Hodesden's wife. A Jenkins daughter later became a Quaker, and Nicholas Hodesden had been accused of entertaining Quakers in May 1660. If these non-Quakers were in fact members of the meeting and had escaped the earlier citations in 1663, their inclusion here would confirm the various motives for punishment as I have described them. That is, punishment for heterodoxy occurred only under unusual circumstance. Political conflict was one unusual circumstance; the demand by the town that others share in the support of the minister, another. Stackpole, Old Kittery, pp. 115, 549; Salem Monthly Meeting Records, 1672-94, pp. 7-8, New England Yearly Meeting of Friends Manuscript Collection, Rhode Island Historical Society Library, Providence. Libbey, Maine Court Records, 2:80, 175, 183, 256, 263, 273, 346.

34. Libbey, Maine Court Records, 2:306-7.

35. Stackpole, Old Kittery, pp. 123-28. Reid, Maine, Charles II, and Massachusetts, pp. 2-12.

36. Answer of Edward Randolph to Heads of Inquiry Concerning New England, 12 October 1676, Calendar of State Papers: Colonial, 1675-1676, ed. W. Noel Sainsbury (London, 1893), no. 1067. Sargeant, Maine Wills, p. 50. Libbey, Maine Court Records, 2:170, 331, 3:41; Deposition of Humphrey Chadbourn, 5 April 1653, Massachusetts Archives, 60:58; Stackpole, Old Kittery, p. 312.

37. Stackpole, Old Kittery, pp. 312, 453-54.

38. Ibid., pp. 549, 625-27.

39. Libbey, Maine Court Records, 1:333-34, 2:119, 223-34, 288; Samuel Eliot Morison and Zachariah Chaffee, eds., Records of the Suffolk County Court, 1671-1680, Publications of the Colonial Society of Massachusetts, vols. 29-30 (Boston, 1933), 29:488. Samuel Sewall, Diary 1674-1729, 2 vols., ed. M. Halsey Thomas (New York, 1973), 1:44.

40.   See, for example, the county court's frequent
injunctions to support organized religion.   Libbey, Maine
Court Records, 2:67, 80-81, 290n.

41.   Before the political disputes of the sixties,
judges of the county court were drawn from three towns:
Dover, Scarborough, and Kittery.   Only Dover continued
to have representation at the court in the decade following the return to Bay authority.   Representatives from
Wells, Falmouth, and York, hitherto unrepresented, generally replaced the Scarborough representative.   Kittery
had someone present seven of the ten years, but the town
would have been hard to ignore; it was, for tax purposes,
the highest rated town in the county.   Libbey, Maine
Court Records, 2:171, 186, 273, 312, 333, 340; Warrant
for the Support of Fort Loyal, 24 May 1682, vol. P.,
Willis Manuscript Collection, Maine Historical Society,
Portland.

42.   See, for example, John Norton, The Heart of New
England Rent (Cambridge, Mass., 1659), pp. 52-53; and
chapter 3.

7
Quakers in Salem

"A Company of Quakers wee have in severall
townes which neither severity nor leniency
will keepe in order." - Simon Bradstreet -

The General Court of Massachusetts should have expected
that, unlike York, the remaining major Bay county courts
would have suppressed local Quakerism systematically.
There was good cause to believe that the actions of the
inferior courts would be consistent with those of Boston.
After all, Suffolk, Middlesex, Norfolk, and Essex were
the four oldest, most centrally located, and presumably
most Puritan of the Bay counties, and they provided the
General Court with most of its membership. Also county
judges were selected from the Court or were its appointees.
Yet suppression of Quakerism in these four counties was
subject to the peculiarities of the locality and the individual. The Middlesex County Court cited eight persons
between 1663 and 1680 for Quaker-related crimes. For the
most part, the citations were of individuals whose behavior the court felt was eccentric and disorderly. In Suffolk, an active Boston meeting went virtually unpunished
from 1662 to 1673. During the same period, the pattern of
punishment in Norfolk County was irregular and apparently
prompted by local reaction to demonstrations of faith that
were deemed to be excessive.[1] Essex alone seemed to reflect the desires of the General Court as it attempted to
suppress Quakerism in the town of Salem. Beginning in
1658, thirty-four resident Friends were indicted, and
annual mass citations and fines involving fifty-seven
Quakers continued until 1670.[2] Yet even in this apparently systematic pattern of punishment, Essex demonstrated
an accommodation to General Court policies that reflected
the serving of local interest for local ends, and, ironically, the emergence of a crude form of religious toleration.

To stop conversions in Salem, the county's largest
town, Essex did not use the legislation specifically designed by the General Court to regulate Quakerism. Although the colony prescribed ten-shilling fines for attendance at a Quaker meeting and possible banishment for
continued association with it, the county court substitu-
ted an older, 1646 law levying fines of five shillings for
failing to attend orthodox worship.[3] The application of
the 1646 law may have been initiated because of the fear
of visiting Quakerism in the late 1650's, but Essex's continued use of it through the next decade cannot be attributed solely to a sustained desire to compel religious conformity. Indeed, the substitution of specific, anti-Quaker legislation with the compulsory attendance regulation
muted and deflected the harsher attributes of General
Court justice. The county court chose to apply a legal
device enabling it to restrict Quakers' criminality to
misdemeanor levels and thus to maintain jurisdiction over
them. This ensured a larger role for the play of local
influence and lessened the possibility that local offenders would become fully liable for the consequences of
their heterodoxy.[4]

While the general use of fines did not preclude corporal punishment of Quakers in Essex, the few times the
county court resorted to it suggests a pattern of dealing
with isolated, petty disorder and not the singling out of
Quakers for persecution. When, for example, John Burton
was placed in the stocks in 1661, it was not because he
was a Quaker. He was punished for his contempt by refusing to be silent and failing to show proper deference to
the magistrates. The following year, 1662, the court
ordered Deborah Wilson to be whipped for public nudity.
The court did not see her exhibition as a form of religious protest in need of suppression. Rather, it punished
a disorderly woman.[5] Whipping, in fact, was a way of
reducing one's financial obligations to the county. Quaker Ann Needham apparently elected to be whipped instead of
paying a fine of three pounds, fifteen shillings. She
received twelve lashes, only two more than Harvard presi-
dents were empowered to give students for their "misdemeanours of youth."[6]

Still, a systematic application of fines could have
produced severe economic distress. Had the county court
chosen to apply the fines for absence conscientiously,
Quakers could have been reduced to poverty or deterred
from attending the meeting. When Friends chose to absent
themselves from regular worship, they became liable to a
minimum annual fine--presuming that they were cited only
for absence from Sunday services--of thirteen pounds per
annum. The magnitude of this punishment and its potential
for seriously weakening Quakers' economic position can be
seen in the data compiled by James Henretta: thirteen
pounds is more than the assessed wealth of two-thirds of
Boston taxpayers in 1687.[7]

In general, however, the Essex County Court did not fine Quakers to the full extent allowable by law. While Daniel Southwick was one of the few Quakers to be cited every year between 1658 and 1670, he was sentenced to pay fines totalling only fifty-five pounds, not the 169 pounds the law demanded for the period of his absence. The disparity between his actual and theoretical fines was seemingly deliberate; in 1661, Southwick was sentenced to pay fines for missing twenty services for a period covering thirty-two sabbaths. There is further evidence to indicate that Southwick may not have paid all the fines to which he had been sentenced. In 1659, he and his sister Provided were ordered to be sold into indentured servitude for failing to pay their fines. This was, however, an order from the General Court and not the county. In 1661, after the deaths of their parents, both were still living in Salem and owed the county court nine pounds. At the time, Daniel was negotiating the probate of his parents' will, and despite the legally ambiguous nature of the unsworn document, the county made no effort to use the occasion to extract payment from Daniel and Provided, the two principal heirs of the estate.[8] The Southwicks were not the only individuals to benefit from the apparent leniency of the county court. Quakers John and Elizabeth Kitchin were sentenced to pay fines of three pounds for having missed public worship for one and two years respectively. The three-pound fine could not have covered their missing services since the previous court session.[9]

By 1665, the county court, without authorization by the General Court, reduced the annual fines for absence. First the court limited the fine for a year's absence to a maximum of forty shillings. The next year, 1666, the court again reduced the fines, this time to a maximum of twenty shillings for men and ten for women.[10] The reductions may have been attempts to make the collection of the fines easier and to reduce local resistence to what might seem extraordinary fiscal penalties, but they were still an open admission of an increasingly erratic and lazy mechanism of law enforcement. Not only did the quasi-official cost of Quaker heterodoxy drop precipitously after 1667, indictments became highly erratic. For example, the court cited Joshua Buffum, one of the most ardent and enthusiastic of local Quakers in 1668 and 1669 but not in 1670. In 1667, twenty-seven Quakers were assessed fines totalling nineteen pounds, ten shillings; in 1670, only eleven Quakers, for seven pounds, ten shillings. The decline in the number and size of the fines after 1667 reflected either the court's general inability or its lack of desire to collect previous fines. As far as can be determined from the extant file papers and records of the Essex County Court, Quakers only paid about one-third of the amount assessed them, a figure already far lower than the one to which they should have been subject.[11]

The absence of additional fines may be attributable
to gaps in the extant court records, but the possibilities
of this are slight. The Essex manuscript court records
and files are the most complete for Massachusetts in this
period. More significant, however, is the fact that the
fines were neither confiscatory nor seemingly punitive,
characteristics one might expect of any sustained effort
to suppress a heterodoxy that lasted over a decade. The
fines appear to have had little effect upon Quaker wealth.
Throughout the sixties and the remainder of the century,
Quaker fortunes seemed to have been unaffected by the
actions of the county court. Beyond the last half of the
seventeenth century into the early eighteenth, Quakers
cited by the county court maintained an economic position
among the middling to moderately wealthy members of the
town. William Davisson has estimated that between 1640
and 1681 only about twenty-five percent of all decedents
used the probate process, and they were generally rich,
long-lived white males. Five-eighths of all male Salem
Quakers (62.5 percent, twenty of thirty-two) had probated
wills or inventories with an average value of more than
300 pounds, a figure that set these Quakers in the upper
economic strata of the town.[12]

Quaker tax rates in 1683 further suggest the minimal
effect that the fines seemed to have had upon Quaker
wealth. In the 1683 tax census, 43 percent of all Salem
taxpayers paid colony rates of two shillings, six pence
or more; thirteen of the seventeen Quakers (77 percent)
on the tax rolls were in this category. The average tax
paid by everyone was 2.8 shillings; that paid by Quakers,
slightly more than four shillings. Two Quakers, Josiah
Southwick and Robert Stone paid rates of eight shillings.
While this was not the highest tax paid, it is, according
to Richard Gildrie, indicative of an estate worth about
1,100 pounds.[13] Thus, like their probate records, the
Quakers' tax records indicate a group likely to rank among
the middling to upper levels of the town's economic
structure.

Admittedly, this evidence is somewhat circumstantial,
and the tax and probate data are a more accurate reflection of Quaker economic standing after the fines had
ceased. But they raise a distinct question about the
allegedly enervating nature of the court's treatment of
the Salem Quakers. Reducing fines or being lackadaisical
in their collection does not absolve the county court of
charges of persecution, but they do raise questions about
the underlying motives that prompted and sustained the
punishment of the Quakers. In light of the probate and
tax data, the fines could only have been damaging if the
fines were far greater than reported and either Quakers
were among the wealthiest members of the town and had been
forced back into its middling ranks; they, as a group,
demonstrated enormous talent and resilience in reviving
shattered fortunes in a mixed economic situation; or the

records are reasonably accurate, and the fines had a
negligible effect upon Quaker wealth.

The first two explanations are the least plausible.
Before 1658, the Quakers were not among the wealthiest
residents of the town. Except for connections by marriage
to the Gardner family, Quakers did not seem to have unusually large grants of land or hold the kinds of political office that might imply significant wealth. Quite the
contrary, Quakers did not command the kind of recognition
that denoted wealth. Most were relatively young, and none
served in any town or county offices of consequence before
1657 when Joseph Boyce was elected a selectman. Before
their conversions disqualified them from holding colonial
office, Quakers were members of juries or noncommissioned
officers in the town militia, indicating a relatively low
level of political influence and a more middling place in
the community.[14] Under these circumstances, it is unlikely that Quakers possessed extraordinary estates prior to
being fined.

For the fines to have had a significant impact upon
their fortunes, Quakers would have had to have been al-
chemists as well as shrewd, diligent businessmen. Fourteen of the thirty-two male Quakers had agricultural oc-
cupations, and while they had smaller estates than their
mercantile and artisan brethren in the meeting, the value
of their assets averaged 196 pounds, a figure that com-
pares favorably to the 124 pound mean for the entire town
during the 1662-81 period. Furthermore, farming was the
slowest growing sector of the Salem economy, making a
rapid recovery by this means most difficult during the
seventies and eighties. But if John Southwick was representative of the group, Quakers prospered during the most
intense period of the fines. Southwick died in 1672
leaving an estate valued at just over 600 pounds, one of
the dozen largest estates listed in the probate records
before 1681. The bulk of his fortune had to have been
accumulated precisely during the period of the fines.
When he arrived in Salem on the verge of adulthood in
1639, he could expect little help from his father Lawrence.
The senior Southwick had a wife and three other children
to support and had become involved in a disastrous attempt
to build a glassworks in Salem. John's success can be
explained only by a long period of diligent husbandry
sustained through, not revived after, the fines. His
assets were not the stuff of quick wealth. He did not
have the tools of an artisan or the inventories of a
merchant; he had the assets men accrue when they tend
to fields and animals. It would have been extremely unlikely that John Southwick accumulated a fortune by age
thirty-eight, witnessed its dissipation through fines,
and amassed another in the four years between his last
citation and death.[15] While economic recovery among Quaker artisans and merchants may have been more likely, the
rate in some instances would have had to have been

miraculous.   Joshua Buffum's 1671 rates, the year after
the fines ceased, were eight-shillings, three pence, a
substantial sum for a young man who had yet to receive
his double portion from his father.[16]

The simplest explanation for the patterns of Quaker
wealth in the fifties and sixties is that the records
accurately report the fines actually assessed and collected and that the fines had a negligible effect upon Quaker
economic status.   The laborious duplication of the bills
of indictment, constable arrest warrants, and trial judgments argues against fines being underreported because of
sloppy bookkeeping or the subsequent destruction of
records.   Nor is it feasible to suggest that underreport-
ing the number of offenses from year to year was the
result of not knowing who the Quakers were.   The local
composition of bench and juries, the stability of their
membership, and the same painstaking detail characteristic
of the Essex records indicate an almost deliberate pattern of selective punishment.[17]

Although other Bay courts adjusted fines to suit local
cirumstances, Essex's methods raise questions about the
motives historians have traditionally imputed toward its
punishment of the Salem Quakers.[18]   The reduction of fines
occurred relatively frequently in seventeenth-century
Massachusetts and were intended seemingly to alleviate
the burdens of the poor.   Reductions had significant ad-
vantages; a strict accounting might force an individual
to become dependent upon town charity.   A reduced fine
would still serve the needs of justice, fixing a punishment more appropriate to one's means without making the
town assume the care of an impoverished offender.   Given
the indicators of Quaker wealth, claims of penury would
not have justified lower penalties for heterodoxy.   The
county court could have required the Quakers to pay larger
fines.   It did not.

The reduced fines were the result of the county
court's adjustment to the existence of a permanent Quaker
meeting in Salem and came about in response to local
pressure.   As early as September 1659, John Higginson,
the town minister, and William Browne, the town's leading
merchant, requested the suspension of all the fines levied
against the Quakers.   At the same time, the judges also
ordered the remission of half the fines assessed Quaker
Samuel Gaskin the previous September.   Higginson's and
Browne's action was probably an attempt to heal divisions
within the church and town as the former assumed the Salem
pulpit, but the process of reducing the fines upon the
Quakers continued throughout the next decade.[20]   Later,
when Quakers Hannah Phelps and John Small were fined for
slandering Higginson, William Flint, a non-Quaker and full
member of the church, paid the fines in their behalf.
The fines were not onerous, five shillings, six pence,
including routine court costs of two shillings, six pence.
Flint obviously saw no challenge to order or authority but

a bit of name calling and bickering, and in assessing the
minimal fines the court seemed to share his evaluation.[21]
   Other town members repeated acts like Flint's. William Hathorne's son Eleazar paid Tamosin Buffum's fine,
while Phillip Cromwell paid that of the wife of Richard
Gardner. When the court ordered Samuel Shattock to be
whipped for reviling its magistrates, his step-brother,
John Gardner, a non-Quaker, prevented the whipping by
paying a fine in his behalf.[22] The actions of Gardner,
Hathorne, Cromwell, and Flint satisfied judgments of the
court against Quakers and revealed a base of support
among the scions of the leading citizens of the town that
apparently found even minimal punishments troubling.
Also, the intercession by sons of these prominent men
robbed the legal process of any symbolic value it might
have had.[23] Flint and his non-Quaker fellows permitted
Quakers Phelps, Small, and Shattock to remain openly unrepentant. When presumably responsible and respected
members of town and church saw Quakers as worthy of help,
it would have been most difficult for the county court,
dependent as it was upon local cooperation and participation in the process of enforcement, to continue to
justify the prosecution of Quakers.
   Indeed, the Essex County Court was careful to maintain distinctions between visiting and resident Quakers.
Court officers simply could not be abusive when dealing
with the latter. While one might be permitted to gag a
visiting Quaker as Constable Edmund Batter did with
Christopher Holder, there were limits to what he might do
to a resident. In 1659, Batter tried to confiscate
Elizabeth Kitchin's horse for the payment of fines. According to Quaker commentator George Bishop, Batter forci-
bly removed Kitchin from her horse and so abused her that
she miscarried. Bishop's charges of physical abuse were
overstated; Kitchin gave birth to a son shortly after the
incident. When the county court considered the episode,
it relied on the testimony of Thomas Meeking, eighteen,
and John Ward, twenty, over the testimony of Batter and
his assistant, ironically, Phillip Cromwell. Having
helped Batter, Cromwell was obviously eager to minimize
the extent of his abuse and claimed that no undue force
had been used nor harsh words exchanged. According to
Meeking and Ward, Batter did not use force to get Kitchin
to dismount or to seize her horse, but he had called her
"a base quaking slut with diverse other opprobrious
taunting."[24] The court cited Batter for his excessive
zeal and abusive manner.[25]
   The Essex County Court also observed Quaker legal
rights from the beginning of the fines. After Lawrence
and Cassandra Southwick died in exile on Shelter Island
in 1660, their unsworn will placed the county court in a
legal quandary. The court was willing to distribute the
proceeds of the estate in accordance with the document
that Daniel and Josiah Southwick said was their parents'

last testament, but the two men were unwilling to swear
to its authenticity. While the court probably did not
doubt the veracity of the document, probating it might
establish a legal precedent that weakened the integrity
of the whole process. Ultimately, the court and the
Southwick children arranged a compromise that satisfied
legal requirements and the refusal of Quakers to swear
oaths. Two non-Quakers, William and Thomas Gardner,
testified that Daniel and Josiah had proposed an equitable
distribution of the estate's assets, and the estate was
divided.[26]

Essex soon learned to dispense with attempts to create
compromises for the Quakers' refusal to swear oaths. Instead the court seemed to presume that Quaker testimony
was functionally equivalent to that given under oath. In
1661, Quaker John Kitchin testified in the case of <u>John
Burton</u> v. <u>John Porter</u>, and Joseph Boyce's deposition on
<u>Ingersoll</u> v. <u>Barney</u> was filed with the notation that he
had "attested to this presence of God." Indeed, the
county court clerk noted in 1666 that Quakers John Hill
and Boyce had given their oaths in attesting the validity
of William Trask's will.[27]

These accommodations to the presence of Quakerism
should not have been unexpected. Resident Salem Quakers
were important parts of town life, and they often made
contributions that cut across political, geographical,
and religious differences. They were a significant minority, accounting for approximately nine percent of the
adult population.[28] While they tended to live on the
north and northwest edges of the town, Quakers were not
isolated.[29] Patterns of intermarriage, participation in
local politics, and economic connections provided points
of reference that made Quakers acceptable members of the
local community and explain why the orthodox were willing
to moderate the strict letter of the law.

The assistance of non-Quakers like William Flint reflected a larger social network that connected other members of the town to the Quakers. Flint's widowed sister-
in-law married John Southwick. Quaker Phillip Veren's
father was a member of the church and a former constable,
his brother Hilliard was a deacon and a collector of the
town's port entry fees. Phillip's sister married Constable Batter, one of the few consistently virulent opponents of the Quakers.[30] These connections were of minor
consequence when compared to the Quaker ties to the
Gardner family. The family patriarch Thomas had been a
resident of the town before the arrival of John Endecott
and the Massachusetts Bay Company in 1629. Gardner was
not a Quaker, but his second wife, younger son Richard,
and two daughters-in-law were. His stepson was Samuel
Shattock, the man responsible for bringing the writ that
suspended the hanging of Quakers in Massachusetts.
Thomas's oldest son George, who subsequently became one
of the town's biggest landowners, never became a Quaker,

but his wife did.   This division within a prominent family
did not diminish the town's esteem for George or impair
its confidence in his ability to defend the town.   During
the same court session that he was named lieutenant of the
town militia, his wife Elizabeth received one of her many
citations for absence.[31]
     There was little risk in defending Quaker relatives
or friends.   Local Quakers as a whole had not had personal
histories marked by disorder.   Only four Quakers had ever
had any previous difficulty with the law and then only
for the most niggling offenses.   Phillip Veren and John
Hill were fined forty shillings each on separate occasions
for inadvertently firing their guns in the woods after
dark and alarming the town.   Edward Wharton was indicted
for excessive tippling and idleness.   The court dismissed
both charges.   Perhaps the gravest charge levied against
a future Quaker was the indictment of Michael Shafflin
for withdrawing from the baptismal service in 1646.   Shafflin's problem may only have been his negligence to do
his duty as constable and arrest John Redknap, an avowed
Anabaptist.[32]
     In most other respects, Quakers were law-abiding,
respectable, and contributing members to the town.   Sixteen Quakers had been full members of the regular church,
and six others baptized in it.   Joseph Boyce and Phillip
Veren had been members since 1641; the elder Southwicks,
Lawrence and Cassandra, since 1639; Shafflin and Joseph
Pope, since 1638 and 1635, respectively.[33]   Quakers also
had personal histories of public service.   Lawrence Southwick was deputized to find a suitable master for John
Scott.   In its instructions on him, the town gave Southwick full power to fix Scott's term of service for up to
three years.   Shortly after John Southwick confessed his
Quakerism in court, the county court approved the transfer of the indentures of Baldwin House to him.   Since
neither House nor his former master, George Gardner, were
Quakers, the court probably would not have allowed the
transaction to take place if it feared that House might
be corrupted by an intimate association with Southwick.[34]
     Quaker participation in the political life of town
and county further illustrated their integration into the
larger community.   In 1654, Shafflin, Shattock, and John
Kitchin were jurymen on the county court.   On the eve of
the meeting's difficulties with the county court, John
Smith was a constable and Kitchin was the militia sergeant.
In 1658 and 1659, Quakers Kitchin, Shafflin, Boyce,
Joseph Pope, and Anthony Needham were members of juries
that indicted and convicted Quakers for absence.[35]   Quakers continued to hold local office even after the General
Court had ordered their expulsion from the electorate in
1663.   During that same year, two Quakers served as surveyors of fences and highways for the Glasshouse and North
Fields areas of Salem.   In 1665, Needham became the militia captain, and, in 1672, John Southwick became a
constable.[36]

The most important example of Quaker integration into
local politics is the brief career of Joseph Boyce. Boyce
was a selectman in 1657 and defeated for reelection in
1659. Although probably not a Quaker at the time of his
first election, his defeat after his conversion was only
partially related to his religion. The defeat, though,
was not the beginning of an anti-Quaker purge in town
government. Instead, it signaled a distinct shift in the
balance of political and economic power in the town.
Boyce lost because the specific political and economic
interests he represented were losing ground in Salem.
During the fifties, town government had become increasingly dominated by commercial interests living near the
town center. More traditional agrarian interests living
on the edges of the town, areas like those where most of
the Quakers lived, had come to resent the shift especially
when it became apparent that they did not share equitably
in town services. A small farmer and tanner, Boyce represented the growing reaction to the rise of the influence of the commercial faction.[37]
By 1659, however, two events weakened Boyce's base of
support within the more traditional agrarian interest.
First of all, the calling of Higginson to the Salem pulpit
meant the church's leadership would be in the hands of a
more forceful, influential, and, for the first time in
many years, healthy and active cleric. Because Higginson
favored the Half-Way Covenant and the lessening of the
criteria for admission to full church membership, he divided the congregation and alienated some of the traditionalists like William Hathorne. Hathorne and Higginson were
destined to clash. The calling of Higginson was probably
a rebuke to Hathorne who had assumed much of the leadership of the church during the last years of the ministry
of Edward Norris, the ailing incumbent. The religious
division also had political implications. One of Higginson's supporters was Bartholomew Gedney, an important
leader of the commercial faction who had been denied full
admission into the church while it was under Hathorne's
control. Higginson's first ministerial action reinforced
the political separation between men like Gedney and
Hathorne and helped to divide the latter's agrarian constituency. Upon assuming the pulpit, Higginson asked the
congregation to affirm its 1629 covenant. While this was
not an unusual request, he added an additional clause
warning all to beware the leaven of the Quakers.[38] The
introduction of the clause contrasted with his earlier,
conciliatory gestures toward the Quakers and had subtle
but dramatic effect. Traditionalists who supported
Hathorne and Boyce had to reconsider their political
alliances in the light of their religious obligations.
Affirmation of the church covenant meant the repudiation
of Boyce and Quakers in a public and sacred ceremony, and
this gave the anti-Hathorne, pro-Gedney elements an important indirect endorsement.

Hathorne also had difficulties with those who wished
to moderate his and Governor John Endecott's outspoken
defense of the colonial charter. This moderate position
was clearly in the interests of the commercial faction.
Men like Gedney and Edmund Batter, a former Hathorne ally,
felt that Hathorne endangered trade relations by antagonizing the Crown. Moreover, Hathorne's political preeminence was anachronistic and not fully representative of
the new allocation of economic power in the town.
Hathorne also had rivals for preeminence in the county.
Early in their political careers, he and Simon Bradstreet
had complemented each other in county politics. Hathorne's
center of influence was Salem; Bradstreet's, Andover and
Ipswich. Both men had led the Essex opposition to Winthrop and Boston in the forties, but they had separated
over the charter.[39] For Bradstreet, as well as Gedney
and Batter, one means of supporting the moderates in town,
county, and colony was to undermine Hathorne's local
political influence; however, because of his prominence
and Endecott's support, Hathorne was personally unassail-
able in Salem in 1659. Joseph Boyce was not.

Quaker support was thus a factor that weakened the
political influence of Boyce and Hathorne. Anti-Quakerism
united elements of the moderates in Salem, Essex, and
Massachusetts. Batter's distaste for Quakers struck sympathetic chords among Bradstreet and Boston moderates
like John Hull who had consistently advocated harsh penalties and enforcement.[40] Those holding these common
sentiments were able to use the General Court's anti-
Quaker concerns to weaken Boyce subtly, indirectly, but
with telling effect. In 1659, the General Court banished
five Salem Friends for their excessive zeal in supporting
the visitors. Four of the five were freemen. Their presence in Salem would not have saved Boyce since he lost
by eleven votes, but their exclusion was crucial. Because
Salem probably permitted non-church members to vote in
their town elections, Quakers probably constituted nine
percent of the electorate. If their continued capacity
to participate in local elections depended upon forces
outside local control, that is if the central authority
could disenfranchise Quakers as it did later in 1663,
Boyce probably would have been unable to remain in office
anyway. This hint of weakness, its potential for the
manipulation of local affairs by local factions with the
tacit connivance by elements in the General Court, probably compounded the difficulties of the agrarian faction
and caused a sufficient number of voters to look elsewhere for more successful political connections.[41]

Despite the political setback, Boyce's defeat was
neither the result of persecution nor an event marking
its beginning. It was merely an event that showed the
transfer of political power in the town from one faction
to another. Boyce had been a successful politician because he appealed to both Quaker and non-Quaker; and,

even in defeat, he had had more non-Quaker than Quaker votes. In 1659 he received thirty-five votes; the maximum number of Quaker votes he could have received--that is, all the adult male Quakers in Salem that year--was seventeen.[42] The loss was a narrowly defined local issue shaped by the juxtaposition of different forces in town, county, and colony. Larger forces had been brought into the fray because they provided one faction with levers for changing the balance of power and securing victory. After the election, there was no sustained effort to persecute the Quakers once they had been rendered politically impotent. Quakers neither found themselves harried from the town nor, as we have seen from their wealth, seriously threatened with financial penalties.

The election results of 1659 also illustrate that Quakers had bases for common action with others in the town. Quakers may have been divided between agrarian and commercial interests too. While thirteen of the Quakers were husbandmen or yeomen, fifteen were either tradesmen, artisans, or owners of shipping interests. Some of the Quakers with commercial interests had curious connections and patrons. Edward Wharton, the guide of many visiting Quakers, sold the town fifteen pounds of glass and other materials to repair the church. Joshua Buffum was a shipbuilder and merchant who numbered among his customers Bartholomew Gedney and William Browne, another merchant and prominent moderate. Samuel Shattock had a half interest in a warehouse; Gedney owned the remainder.[43]

Non-Quakers went into business with Quakers because the latter provided the former with larger, trans-Atlantic trade connections. Gedney could use his connection with Shattock as a means for establishing a working relationship with Shattock's Boston partner, Quaker John Soames. Edward Wharton's combination of trade and religion had taken him to Kittery and Salisbury. In Richard Gardner, Friends had a union of Salem's agrarian and commercial interests. The younger brother of the town's largest landowner, Gardner migrated to Newport, where he became a member of the Rhode Island Assembly. A former resident of Salem and, unquestionably, an acquaintance of Rhode Island's Governor William Coddington, Gardner was thus an ideal conduit for trade and influence. Indeed, he was probably the connection that enabled Caleb Buffum, Joshua's younger brother, to make his first Rhode Island investments that grew into his own large fortune.[44]

In light of these connections and concerns, why then did the fines take place? They may have been initiated in 1658 because of the stereotype of Quakers and the missionary activities occurring in the town that year, but they were not sustained for the next twelve years on bigotry alone. Coincidentally, the fines actually paid were comparable to amounts Quakers might have had to contribute to the orthodox church. For the period 1658-70, the total fines averaged about twelve shillings

annually for each household. Extrapolations taken from
the 1683 tax rates for Salem and from the ratios of ministerial to county rates paid during the sixties suggest
that the annual per household rate for the ministry would
have been about twelve shillings, six pence. Since the
fines were supposed to go to the town in which the offender resided, Salem would have benefited directly.[45]

Salem needed the money. During the fifties, the
church incurred new, unexpected expenses while its tax
base shrank. Beverly asked to be allowed to separate
while the Farms established a new parish.[46] In 1659, the
town also committed itself to a ministry beyond its means.
Two years earlier, the town noticed that the years had
begun to take their toll on minister Edward Norris and
hired John Whiting to be his assistant. Whiting's salary
was seventy pounds per annum, ten less than Norris's,
and he required a house. To make ends meet, the selectmen abandoned the practice of voluntary contributions for
maintaining the church; anyone who failed to provide their
portion would be taxed. Although the town managed to
scrape together enough money to buy Whiting a house, the
roof leaked badly. Whiting, sensing the town's economic
difficulties, despaired of having a decent living in
Salem and resigned.[47]

Whiting's resignation was fortunate because it provided the town with the opportunity to call John Higginson to the pulpit. Higginson was especially attractive
to the town because of his father's previous service as
its first and fondly remembered minister and because he
was considered one of Thomas Hooker's proteges. The town
wanted him so badly it offered him 160 pounds annually,
ten pounds more than the combined salaries of Norris and
Whiting. To aggravate the town's financial hardships
even further, the aged Norris clung to life. The economic
crisis struck home in 1659 when the town had to arrange
to pay both Norris and Higginson. Rather than pay Norris
for the whole year, the town gave him only six months'
salary. In addition, the town repeated the taxation of
those who refused to make voluntary contributions to the
church.[48]

Although Norris's death in 1660 relieved the town of
part of its economic liabilities, Higginson's salary
still posed problems. Between 1664 and 1667, the town
failed to pay his salary in full and had to order a special tax to pay Higginson forty pounds in back salary.
To eliminate the chronic problem of Higginson's arrears,
the town tried a new means of collection. In 1670, it
decided to farm out the tax collection to William Browne.
Browne was supposed to advance Higginson his salary and
then collect the minister's rate. In practice, the new
method meant a reduction in the cost of the ministry.
Browne obtained Higginson's consent to reduce his salary
to 100 pounds and forty cords of wood.[49]

The town's difficulties with meeting its ecclesiastical obligations coincided with the county's demands

upon the Quakers. Shortages in Higginson's salary appeared after the county court reduced the maximum fine
for absence in 1665 and 1666. As the town reached its
accommodation with Higginson after 1667, the county reduced its demands upon the Quakers, not only through its
increasingly erratic system of citation but by the total
amount of fines. Of all the fines assessed from 1658 to
1670, only ten percent were levied after 1667.[50] Even
when the town proved its inability to meet its obligations in 1667, it tried to exempt Quaker contributions
to the special levy. Unfortunately for the Quakers, the
town was unable to raise sufficient funds and had to demand contributions from everyone. While Quakers did not
keep their blanket exemption, individuals received tax
relief. In 1668, John Smith received an abatement of
five shillings, and the next year William Marston received a return of six shillings. By 1670, the town felt
sufficiently solvent to grant Quakers permanent relief
from all rates for the ministry; that was the same year
that the county court ceased to cite Salem Quakers for
absence from church services.[51]
    The evidence that the fines served in lieu of eccles-
iastical taxation is admittedly circumstantial, but the
process was appropriate to the situation and provides the
best possible explanation for the Essex County Court's
treatment of local Quakers. Quakers would not have had
to make direct payments to a Puritan minister, and the
town would have had legal judgment against them to ensure
the collection of funds. Even though the connections between the fines and Salem's fiscal problems are tenuous,
the town's need for the money and its relative restraint
in its fiscal demands upon the Quakers are clear. If the
Quakers refused to conform, the cost of nonconformity was
still manageable, and they were, in general, liable to
punishment only in institutions where their local influence was most useful. As long as they kept their dissent
within the jurisdiction of the local courts, that is, as
long as they refrained from behavior that seemed dangerous
and too much like the visitors, they would not be subject
to the harsher attributes of General Court justice.[52]
    Certainly, the minimal effect the fines had on in-
dividuals, families, political affiliations, and economic
relations illustrates an accommodation to Quaker heterodoxy that in turn demonstrated the emergence of religious
toleration in seventeenth-century Salem. During the
third quarter of the seventeenth century, Salem Puritans
adjusted to the presence of a Quaker community. Indeed,
they found that tolerating Quakerism was less disruptive
to the fabric of their lives than making a systematic
attempt to persecute it. As they had in the fifties and
sixties, resident Quakers provided an important source of
responsible manpower in the seventies and eighties. Not
using them because of General Court prohibitions against
the use of nonfreemen would only have increased civic

burdens upon the rest of the town, especially as Salem
expanded geographically and required the distribution of
services to the Glasshouse and North Fields. In the
seventies, the town authorized the payment of bounties to
Quakers to help eliminate wolves and began to cull the
town's common forests. Quaker Anthony Needham supervised
the latter effort and, with the consent of the town, the
allocation of some of the wood to John and Josiah Southwick.[53] Samuel Gaskin, Joshua Buffum, and Josiah and
Daniel Southwick periodically served in the minor offices
of surveyors of fences and highways during the seventies
and eighties.[54] They do not appear to have been relegated
to lesser offices because their previous history of Quakerism disqualified them for other, higher posts; rather,
they seem to have been younger men serving in minor office
until age, experience, and esteem qualified them for
higher posts. Born in 1637, Daniel Southwick first served
as a surveyor of fences at thirty-nine. By 1684, he had
been surveyor of fences and of highways twice. In his
second term as surveyor of highways, he supervised extensive road work involving thirteen days of his own time
and twenty-seven other men. He served an additional term
as surveyor of highways in 1690, and then became town
constable in 1694 and a collector of taxes in 1695.[55]

Older and wealthier than his brother Daniel, John
Southwick became a constable in March 1672 at age fifty-
two. His selection indicated the importance the town
placed upon his personal character and the lack thereof
upon his religious beliefs. Although far less active in
the Quaker meeting than his family, his Quakerism was
still beyond question. He was one of the first to confess
to being a Quaker, and, in 1660, he had stood surety for
two visiting Quakers, Joseph and Jane Nicholson.[56] His
assumption of the post of constable caused no apparent
break between him and the rest of the Southwicks despite
his willingness to collect Reverend Higginson's rates.
After John's death in 1672, Daniel and Josiah became the
executors of his will.[57]

Ironically, the nature of Quakers' faith may have
contributed to making them appear sober, responsible
members of the Salem community. Begun as early as 1656,
the meeting probably developed because the center of
would-be Quaker population was beyond the North Bridge
and too distant or inconvenient for regular attendance.
The situation may also have been aggravated by problems
associated with Norris's distaste for more Antinomian
strains of belief and his increasing infirmities.[58] Holding silent meetings in Quakers' homes may have resolved
some of these difficulties, rationalized doing without a
minister, and, in a small way, reduced conflict and
tension.

While some Quakers may have been caught up in the
initial excitement of conversion and been extraordinarily
enthusiastic, most probably exhibited forms of faith that

were sedate and understandable if not entirely acceptable
to Puritans. Quakerism addressed itself to familiar
Puritan doctrine; the search for God's free grace could
be construed as being analogous to the discovery of the
inner light. The sixteen former full church members
demonstrated that many Quakers had already shown an abiding concern in matters of faith, and the willingness of
the entire meeting to endure patiently the disadvantages
of their faith confirmed a pattern of religious idealism.
Moreover, as that idealism was sustained, it probably was
not seen by Puritans as excessively enthusiastic. Josiah
Southwick's career provides an important illustration of
the evolution of the meeting. Exiled with his parents,
Samuel Shattock, and Joshua Buffum in 1659, Southwick
returned to a quiet, if heterodox, life in Salem in 1662.
During the seventies, he became one of the most weighty
members of the meeting. The rise of his influence par-
alleled the domination of Quakerism by George Fox and the
practice of more quiescent forms of belief. In the sixties, Fox had broken with John Perrot and urged that
greater discipline over individuals ought to be exercised
by meetings. By 1672, Fox was firmly in control in
England and had begun to extend to New England the structure of monthly and yearly meetings for business that
gave the sect a more structured, disciplined, and centralized denominational cast.[59] In the early eighties, Southwick first led the monthly meeting in disciplining Quakers for "disorderly walking" and then in excommunicating
Samuel Shattock and Joshua Buffum. Both men, as Perrot
had done, maintained that they could wear their hats
during worship. Their expulsion from the meeting meant
the supremacy of the more quiet, less visibly challenging
but nonetheless sustained faith of Quakers like Southwick
and Fox.[60] Indeed, in the practice of faith, Southwick
probably presented Puritans with a demeanor not significantly different from the outward faith of others and
equally worthy of toleration if not acceptance.

Moreover, the Salem church had never been strict in
its pursuit of doctrinal orthodoxy among its members.
The Old Planters, those who had settled the town before
the arrival of the Massachusetts Bay Company, had probably
been admitted without a stringent test of faith, and
Higginson, in pressing for the Half-Way Covenant and
looser admission requirements, followed in this tradition.
In 1663, Higginson also petitioned the General Court for
looser religious requirements for admission to the franchise. The vote should be given, he declared to those
non-church members who were "orthodox in religion and
unblameable in conversation."[61]

In 1672 these ambiguities over the religious criteria
for political participation led to deep division over the
appointment of Charles Nicholet to the post of assistant
pastor. Higginson opposed the call and complained at the
end of Nicholet's first year that "he found no assistance

nor help from him, but much affliction and oppression."
In response, the town voted to extend Nicholet's temporary
appointment an additional year. The following year, the
town extended the appointment for life. To Higginson and
his supporters, the actions of the town were especially
insulting. First, it had forced him to accept a cut in
pay, and now it was blatantly interfering in the affairs
of the church. When Higginson and his supporters appealed
to the General Court for help, the Court declined taking
any action and suggested feebly that both town and congregation live in harmony. Victory for the town was
short lived; Higginson and the congregation made life in
Salem so unbearable for Nicholet he left in 1676.[62]
     The role of the Quakers in the controversy was ambig-
uous. To the members of the church, Quakers were a sizable faction, twenty-one adult males out of an approximate
town population of 300, who, while they might have no
opinions on Nicholet, would be unwilling to have the town
bear the costs of an additional minister.[63] On the other
hand, the non-Quaker, non-church members opposing Higginson and the church could not prohibit Quaker political
participation without conceding the legitimacy of their
own exclusion from the decision-making process. Furthermore, because of the previous tension between Higginson
and the Quakers, there was always the possibility that
they might vote against him.
     Whatever the range of possibilities, that Quakers
could be seen in a context favorable to the two opposing
factions demonstrated the complexities of Salem life and
the ease with which local Quakerism could shed its harmful image. As the Nicholet controversy grew, it could
only work to the advantage of the Quakers by placing them
in the background of town concerns. For when the Nicholet
controversy damaged the relationship between church and
state, did it not follow that those who had promoted it
were more destructive of moral order than Quakers who
merely withdrew from services? Conversely, the evolution
of Salem life with its periodic and religious upheavals
may have provided the town with a more subtle understanding of the nature of change. The town need not have perceived change as a decline in consensus or something in-
nately destructive to daily life. Rather, the town may
simply have been coping with everyday events that required adaptations or adjustments to preserve, to the
best extent possible, the overall peace of the community.
Within this context, divergent political and religious
interests need not equal cataclysmic dissension and dis-
harmony; they might merely be small, specific areas of
disagreement that required mutual adjustment and adapta-
tion for the satisfaction of all.
     The experience of Quakers in Salem and in the Essex
County Court was one example of legal institutions ad-
justing to conflict and differences while affirming a
larger consensual community. In 1678, when the General

Court asked nonfreemen of the colony to take the oath of allegiance, sixteen of twenty-two Quakers complied without any apparent difficulty.[64] The Quakers' compliance, like their other attributes of civil behavior and economic standing, again confirmed their place in the larger Salem community. Once it was clear that Salem Quakers were different from the visitors, Higginson and the orthodox church found that it was impossible to compel the town or the county court to suppress an illegal but peaceful meeting. The fines that other historians have seen as originating solely in the desire to produce conformity were more likely a series of adjustments made to determine who would rule the town and pay for town services, the benefits of which were not used by everyone. That Quakers were ostensibly punished for religious reasons does not necessarily mean that they were considered to have committed vicious criminal acts or that the impulse for conformity was crucial. Quakers in Salem were different, and they paid for their differences with compulsory and, from the modern perspective, discriminatory ecclesiastical taxation and in diminished political influence. But the price they paid for those differences was one paid, however reluctantly, by all nonconforming seventeenth-century Englishmen.

Despite the encouragement the local conversions gave to the visiting Friends, the mechanisms designed to suppress heterodoxy were muted in Salem, revealing the dependence of the General Court upon local cooperation in governance. However much the central government in Boston might desire the suppression of Quakerism, the need to use local secular authorities limited the capacity of the colony to enforce Quaker conformity. For the policy of the General Court to be carried out effectively, there could be no disagreement with the policy at the local level. Salem magistrates and townsmen had to have the same opinion of Quakerism as the bulk of the members of the General Court.[65] To complicate matters further, the magistrates and juries could only act if they perceived a specific threat to secular peace. Civil governments could not rely upon religious tests, however accurate they might appear. To do so would have enabled a centralized civil authority to command orthodoxy.

Few Puritans questioned a case like Mary Dyer, who repeatedly and defiantly flouted the General Court to preach the Quaker faith. Most thought she deserved to hang for her contempt of all authority; but what were magistrates to make of others who said they held similar religious beliefs but who, besides their beliefs, possessed other indicators that made it difficult to distinguish them from other valuable, well-behaved members of their local communities? To the town and county magistrates concerned with the case of the Salem Quakers, the distinctions between the visiting Quaker incapable of controlling his passions and the resident, heterodox in

belief but sober in conduct, were all too apparent. The
local Quakers often proved to be part of an industrious
middling class, a business associate who offered opportunities for mutual profit, or a good friend, neighbor,
cousin, sister, or brother. In short, in all those areas
that touched men's lives six out of seven days of the
week, the positive value of Quakers in Salem counted for
more than their refusal to attend Mr. Higginson's church.

NOTES

1. The only recorded mass citation of Quakers in
Middlesex occurred in 1633. Four residents were convicted
of reviling local ministers and entertaining visiting
Quakers. One of the residents, Ursula Cole, was an obvious example of a persistently troublesome person. In
addition to Quakerism, she was also convicted for selling
beer illegally, receiving stolen money, and entertaining
men at unseasonable hours. Benanual Bowers was the only
person cited repeatedly for religious crimes. Before becoming involved with Quakers, he supported the Charlestown Anabaptists. Upon investigating charges that Bowers
was living with Elizabeth Holman without being married to
her, Daniel Gookin concluded that he was a "perverse
Quaker." See the David Pulsifer transcription of the
Middlesex County Court Records, 1:102, 287, 296-97, 301,
2:257, in the New Middlesex County Court House, Cambridge,
Mass.; Middlesex County Court Files, no. 34, New Middlesex County Court House, Cambridge, Mass. William G.
McLoughlin, New England Dissent, 1630-1833: The Baptists
and the Separation of Church and State, 2 vols. (Cambridge,
Mass., 1971), 1:17, 60-63.
In Boston, only, two residents had any difficulty
with the county court before 1673. Anne Gilliam was
threatened with deportation in 1662, but the petition of
her aged husband and Shattock's return with the king's
writ prevented her exile. With the exception of Nicholas
Upshall, no other Boston residents were identified or
punished as Quakers until 1673. Between 1673 and 1678,
the Suffolk County Court cited seventeen Quakers, including Gilliam. These citations seemed linked to the
arrival of Nicholas and Christian Moulder (see chapter 5)
and not to persecuting sentiments. At least twelve were
residents of Boston before 1666. There are, in fact,
indications of some toleration of local Quakers. Edward
Shippen, the founder of the famous Philadephia mercantile
family, reportedly converted to Quakerism when he married
in Boston in 1671. There are extant county court records
for that period, and they do not show any citations of
him for Quaker-related crimes. Randolph S. Klein,
Portrait of an Early American Family: The Shippens of
Pennsylvania across Five Generations (Philadelphia, 1975),
pp. 10-12. John Noble, ed., Records of the Courts of

Assistants of the Colony of the Massachusetts Bay, 1630-
1692, 3 vols. (Boston, 1901-28), 2:64-66, 79. Samuel
Eliot Morison and Zachariah Chaffee, Jr., eds., Records
of the Suffolk County Court, 1671-1680, Publications of
the Colonial Society of Massachusetts, vols. 29-30
(Boston, 1933), 29:438-39, 488, 630, 868, 917. Suffolk
County Court Records, 1680-92, pp. 17, 25, Old Suffolk
County Court House, Boston, Mass. Benjamin Gilliam to
the General Court, 9 May 1662, Massachusetts Archives,
10:278a, 279, State House, Boston. Also see George A.
Selleck, Quakers in Boston, 1656-1964: Three Centuries
of Friends in Boston and Cambridge (Cambridge, Mass.,
1976), pp. 26-28.
    In Norfolk, Quakers were indicted in 1662, 1663, 1668,
1669, 1670, and 1674. Each instance seemed to be prompted
by visitor-like behavior or by the presence of a visitor.
In 1663, Eliakim Wardell charged magistrate Simon Bradstreet with acting maliciously for punishing his wife for
public nudity and for executing the Quaker martyrs. When
asked why he did not attend church services, Wardell
informed the county court that Seaborn Cotton, the Hampton
minister, was "a hireling preaching false worship." In
1674, thirteen adult males were admonished for being at
a Quaker meeting presided over by visiting Quaker John
Stubbs. Norfolk County Court Records, 1648-78, pp. 52,
56, 58, 59, 60. 64-66, 100, 114, 120, Essex Institute,
Salem, Mass.

    2. Historians disagree on the numbers of resident
Quakers in Salem. In Wayward Puritans: A Study in the
Sociology of Deviance (New York, 1966), p. 176, Kai T.
Erikson used George F. Dow and Mary Thresher, eds.,
Records and Files of the Quarterly Courts of Essex County,
Massachusetts, 1636-1692, 9 vols. (Salem, 1911-75) to
identify fifty-one resident Quakers; Richard P. Gildrie,
in Salem, Massachusetts, 1636-1683: A Covenant Community
(Charlottesville, Va., 1975), p. 131, found sixty-three
(thirty-seven men and twenty-six women); and I discovered
thirty-two men and twenty-five women. My differences with
Erikson stem from my use of the manuscript court records
and files instead of the printed records. Dow understandably wearied of the constant lists of Quakers and edited
them quite severly for the years 1663-70. My differences
with Gildrie are the result of using different criteria
for identifying Quakers. See Appendix 1.

    3. Thomas G. Barnes, ed., The Book of the General
Lawes and Libertyes Concerning the Inhabitants of Massachusetts (1648; rept. San Marino, Calif., 1975), p. 20.
Salem Court Records, 1655-66, June Term, 1657, no. 44,
Essex Institute, Salem, Mass. Nathaniel B. Shurtleff,
ed., Records of the Governor and Company of the Massachusetts Bay in New England, 5 vols. in 6 parts (Boston,
1853-54), 4, pt. 1:277-78 (hereafter referred to as
Mass. Records).

4. By going to Boston and supporting the visitors, Salem Quakers changed the venue of their actions and made themselves subject to the jurisdiction of the General Court. See chapter 3. Shurtleff, Mass. Records, 4, pt. 1:345-47.

5. Salem Court Records, 1655-66, November Term, 1661, no. 36; November Term, 1662, no. 35.

6. The king's letter of 1661 ordering the suspension of capital punishment for Quakers in Massachusetts had little effect upon the treatment of local Quakers. Magistrates could still use corporal punishment because Quakerism was a form of criminal disorder. The king's letter raised problems because it posed a possibility that appeals for royal intervention in local cases might make the local administration of justice problematical. See chapter 4.

7. James Henretta, "Economic Development and Social Structure in Colonial Boston," William and Mary Quarterly, 3d ser., 22 (1965):80.

8. Dow and Thresher, Records of the Essex Quarterly Courts, 2:224-25, 3:412.

9. Salem Court Records, 1655-66, June Term, 1661, no. 14; November Term, 1661, nos. 53, 54.

10. Ibid., September Term, 1665, no. 36. Essex County Court Files, 11:140, Essex Institute, Salem, Mass.

11. The fines were noted in the records or on indictment papers. According to the records, the total of Quaker fines through 30 April 1667 was 922 pounds. The county treasurer's accounts for that date indicated that 644 pounds were still outstanding. Also note the indictment of 27 June 1665: "We present the Quakers which were presented at the last Court except Roberd Willson." Essex County Court Files, 10:150, Salem Court Records, 1667-79, June Term, 1670, nos. 54, 55; Dow and Thresher, Records of the Essex Quarterly Courts, 3:412; Appendix 2.

12. The large number of Quakers using the probate system indicates that, as a group, they were generally well off. While the data presented here use wills and inventories that extend into the eighteenth century (see Appendix 3), the material directly comparable to statistical data for the years 1661-81 places them firmly among the middling class. In this period, Quakers accounted for slightly more than seven percent of all the wills and inventories filed, a figure roughly equal to their proportion of the town population. The average value of Quaker wills in this period was 327 pounds, of town wills

as a whole, 330 pounds. Essex Probate Files, nos. 2646,
3977, 4240, 4403, 10607, 11627, 15820, 17862, 25127,
25413, 25919, 18015, Essex Probate Court, Salem, Mass.
Donald Warner Koch, "Income Distribution and Political
Structure in Seventeenth-Century Salem, Massachusetts,"
Essex Institute Historical Collections, 105 (1969):57-58;
William I. Davisson, "Essex County Price Trends: Money
and Markets in Seventeenth-Century Massachusetts," and
"Essex County Wealth Trends: Wealth and Economic Growth
in Seventeenth-Century Massachusetts" both in Essex Institute Historical Collections, 103 (1967):144-85, 291-
342 respectively; George F. Dow, ed., Probate Records of
Essex County, Massachusetts, 3 vols. (Salem, Mass., 1916-
20), 1:318-19, 2:92-93, 3:78-80, 201-8, 368-70, 401-2,
431-32; Dow and Thresher, Records of the Essex Quarterly
Courts, 3:116; Sidney Perley, The History of Salem, Massachusetts, 3 vols. (Salem, Mass., 1924-27), 1:68.

13. For comparative tax rates for 1683, see Appendix
4. For estimates derived from tax assessments, see Gildrie, Salem, p. 155, and Harold H. Burbank, "The Taxation
of Polls and Property in Massachusetts, 1630-1775,"
(unpublished manuscript, n.d.), pp. 10-11a, Burbank Papers, Baker Library, Harvard University, Boston.

14. See below, this chapter.

15. Dow, Probate Records of Essex, 1:318-19, 2:136-
40; for a description of the problems connected with the
glassworks, see Perley, The History of Salem, 2:53-58.
For the economic conditions in the farm sector, see
Davisson, "Essex County Price Trends," pp. 144-85, and
"Essex County Wealth Trends," 291-342.

16. Buffum's estate at his death was valued at 604
pounds, 10 shillings. His father left an estate of 270
pounds, 19 shillings to be divided among his widow and
children. None of this was available to Joshua until
1678 because his father died intestate in 1669, and the
portions given to the four daughters were contested.
Dow, Probate Records of Essex, 2:174-76; Joshua Buffum
Account Book, p. 1, Buffum Family Papers, Essex Institute,
Salem, Mass. Compare Buffum's rate to the 1683 distribution in Appendix 4.

17. See, for example, Salem Court Records, 1655-66,
November Term, 1662, no. 61; November Term, 1663, no. 46.

18. See, for example, Rufus M. Jones, The Quakers in
the American Colonies (1911; rept. New York, 1962), pp.
103-4, and Erikson, Wayward Puritans, pp. 107-36.

19. According to Barbara Dailey in "John Cotton's Abstract of the Laws of New England" (seminar paper, Boston University, 1977), forty-three percent of some 200 fines levied between 1630 and 1641 were remitted wholly or in part. The system, Dailey believes, was dependent upon constables who tended to avoid difficult collections and upon an apparent understanding that bankrupt men would only require increased support from the town (p. 12). Shurtleff, Mass. Records, 2:153-54, 3:52, 69, 340, 341.

20. Salem Court Records, 1655-66, November Term, 1659, nos. 43-44.

21. Essex County Court Files, 5:128; Salem Court Records, 1655-66, June Term, 1660, no. 75.

22. Salem Court Records, 1655-66, November Term, 1663, no. 35; June Term, 1661.

23. For a contrasting opinion, see Erikson, Wayward Puritans, pp. 107-36.

24. George Bishop, New England Judged by the Spirit of the Lord (1661; rept. London, 1703), pp. 390-91; Vital Records of Salem, Massachusetts to the End of the Year 1849, 2 vols. (Salem, Mass., 1916), 1:496. Essex County Court Files, 5:128.

25. Perley, The History of Salem, 2:244-45. Essex County Court Files, 5:128.

26. At the time, Daniel and Provided Southwick owed the county court ten pounds. Dow and Thresher, Records of the Essex Quarterly Courts, 2:224-25; Essex County Court Files, 5:47, 53, 119.

27. Essex County Court Files, 8:3, 9:134, 14:88-89.

28. My figures were taken from a ratio of adult male Quakers (thirty-two) to adult males in the town according to Robert Wall. The figures are supported by Felt's estimate of a total population of 1,446 and the use of about 300 households as a standard for the assessment of rates. Robert E. Wall, "Decline of the Massachusetts Franchise, 1647-1666," Journal of American History, 59 (1972):304. Joseph B. Felt, Annals of Salem, 2 vols. (Salem, Mass., 1845), 2:410; William P. Upham et al., eds., Town Records of Salem, Massachusetts, 1634-1691, 3 vols. (Salem, Mass., 1868-1934), 3:9.

29. See the William W. K. Freeman map in James D. Phillips, Salem in the Seventeenth Century (Boston, 1933), end paper.

30. Phillips, Salem in the Seventeenth Century, pp. 131-252, 255; Dow, Probate Records of Essex County, 2:136.

31. Ann, the widow of the youngest brother of George, married Simon Bradstreet in 1673; Perley, The History of Salem, 1:68; Salem Court Records, 1655-66, November Term, 1663, no. 46; Dow and Thresher, Records of the Essex Quarterly Courts, 3:16.

32. Dow and Thresher, Records of the Essex Quarterly Courts, 1:70, 99n-100n, 173, 287, 313, 414.

33. Richard D. Pierce, ed., The Records of the First Church in Salem, Massachusetts, 1629-1736 (Salem, Mass., 1974), p. 6.

34. Upham et al., Salem Town Records, 1:144; Salem Court Records, 1655-66, November Term, 1658, no. 4.

35. Lists of local jurymen are to be found in both the county court and town meeting records. Upham et al., Salem Town Records, 1:150, 152, 194, 229, 232; Salem Court Records, 1655-66, June Term, 1658, no. 48. Dow and Thresher, Records of the Essex Quarterly Courts, 1:153, 2:125, 157, 183. On seventeenth-century juries, see John M. Murrin, "Magistrates, Sinners, and a Precarious Liberty: Trial by Jury in Seventeenth-Century New England," in David D. Hall et al., eds., Saints and Revolutionaries: Essays on Early American History (New York, 1984), pp. 152-206.

36. Upham et al., Salem Town Records, 1659-1661, 2:45, 148. For other examples of Quakers holding office after 1663, see ibid. 2:201, 208, 234, 3:2, 62, and Salem Town Records, 1689-1709, typewritten manuscript, n.d., pp. 35, 39, Essex Institute, Salem, Mass.

37. Gildrie, Salem, pp. 133-34.

38. Pierce, Records of the First Church in Salem, p. 8; Gildrie, Salem, pp. 133-34. Richard P. Gildrie, "Contention in Salem: The Higginson-Nicholet Controversy, 1672-1676," Essex Institute Historical Collections, 113 (1977):127.

39. Gildrie, Salem, pp. 89-90. Also see Paul Lucas, "Colony or Commonwealth, Massachusetts Bay, 1661-1666," William and Mary Quarterly, 3d ser., 24 (1967):88-107.

40. In his explanation of the role Quakers played in the life of Salem, Gildrie underplayed the rivalry between Edmund Batter and Hathorne. While Batter had been an ally of Hathorne, they broke over the issue of the defense of the charter. Batter was also the most visible opponent of the Quakers. As county treasurer, he profited from the fines. On the other hand--and here I disagree with Gildrie--Hathorne not only represented the geographical and agrarian interest of which Quakers were a part, he seems to have been more genuinely sympathetic toward them. He was ambivalent over the necessity of hanging the visitors, and in 1665 the county court withdrew from him the authority to hear cases concerning Quakers without the presence of another magistrate. One of Hathorne's rivals on the county bench was Simon Bradstreet, who had little affection for Quakers. As governor in 1672, Brad-street complained of the colony's inability to stop the spread of Quakerism by either lenient or severe means. Gildrie, Salem, p. 136; Dow and Thresher, Records of the Essex Quarterly Courts, 3:266; Upham et al., Salem Town Records, 1:223-24; on Hathorne, see chapter 4. For Brad-street, see his letter to Richard Baxter, 5 February 1672, in Raymond Stearns, ed., "Correspondence of John Wood-bridge, Jr.," New England Quarterly, 10 (1937):583; Petition for Stronger Penalties against the Quakers, October 1658, Massachusetts Archives, 10:46, State House, Boston; John Hull, "Diary," Archaelogia Americana, 3 (1857):213.

41. Gildrie, Salem, pp. 133-34.

42. See Appendix 1.

43. Buffum Account Book, pp. 15, 39, 41. Essex Probate Files, no. 25127; Upham et al., Salem Town Records, 1:223-24; also see Carl Bridenbaugh, Fat Mutton and Liberty of Conscience: Society in Rhode Island, 1636-1690 (New York, 1974), pp. 107-10.

44. Perley, The History of Salem, 2:68n.; Walter Buffum, "Notes Related to Robert Buffum and His Children" (unpublished manuscript, n.d.), pp. 1-5, Buffum Family Papers.

45. Because of the limited evidence available on Salem taxes during this period, I have tried to be ex-tremely careful in estimating probable payments. In 1683, the minister's rate was three times the colony rate. Using tax figures for 1659, 1667, 1668, and 1669, I arrived at a ratio of 1.88. I used this figure for computing tax payments for the sixties. The few reports of Quaker rates seem to confirm my estimates. In 1657, John Kitchin and Phillip Veren paid colony rates of five shillings, while Henry Trask paid sixteen shillings.

Using these figures, their estimated ministerial rates
would have been nine shillings, five pence for Kitchin
and Veren and thirty shillings for Trask; and their
average rates sixteen shillings. In 1671, the estimated
rate for Joshua Buffum would have been sixteen shillings,
eight pence; in 1683 he would have paid twelve shillings.
Also, Buffum was only the fifth (of seventeen) highest
Quaker taxpayer. Upham et al., Salem Town Records, 1:217,
226, 2:82-84, 95, 98, 103; Buffum Account Book, p. 46;
Essex County Court Files, 9:349-91; Shurtleff, Mass.
Records, 4, pt. 1:88, 184-85.

46. For a more complete discussion regarding the
separation of the Farms and Beverly from Salem, see Paul
Boyer and Stephen Nissenbaum, Salem Possessed: The
Social Origins of Witchcraft (Cambridge, Mass., 1974),
pp. 40-41, and Phillips, Salem in the Seventeenth Century,
pp. 191-92.

47. Upham et al., Salem Town Records, 1:203, 215,
222; Phillips, Salem in the Seventeenth Century, pp. 191-
92; for a more detailed account of Salem's problems in
supporting its ministry, see Gildrie, "Contention in
Salem," pp. 117-39.

48. Upham et al., Salem Town Records, 1:97, 2:1.
In comparison, sixty years later, the towns of Dartmouth
and Tiverton paid their ministers 100 pounds and 72 pounds
per annum, respectively, and they also demanded that
resident Quakers contribute to the support of the church.
Susan M. Reed, Church and State in Massachusetts, 1691-
1740 (Urbana, Ill., 1914), p. 129. The difference between
compulsory and voluntary support of the ministry could be
as much as 50 pounds per annum. In 1693, Higginson complained that Andros's nullification of compulsory rates
cost him that much. Letter to his son Nathaniel, 31
August 169[3], Higginson Papers, Essex Institute, Salem,
Mass.

49. Upham et al., Salem Town Records, 2:79, 87, 128,
158.

50. Before 1667, 922 pounds, fifteen shillings of
1,020 pounds, fourteen shillings, six pence were assessed.
Furthermore, included among the post-1667 fines is one of
50 pounds assessed on Edward Wharton in 1669. The court
ultimately accepted a settlement of 20 pounds. See Appendix 2. Dow and Thresher, Records of the Essex Quarterly
Court, 4:204.

51. Upham et al., Salem Town Records, 2:99, 105;
Essex County Court Files, 12:119.

52. Shurtleff, Mass. Records, 4, pt. 1:349.

53.   Upham et al., Salem Town Records, 1:116-18, 140, 160.

54.   Ibid., 2:148, 160, 186, 201, 208, 234.

55.   Ibid., 3:2, 106, 119, 215; Salem Town Records, 1689-1709, pp. 25, 39, typescript, Essex Institute, Salem, Mass.; Perley, The History of Salem, 2:53.

56.   Upham et al., Salem Town Records, 2:140.

57.   Ibid., 2:147-49; Dow, Probate Records of Essex County, 2:136-40.

58.   John Rous to Margaret Fell, 2 September 1658, quoted in James Bowden, The History of the Society of Friends in America, 2 vols. (London, 1854), 1:120; see Freeman map in Phillips, Salem in the Seventeenth Century, end paper.   On Norris, see Philip F. Gura, A Glimpse of Sion's Glory: Puritan Radicalism in New England (Middletown, Conn., 1984), pp. 56-58.

59.   Arthur J. Worrall, Quakers in the Colonial Northeast (Hanover, N.H. and London, 1980), p. 29.

60.   Ibid., pp. 29-31.

61.   John Higginson to the Governor of Massachusetts, 6 June 1663, typewritten copy of the manuscript, Higginson Papers, Robert E. Wall, Jr., Massachusetts Bay, The Crucial Decade, 1640-1650 (New Haven, Conn., 1972), pp. 35-40.

62.   Pierce, Records of the First Church in Salem, p. 130.   Upham et al., Salem Town Records, 1:145, 157, 186, 195, 202, 204.   Gildrie believes that part of Higginson's problem was his desire to restore his ministerial authority.   An additional factor in Higginson's distaste for Nicholet may also have been the latter's Presbyterian inclinations.   "Contention in Salem," p. 127.

63.   See Appendix 1.

64.   Essex County Court Files, 30:51-56.   For a list of those Quakers who took the oath, see Appendix 1. Whether taking the oath caused problems for the Quakers is not clear.   Only one Quaker, Robert Gray, actually refused to take the oath.

65. For a discussion of this theme, see Timothy H. Breen, "Persistent Localism: English Social Change and the Shaping of New England Institutions," <u>William and Mary Quarterly</u>, 3d ser., 32 (1975):3-4, 27; Darrett B. Rutman, <u>American Puritanism: Faith and Practice</u> (Philadelphia, 1970), pp. 4-10, especially p. 7n.; David T. Konig, "Origins of Local Government in Northern Massachusetts," in Bruce C. Daniels, ed., <u>Town and Country: Essays on the Structure of Local Government</u> (Middletown, Conn., 1978), pp. 3, 6, 37.

8

They Are a Trouble unto Me;
I Am Weary to Bear Them

Near the steps leading to the State House, not far from
the site of the Quaker executions, rests the Bay State's
memorial to Mary Dyer. The depiction of Dyer in quiet
contemplation of her impending martyrdom and her commem-
oration as an early defender of religious liberty is an
ironic footnote to the experience Quakers had in seventeenth-century Massachusetts. The statue illustrates the
way in which the reactions of the General Court to the
visiting Quakers came to epitomize the confrontations
between Puritan and Quaker. Thus, the adjustments of Bay
institutions to Quakers are supposed to be seen either as
the reprehensible product of Puritan bigotry or as the
understandable, though regrettable, reaction of those in
authority to a group generally associated with factious-
ness, disorder, and sedition.[1] Yet Quakerism in Massachusetts encompassed more than the visiting missionaries.
For every Mary Dyer there were residents like Joseph
Boyce, John Southwick, or Nicholas Shapleigh, and the
Bay Colony was less sure of what its reactions to the
latter ought to be. It is the story of the Boyces, Southwicks, and Shapleighs that should be the central focus of
the confrontation between Puritans and Quakers. Their
experiences explain the General Court's inability to
suppress religious dissent and demonstrates the range of
factors that influenced policy through the layers of
government in Massachusetts.
     When the General Court hanged Quakers like Dyer, it
believed it had good cause. The Court presumed that
religious dissidence weakened men's obedience to government and authority. Good Protestant Englishmen had always assumed that Catholicism, for example, denoted a
foreign allegiance that encouraged treason and rebellion.
A good many other Englishmen on both sides of the Atlantic
also deplored the rise of enthusiastic religions that

threatened order in society. While Quakers attempted to
disassociate themselves from sects like Ranters and Fifth
Monarchists, they still seemed to be part of the enthusiast tradition that had made Muenster anathema to Western
Christendom.[2] Although Massachusetts magistrates had
acted quickly to prevent Quaker proselytizing, the stubborn nature of the early visiting Friends confirmed their
image as sowers of sedition. Their sustained and continued defiance of duly constituted authority in Massachusetts when faced with increasingly severe physical punishments and their refusal to permit any regulation of their
behavior convinced the magistrates that Quakers were mad
with spiritual pride and moved by ungovernable passions.
Perfect examples of the visitors' uncontrollable nature
were their defiance of magistrates and ministers in seemingly strange and bizarre ways and their willing acceptance of pain and death under the belief that they acted
for conscience' sake.

In contrast to the visitors, local Quakers could be
seen within a context that worked against the presumption
that their religious beliefs would produce discord. Fear
of Quakerism in the abstract may have helped to initiate
the punishment of local converts, but they could not be
sustained in secular courts without specific evidence of
disorder. For the most part, that evidence was lacking.
Personal histories of reasonably civil behavior, of substantial contributions to town life, and of participation
in positions of moderate responsibility had earned residents a considerable reservoir of regard contradicting
the assumptions that Quakerism necessarily produced
sedition and disorder. Furthermore, residence provided
traditional measures for evaluating behavior and customary
institutions for controlling individuals. The very fact
of residence, of the real and personal ties that residence
entailed, indicated an interest and a stake in the order-
liness of the locality. Fines could be assessed with the
confidence that they would be collected, the stigma of
jail could be real punishment, and a range of informal
but no less effective economic and social pressures could
be brought to bear in a systematic and omnipresent way.

Yet even when local residents adopted the manner of
the visitors, the fact of their residence tempered the
perception that Quakers were threats to the ordering of
the community. When Deborah Wilson walked naked down
Salem's main street, the Essex County Court did not see
obstinate and persistent contempt, it saw a young woman
"distempered of mind." In Wilson's action the county
court saw nothing seditious--shocking perhaps, disorderly
certainly--but nothing worthy of extraordinary alarm.
The court had little doubt as to the best remedy for this
kind of behavior: it remanded her to the custody of her
Quaker husband.[3]

Not even the remarkable prominence of women in the
movement made local Quakerism a threat to individual Bay

communities. In Salem, for example, the path of Quaker
conversion followed women. Gardner, Southwick, and Buffum
women accounted for thirteen out of twenty-five women in
the meeting. In June 1658, John Smith had helped the
Salem constable arrest Quakers at the homes of Lawrence
Southwick and Nicholas Phelps. One of the Quakers was
Tamosin Buffum. Within a year Smith himself was in jail
with his wife for Quaker-related crimes. His wife was
Tamosin's daughter; another daughter was Deborah Wilson.
In addition, Buffum's two sons, Joshua and Caleb were
very active in the sect.[4]

Women in the Quaker meeting probably had functions
that were similar to ones held by their Puritan sisters.
Robert Pope has suggested that because women were responsible for introducing children into the larger community
and because the church was an important institution for
bridging the gap between the family and the larger community, religion was of special interest to women. Thus,
according to Pope, women church members outnumbered men.
Generally, men outnumbered women in the Quaker meeting.
The only exception appears to have been in Boston. But
if the point of comparison is one of function--that is,
seeing the church as a bridge from the family to a larger
social universe--the highly visible role of Quaker women
in conversion would correspond to the comparable one
women held in Puritan congregations.[5]

Where Puritan authorities may have had more reason to
be concerned was the possibility that such activities
diminished paternal authority and produced division within
families. Yet Bay households frequently maintained two
faiths or different degrees of belief. Nearly a quarter
of the married women in the Boston and Salem meetings,
eight of thirty-four, had non-Quaker husbands. Here
again, however, was another point of favorable comparison
to orthodox congregations; the disproportionately high
numbers of women full church members also suggests that
there were considerable numbers of Puritan families with
varying levels of belief.[6] Furthermore, the husbands of
Quakers did not seem to be disturbed by their wives'
heterodoxy. Most of the Boston non-Quaker men with Quaker
wives seemed indifferent on religious matters. Most were
not listed among the full members of the Boston First
Church and seemed to prefer to have the births of their
children registered in the town records. One orthodox
church member, Benjamin Gilliam, seemed more troubled by
the thought of losing his wife's services than by her
Quakerism. In 1662 the General Court ordered the deportation of Anne Gilliam because of her Quaker activities.
Benjamin successfully petitioned to have the order suspended, arguing that Anne's deportation would leave no
one to see to his needs. Other than his petition to the
Court, Gilliam apparently made no other effort to curb
his wife's activities.[7] In Salem, Robert Buffum and
George Gardner illustrated the different ways in which

non-Quaker husbands responded to their Quaker wives. Buffum, Tamosin's husband, was probably apathetic in religious matters. He was not a full member of the church and never joined the meeting. Clearly, Tamosin's religious sentiments were dominant among the couple's four Quaker children. In contrast, while Gardner could not keep his wife orthodox, his children remained under the supervision of the Salem church.[8]

The paternalistic nature of seventeenth-century Massachusetts may also have militated against the belief that Quaker residents were as dangerous as the visitors. Even if Quaker women were seen to be unusually important in religious affairs, they did not have to be seen as outside the control of an indulgent, paternalistic society. The General Court did not seem to assume that the presence of women at Quaker administrative meetings indicated a desire to turn Bay society upside down. Visibility did not necessarily mean an active policy-making role, and it would appear that the General Court recognized that women had a subordinate position. When the Court banished local Quaker leaders in 1658, only one of the six was a woman. Also, although women were present at disciplinary meetings after 1672, actual control seemed to be vested in men. Alice Shapleigh and Anne Needham only endorsed the first disciplinary actions recorded in the minutes of the Salem Monthly Meeting. The actions themselves had been initiated by men. Indeed, during the censures, John Blevin's apology was sufficient to free his wife Jane from further discipline.[9]

John Blevin's actions further demonstrated familiar attributes of male control over women that made Quakers appear to be more like Puritans. If one presumed that an indicator of the sect's danger could be seen in the disorder of its women, the fact of their husbands' or fathers' presence provided the state with another mechanism of control so obviously lacking with a visitor like Mary Dyer. Dyer had escaped her husband's control, as evidenced by her presence in Boston; yet with resident women, the state still had implicit guarantors of order in reasonably well-behaved husbands. One such guarantor was someone like George Gardner; but Bay institutions did not limit sureties to full church members. After all, when Deborah Wilson's nude walk through Salem was found to be the product of a disordered mind, the solution was a traditional, paternalistic one, the supervision of her Quaker husband. While the mechanisms were not always effective, as the problems of Salem Quaker John Smith indicated, the supervision of a father or husband was still a reasonable check upon the activities of potentially errant resident women and an implication that the sect could co-exist with Puritanism.

Other attributes of Quaker family life tended to diffuse criticism of the sect. The structure of the meeting also affirmed the traditional social utility of the

family. To be a Quaker meant the assumption of legal and
political disabilities, and Quaker families seemed more
tightly knit because of the demands entailed by their
selection of faith. Although some families were split,
a Quaker meeting was essentially a family affair. Male
Quakers generally brought their entire families into the
meeting. Twenty-one of the twenty-three married men in
the Salem meeting had wives who were also Quakers; and
six families--the Boyces, Buffums, Shafflins, Gardners,
Popes, and Southwicks--accounted for thirty-one of the
fifty-seven adult members of the meeting.[10]
     Furthermore, just as customary patterns of authority
of families denoted Quaker similarities with more orthodox members of the community, the Quakers' application
of discipline narrowed their difference with Puritans.
During the seventies and eighties, Quakers purged themselves of their more Antinomian, enthusiastic elements.
Thus, English Quakerism became more quiescent and orderly.
As they developed an institutional structure to cope with
legal and economic difficulties, English Quakers had to
differentiate between real and false Friends; but as
they formed the meetings for sufferings and discipline,
Friends divided, becoming in the process less tolerant
of individual eccentricities. To John Perrot, the new
meetings inhibited the operations of the inner light.
Perrot complained that the meetings subordinated the individual to a larger corporate discipline. He was right;
and for his pains was disowned in 1662, a victim of Quakerism's evolution into a denomination.[11]
     Notwithstanding the enthusiasm that had been charac-
teristic of early Quakers, a more sedate form of the sect
came to prevail on both sides of the Atlantic. Beginning
with the early meetings for sufferings, Quakers created a
hierarchical, presbyterian structure capable of suppressing dissent. Perrot was not the last Friend to be disowned for individualistic behavior. John Wilkinson and
John Story similarly claimed that the creation of the
yearly meetings in London and New England restricted and
suppressed Quaker abilities to respond to the demands of
the inner light. George Fox and Margaret Fell had
Wilkinson and Story disowned by the meeting and further
cemented their hold on the institutional structure of
Quakerism.[12] In 1672, Fox created the yearly meeting
structure in New England. Under its umbrella were brought
the Quaker meetings in Massachusetts Bay, New Plymouth,
and Rhode Island. Through his frequent general epistles,
moreover, Fox imposed his particular view of Quaker doctrine upon New England Friends.[13]
     Like their English brethren, Massachusetts Quakers
repudiated the more individualistic and enthusiastic
members who might side with the likes of Perrot, Wilkinson, and Story. To orthodox Bay Quakers, Perrontonians
like John Chamberlain seemed to have succumbed to madness.[14] While Perrotonian ideas persisted in Salem

through the seventies, Bay Quakers aligned themselves with
Fox. In 1680, twelve Salem Quakers were censured for disorderly walking and two, Joshua Buffum and Samuel Shattock,
were subsequently disowned. The ostensible issue was the
failure of Buffum, Shattock, and the others to remove
their hats during prayers. When Perrot had raised the
issue earlier in England, he had been supported by Buffum,
Shattock, and Josiah Southwick. By 1675, however, Southwick had responded to the Fox directives and, breaking
with his former comrades, called for the removal of hats.[15]
Thus, the expulsion of Buffum and Shattock secured control of the meeting for the more quiescent, corporate
elements of the meeting, and this in turn further substantiated the fact that these particular Quakers seemed
to have no wish to recreate Muenster in Massachusetts Bay.

This increasingly quiescent Quakerism forced Bay
authorities to reconsider the assumptions that shaped
their first reactions to the denomination. The creation
of a separate category of punishment for resident Quakers
reflected the General Court's early ambivalence toward
them, and once local courts demonstrated their minimal
fear of the domestic variety by their haphazard and diffident enforcement of anti-Quaker laws, the justification
for continued suppression of the sect at any higher jurisdictional level became increasingly difficult. Unless the
threat of subversion was evident to all, civil authorities
did not have the power to punish Quakers for heterodoxy
alone. Charging them without actual evidence that sedition was present or disorder imminent would mean punishing
men on purely religious grounds and be a violation of
another, more deeply held value: the wisdom of separating
civil and ecclesiastical authority.

Puritans had purposely split the institutions of
church and state to prevent the latter from dictating
matters of conscience to the former. While the General
Court had interfered in religious affairs before its
confrontations with Quakers, the justifications for involvement had rested upon its belief that the particular
form of heterodoxy obviously was seditious. Sedition was
being punished and not heterodoxy. Magistrates could
prosecute John Wheelwright and Roger Williams because the
church lacked the capacity to save both it and the state
from anarchy and disorder and, hence, the destruction of
godliness. But once the link between sedition and heterodoxy was severed, as with the Quakers, religious dissidents were beyond the power of the state.

Furthermore, there were institutional barriers within
the civil polity preventing the General Court from acting
unilaterally. Migration from England had been spurred by
the desire to escape the extension of centralized Stuart
government. So preoccupied was Massachusetts with the
problem of obstructing the extension of royal power into
local life that it created a polity resistent to direction
from a central source. Although the judges of county

courts were magistrates or appointees of the General
Court, there were considerable opportunities for the more
particularistic of them to disagree with the will of a
General Court majority.16 More importantly, the enforcement of justice rested upon local officials. Justice
required the use of constables and jurymen selected from
the town in which the alleged crimes took place and in
which accused, accuser, jury, and, often, judge resided.
And because circumstances required placing the burden of
suppressing local Quakerism upon the local machinery of
law enforcement, the General Court had to rely upon individuals most susceptible to local influence, most
likely to use criteria of personal reputation in judgment,
and least likely to see seditious implications in the
behavior of long-time valued neighbors.

The concern for the integrity of local institutions
also increased the difficulty of seeing Quakers as a
potential threat to the ordering of communities when the
same communities divided over other issues. During the
late fifties and early sixties, Massachusetts orthodoxy
faced two major issues: the extent to which church membership could be broadened and the extent to which the
General Court should assert its autonomy. Although the
two issues might seem to be mutually exclusive--one
essentially a religious question, the other political--the
issues produced two discrete factions. On the one hand,
those who favored the lowering of standards for admission
to full church membership also tended to be more moderate
in their demands for autonomy from royal interference in
colonial affairs. The other faction was more resistent to
change in the standard of church membership and more extreme in its defense of the autonomy its supporters saw
guaranteed by the colony's charter. Ironically, those
who were liberal and flexible on admissions policies--who
favored the Half-Way Covenant--and were moderates in defending the charter tended to be far less tolerant toward
religious dissent than their opponents. Meanwhile, the
traditionalists on church membership and the ardent defenders of the charter privileges, the commonwealthmen,
tended to be sympathetic to religious dissidents.17

The reaction of supporters of the Half-Way Covenant
and the moderates toward heterodoxy was not surprising.
The challenge to heterodoxy in general and to Quakerism
in particular provided a test of orthodoxy and a means
for justifying the colony's request to be free of interference without openly rejecting the authority of the
Crown. The latter issue, as we have seen, was one of
practicality, of demonstrating to the Crown that the interests of king and colony would be better served by
local retention of legal jurisdiction.

By far, the most significant reaction occurred among
the traditionalists and commonwealthmen. Instead of
providing a point of reference that confirmed the unity
of Bay Puritanism, local Quakerism raised an issue in

which traditionalists and commonwealthmen had more in
common with some dissidents than other Puritans.[18]   One
might have expected that traditionalists and commonwealthmen would have been intolerant of those who rejected the
regular church outright and who were connected to groups
like the English Quakers. Would the traditionalists not
have despised the Quakers' rejection of their faith, and
would not the commonwealthmen have seen Quaker attempts
to influence the king as a call for interference in
colonial affairs? Would not the Quakers' call for toleration have been a deliberate attack upon the autonomy supposedly guaranteed by the charter?[19] Yet this was clearly
not the case. Traditionalists and commonwealthmen were
far less zealous in trying to root out the evil that
religious dissent and Quakerism were supposed to be. One
reason for this may have been a rough similarity in doctrine.[20] For Quakers, the central test of saving faith
was not outwardly civil behavior but the realization of
a state of grace or, in Quaker terms, the discovery of
the inner light. If Quakers erred by accepting the evidence of their spiritual state all too easily, their
emphasis upon an individual union with God derived from
a traditional and familiar strain of Reformed Protestant-
ism. Moreover, Quakers' stress upon the spirit avoided
the legalistic, Arminian implications that inhered in the
attempt to establish criteria for Half-Way membership.[21]

Secular institutional reasons were also crucial to
the commonwealth's adjustment to Quakerism. To the commonwealthmen, the General Court's attempt to punish Quakers could be seen as interference with the affairs of
local communities. The preoccupation of the colony with
the integrity of town and congregation explains the co-
incidence of commonwealth sympathies of John Endecott and
William Hathorne and their relatively lenient treatment
of Quakers. Both had suffered as a result of the General
Court's meddling in Salem life--Endecott when he supported
Roger Williams and Hathorne when the moderate General
Court helped his local political opponents. Similarly,
anti-Quaker legislation had been manipulated to pervert
election results in Kittery. Endecott and Hathorne could
have been afraid not only of royal interference with the
charter but more generally of the extensions of centralized state power into local affairs. Just as the intrusion of royal government upon the charter was a violation
of the autonomy of the colony, the General Court had
infringed upon the local jurisdiction of Kittery and Salem
when it disenfranchised resident Quakers.

In light of the adjustments Puritans made to local
Quakerism, the concern for the integrity of local communities was widely shared. Once local authorities were
assured that their particular Quakers did not share the
disorderly characteristics of the visitors, they could
try to sustain the cohesion of their individual communities based upon secular affinities. Quaker behavior and

the Puritan acceptance of it demonstrated a degree of
cohesion based upon the locality and the complex of kin-
ship, geographical proximity, and economic and political
interests.22 In Hampton, the processes of adjustment and
integration took place with even less acrimony than in
Salem and Kittery. While the Quaker meeting was forming
between 1662 and 1674, the town created distinct classes
of membership; but the distinctions were not between Quaker and Puritan. They were between old and new inhabitants. In 1662, the town tightened the criteria for becoming an inhabitant and holding town office. The ex-
clusionary policy had no effect upon Friends. Two land
divisions, in 1662 and 1669, gave allotments to Friend
and Puritan alike. The criteria for distribution were
previous grants and favored first generation settlers,
among whom were Quaker families like the Hussys, Marstons,
Chases, and Wedgewoods. In 1669, Christopher Hussy, a
frequent town deputy, selectman, and militia officer,
received one hundred acres, the largest size grant made;
his son John, the first Quaker convert in the town, received eighty acres.23

Christopher Hussy personified the difficulty Puritans
had in drawing lines between themselves and Friends.
Hussy was not one of the first Quakers to appear in the
court records; he was not cited until 1673. Notice of
Quaker activity in Hampton by the Norfolk County Court
was at best haphazard, but Hussy should have been sus-
pected of conversion much earlier.24 Hussy's holding of
political office, his Quaker children, and his eventual
conversion illustrated the shadings of place and belief
that made toleration, however rudimentary, more likely.
A man of moderate means, Hussy had been the son-in-law
of Stephen Batchelor, the town's first, although contro-
versial, minister. His children and grandchildren married in both church and meeting house and further blurred
the religious distinctions between Quaker and Puritan.25
A sometime deputy to the General Court and a frequent
member of the Norfolk County Court bench, Hussy was also
a member of the militia, becoming its captain in 1664.
His militia service further cemented an intimate and
surprising, for a Quaker in the Merrimack River region,
relationship with Richard Waldron, the old adversary of
the Kittery Friends. Like Waldron, Hussy opposed Robert
Mason's attempts to restore his proprietary in New Hampshire; like Waldron, he supported the continuation of
Bay Colony jurisdiction in the area; and like Waldron,
he served on the first provisional New Hampshire council.
Indeed, Waldron and Hussy became so close that Hussy
named Waldron the executor of his estate.26

Furthermore, membership in the meeting was not fixed
for eternity. Not only did subsequent generations like
the Hussys marry back into the church, some Quakers returned to orthodoxy. In Salem some of the same moderate
elements that purged the Perrotonians became Puritans

again. Anne Needham endorsed the disowning of Buffum and
Shattock; but she had more in common with the orthodox.
She left the Quaker meeting to join with a number of other
former and second generation Quakers to form Peabody's
Old South Church. Other members of the new church were
John Burton, a former Quaker, and Alice Shafflin, the
widow of another. In addition, the sons and namesakes of
first generation Quakers Joseph Boyce and John Southwick
also owned pews in the new church.[27] How were these former Quakers--or for that matter the Quakers themselves--
functionally different from those Puritans who formed
separate congregations? In Salisbury during the fifties
and sixties, men and women who were clearly orthodox insisted upon absenting themselves from services until they
were permitted to form their own orthodox church.[28] In
Boston, the Half-Way Covenant led to the formation of the
Boston Third Church.[29] The phenomenon of separating
congregations was a reality to which Bay residents had
to grow accustomed during the course of the seventeenth
century.

To have insisted upon religion as a test of communal
    When viewed in this context, the experience of Quak-
ers in Massachusetts was hardly surprising. The assimila-
tion of local Quakers and the expulsion of the visitors
reflected older English traditions that had been given
added importance by the creation in the New World of a
polity designed to obstruct the growth of central secular
authority. Its primary purpose had been to assert the
intensely local nature of English and Puritan community
life. Far from weakening characteristically Puritan
communitarian and consensual impulses, towns made pragmatic adjustments to heterodoxy. Reflected in the treatment of Quakers was a practical accommodation to a more
diverse religious community. Towns like Kittery, Hampton,
and Salem affirmed the virtues of town life by weighing
specific criteria of communal worth, and they discarded
religion as a test of common identity once it appeared
anachronistic. Once done, the town reformulated the
terms of commonality and allowed men to live together in
mutual affection and abiding love on the basis of other
common interests.

    To have insisted upon religion as a test of communal
ties would have also meant abandoning the assumption of
the separation of church and state and denying the obvious. Even the most critical opponents of Quakerism
sensed the evolution of Massachusetts religious life
during the last half of the seventeenth century. In 1681,
noting that they had not been exercised for "diverse
years," the General Court belatedly suspended all the
laws against Quakers.[30] On a more personal level, Samuel
Sewall, a moderate on charter issues and a supporter of
the Half-Way Covenant, might argue with Lynn Quaker John
Burrell during a venison dinner, finding, in the process,
the man overbearing and proud; but Burrell was hardly a
wild-eyed Quaker enthusiast. That the man could discourse,

as Sewall phrased their dinner conversation, was ample
evidence of a kind of common association. Burrell was
far different from Margaret Brewster. Sewell noted the
contrast when he applauded her arrest for appearing before the Boston Third Church dressed in a canvas shift
and her face smeared with ashes. Next to his account of
the arrest in his diary, Sewall noted cryptically,
"Isaiah I:12, 14." Sewall's failure to write the passages
in full symbolically confirmed the contrast of his adjustment to the Quakerism exemplified by Burrell and his ex-
asperation with the kind represented by Brewster. For
Sewall's scriptual citation asked Brewster, "Who hath
required this at your hand to tread my courts?...Your
appointed feasts my soul hateth: they are a trouble to
me; I am weary to bear them."[31]
        What made Quakerism in Massachusetts vulnerable to
punishment was that the early disruptive nature of the
visiting Quakers gave credence to the assumption that
heterodoxy was inimical to public peace. In drawing the
conclusion that Quakers were dangerous, Massachusetts
Bay was no different from the rest of England. Moreover,
there was some truth to the charges from the colony's
point of view. Quakers from abroad said they intended
to level all the distinctions of social hierarchy in
Massachusetts; they denied the rights of magistrates to
regulate their activities; and they were aggressive,
abrasive, and most insistent that all men follow their
lead. Yet the confrontations between Quakers and Puritans in Massachusetts involved more than the visitors.
For if the movement included the obviously seditious and
disorderly, it also encompassed persons of long residence
who were resonably well behaved. The first inclination
of the General Court of Massachusetts was to tar the
inhabitant with the brush of the disorderly visitor. But
to the town and county magistrates the distinctions between a visiting Quaker who seemed incapable of controlling his passions and enthusiasms and the sober, industrious inhabitant who only absented himself from regular
church services were all too apparent. The institutional
structure of Massachusetts gave those magistrates an
arena for the exercise of judgments resting upon those
distinctions and, by the 1670's, the result was the
toleration of religious dissent. In the end, Massachusetts Puritans had learned to distinguish among neighbors,
friends, and visiting madmen.

NOTES

1. See, for example, Thomas Jefferson Wertenbaker, The Puritan Oligarchy: The Founding of American Civilization (New York, 1947), p. 340. Ralph Barton Perry, Puritanism and Democracy (1944; rept. New York, 1964), pp. 98-99.

2. Hugh Barbour, The Quakers in Puritan England (New Haven, Conn., 1964), pp. 120-26. Christopher Hill, The World Turned Upside Down: Radical Ideas during the English Revolution (New York, 1973), pp. 204-7.

3. Salem County Records, 1655-66, November Term, 1662, no. 35, Essex Institute, Salem, Massachusetts.

4. See chapter 4.

5. Women outnumbered men in the Boston meeting twelve to ten. John Noble, ed., Records of the Courts of Assistants of the Colony of Massachusetts Bay, 1630-1692, 3 vols. (Boston, 1901-28), 1:12. Samuel Eliot Morison and Zachariah Chaffee, eds., Records of the Suffolk County Court, 1671-1680, Publications of the Colonial Society of Massachusetts, vols. 29-30 (Boston, 1933), 29:438-39, 488, 868, 917. Suffolk County Court Records, 1680-92, pp. 17, 25, Old Suffolk County Court House, Boston, Massachusetts. Robert Pope, The Half-Way Covenant: Church Membership in Puritan New England (Princeton, N.J., 1969), pp. 214-15, 217-18. Mary Maples Dunn, "Saints and Sisters: Congregational and Quaker Women in the Early Colonial Period," American Quarterly, 30 (1978):588-92.

6. Dunn argues that during this period Puritan churches were women's places. She estimated that women may have comprised sixty-three percent of the full church members in Salem. "Saints and Sisters," pp. 590-92. On the other hand, Carla Gardina Pestana argues that the elevation of Quaker women seemed corrosive to the Puritan social order because they deprived fathers of their special place in the family. The potential for similar occurrences in orthodox churches, however, posed like problems for Puritans. "The City upon a Hill under Siege: The Puritan Perception of the Quaker Threat to Massachusetts Bay, 1656-1661," New England Quarterly, 56 (1983): 350. See also Pope, The Half-Way Covenant, Tables 1-5.

7. Petition to General Court, 9 May 1662, Massachusetts Archives, 10:278a, State House, Boston. Upon Benjamin's death, Anne Gilliam married a Quaker, Giles Sylvester. Samuell Sewall, Diary, 2 vols., ed. M. Halsey Thomas (New York, 1973), 1:78, 78n. Pestana disagrees on the

extent of family division.   "The City up on a Hill under
Siege," p. 351.

    8.   Richard D. Pierce, ed., The Records of the First
Church in Salem, Massachusetts, 1629-1736 (Salem, Mass.,
1974), p. 26.   Dunn, "Saints and Sisters," pp. 595-600.

    9.   Salem Monthly Meeting Records, 1672-78, pp. 6-8,
New England Yearly Meeting of Friends Manuscript Collection, Rhode Island Historical Society Library, Providence.

    10.   Appendix 1.

    11.   Kenneth L. Carroll, John Perrot, Early Quaker
Schismatic (London, 1971), pp. 85-94.

    12.   Ibid., pp. 66, 144.   Hill, The World Turned
Upside Down, pp. 204-6.   Arthur J. Worrall, Quakers in
the Colonial Northeast (Hanover, N.H., and London, 1980),
pp. 29-31.

    13.   See Ancient Epistles, Minutes, and Advices on
Discipline, 1672-1735, p. 1, and Minutes of the Yearly
Meeting, pp. 1-2, New England Yearly Meeting of Friends
Manuscript Collection, Rhode Island Historical Society
Library, Providence.

    14.   Elizabeth Hooten to George Fox, circa 1662,
quoted in George A. Selleck, Quakers in Boston, 1656-1964:
Three Centuries of Friends in Boston and Cambridge
(Cambridge, Mass., 1976), p. 26.

    15.   Salem Monthly Meeting Records, 1672-1778, pp.
6-8.   Selleck, Quakers in Boston, pp. 26-28.

    16.   Timothy H. Breen, "Persistent Localism: English
Social Change and the Shaping of New England Institutions,"
William and Mary Quarterly, 3d ser., 32 (1975):6, 18-19,
20-24.

    17.   Paul Lucas, "Colony or Commonwealth, Massachu-
setts Bay, 1661-1666," William and Mary Quarterly, 3d
ser., 24 (1967):88-102.   See chapter 3.

    18.   See Edward Drinker's comments to John Clark
about the efforts of the Boston First Church ministers
in behalf of Baptists, 30 November 1670, Massachusetts
Archives, 10:228, State House, Boston.   E. Brooks Holifield, "On Toleration in Massachusetts," Church History,
38 (1969) 188-200.   Also see chapter 5.   Furthermore, Bay
institutions permitted the expression of disagreement by
entire counties on certain issues.   Robert E. Wall, Jr.,
Massachusetts, the Crucial Decade, 1640-1650 (New Haven,
Conn., 1972), pp. 36-41.   The phenomenon may also be seen

within the context of the English attempt to reconcile
local manorial custom with the growth of the Common Law.
George Lee Haskins, Law and Authority in Early Massachu-
setts: A Study in Tradition and Design (New York, 1960),
pp. 165-68. David Grayson Allen, In English Ways: The
Movement of Societies and the Transferral of English Local
Law and Custom to Massachusetts Bay in the Seventeenth
Century (Chapel Hill, N.C., 1981), pp. 208-13. David T.
Konig, Law and Society in Puritan Massachusetts: Essex
County, 1629-1692 (Chapel Hill, N.C., 1979), pp. 10-11,
20-22. Keith Wrightson and David Levine, Poverty and
Piety in an English Village: Terling, 1525-1700 (New
York, 1979), p. 116.

19. The scapegoat thesis is best seen in Kai T.
Erikson, Wayward Puritans: A Study in the Sociology of
Deviance (New York, 1966), especially pp. 67-71, 125-38.
Also see Richard P. Gildrie, Salem Massachusetts, 1626-
1683: A Covenant Community (Charlottesville, Va., 1975),
pp. 142-45.

20. Mary Cochran Grimes, "Saving Grace among Puritans
and Quakers: A Study of Seventeenth- and Eighteenth-
Century Conversion Experiences," Quaker History, 72 (1983):
24-25.

21. Pope, The Half-Way Covenant, pp. 143-46. Gildrie,
Salem, pp. 144-45. Philip Gura argues that Quakerism both
emerged out of a traditional strain of religious radicalism while at the same time confirming other more conventional Puritans' worst fears of Antinomianism. A Glimpse
of Sion's Glory: Puritan Radicalism in New England, 1620-
1660 (Middleton, Conn., 1984), pp. 144-52.

22. Peter Laslett, "The Gentry of Kent in 1640,"
Cambridge Historical Journal, 9 (1948):148-49. Timothy
H. Breen and Stephen Foster, "The Puritans' Greatest
Achievement: A Study of Social Cohesion in Seventeenth-
Century Massachusetts," Journal of American History, 60
(1973):5-16. Christine Heyrman sees a retention of private prejudice indirectly related to witchcraft accusations in 1692. According to Heyrman, some accused
witches had Quaker connections and possibly thereby increased their susceptibility to being charged with
sorcery. "Specters of Subversion, Societies of Friends:
Dissent and the Devil in Provincial Essex County, Massachusetts," in David D. Hall et al., eds., Saints and
Revolutionaries: Essays on Early American History (New
York, 1984), pp. 38-74.

23. Joseph Dow, History of Hampton, 2 vols. (Salem, Mass., 1893), 1:352. Hampton Town Records, pp. 106-11, New Hampshire State Library, Concord. Order for the Division of Land, 3 March 1669, Hampton Town Miscellaneous Papers, New Hampshire Historical Society, Concord.

24. The court records for this period are complete. In the period under examination there were only three incidents of mass arrests: 1663, 1668, 1674. Unfortunately, the lack of file papers and town records dealing with the arrests preclude the kind of analysis possible for Kittery and Salem. Norfolk County Court Records, 1648-79, pp. 64-66, 114, 120, Essex Institute, Salem, Mass.

25. His daughter married into a large non-Quaker family; another daughter, Huldy, married within the meeting, but her children did not remain Friends. Nathaniel Bouton et al., eds., Documents and Records Relating to New Hampshire, 1623-1800, 40 vols. (Concord and Manchester, N.H., 1867-1953), 31:326-40, 87. Hampton Monthly Meeting Minutes, p. 9, New England Yearly Meeting of Friends Manuscript Collection, Rhode Island Historical Society Library, Providence.

26. Bouton, Documents and Records Relating to New Hampshire, 1:165-67; 31:387, 513-14, 528. Norfolk County Court Records, pp. 56, 81, 111, 121, Essex Institute, Salem, Mass. Nathaniel B. Shurtleff, ed., Records of the Governor and Company of the Massachusetts Bay in New England, 1628-1686, 5 vols. in 6 parts (Boston, 1853-54), 4, pt. 1:321, 364, 416, 449; pt. 2:507 (hereafter referred to as Mass. Records). Charles E. Clark, The Eastern Frontier: The Settlement of Northern New England, 1610-1763 (New York, 1970), pp. 58-60.

27. Bessie Raymond Buxton, "A History of the South Church Peabody," Essex Institute Historical Collections, 87 (1951):60-62.

28. Salisbury Town Records, pp. 189-92, typewritten manuscript, Essex Institute, Salem, Mass. Shurtleff, Mass. Records, 4, pt. 1:321, 328, 378, 393-94. D. Hamilton Hurd, History of Essex County, Massachusetts, 2 vols. (Philadelphia, 1888), 2:1498-99.

29. Shurtleff, Mass. Records, 4, pt. 1:341-42, 351-52, 390. Pope, The Half-Way Covenant, pp. 160-65.

30. Shurtleff, Mass. Records, 5:347.

31. See also Sewall's connection to John Kitchin in Sewall, Diary, 1:176, 377, 600.

Appendix 1

Adult Quakers in Salem, 1658-70

Quakers Year, 16--	58	59	60	61	62	63	64	65	66	67	68	69	70	
Blevin, John			x	-	x	x	x	x	x	-	x	x	-	#
BOYCE, JOSEPH				x	x	x	x	x	x	-	-	-	-	*, #
Buffum, Joshua	x	x	-	-	-	x	x	x	x	x	x	x	x	*, #
Buffum, Mrs. Joshua			x	x	x	x	x	x	x	x	x	x	x	*, exile 1660-62
Buffum, Tamosin	x	x	+	x	x	x	x	x	x	x	x	x	-	*, nee Demaris Pope
Burnell, John			+											*, Mrs. Robert
Burton, Hannah			x	x	x	-	x	x	-	x	x	-	x	
Burton, John Jr.			x	x	x	x	x	x	x	x	x	x		#
Burton, John Sr.			x	x	x	x	x	x	x	x	x	x	x	#
GARDNER, DEMARIS			x	x	x	x	x	x	x	x	x	-	x	nee Shattock, Mrs. Thomas
Gardner, Elizabeth	x	x	x	x	x	x	x	x	x	x	x	x		Mrs. George
Gardner, Richard	x	-	-	-	x	x	x	-	x	x				removed to Newport 1668
Gardner, Mrs. Richard	x	-	x	x	x	-	x	x	x	x	x	x	x	supra, nee Sarah Shattock
Gaskin, Samuel	x	x	x	x	x	x	x	x	x	x	x	x	x	#
Gaskin, Mrs. Samuel	x	x	x	x	x	x	x	x	-	x	x	x	x	*, nee Provided Scuthwick
GRAY, ROBERT	x	x	x	x	x	x	x	x	-	x	x	-	-	refused oath of allegiance
Hill, John	x	-	x	-	-									#
Hill, Mrs. John	x	-	-	-	x		x	x						*, Lydia
KING, WILLIAM	x	x												
King, Mrs. William			x	x	x	x	x	x		x			x	*, nee Katherine Shafflin
KITCHIN, JOHN	x	-	-	x	x	x	x	x	x	x	x	-	x	
KITCHIN, MRS. JOHN			x	x	x	x	x	x	x	x	x	x	x	nee Elizabeth Sanders
Kitchin, Mary										x	x	x	x	aka Mrs. Timothy Robinson
MARSTON, JOHN			x	x	x	x	x	x	x	x	x	x		
Marston, William	x	-	x	x	-	x	x	x	x	x				freeman 1666
Needham, Anthony	x	-	-	-	-	-								see Anne Needham

Appendix 1 -- Continued

Quakers — Year, 16--	58	59	60	61	62	63	64	65	66	67	68	69	70	
Needham, Mrs. Anthony	x	x	x	x	x	x	x	x	x	x	x	x	x	*, nee Anne Porter
Phelps, Nicholas	x	I	I	I	x	I	x	I	I	I			I	exile 1659-61, d. 1664
Phelps, Mrs. Nicholas	x	x	x	x	x	x	x	x	x	x	x			Hannah
POPE, JOSEPH		I	I	I	x	I	I	I	x	I		x		see Gertrude Pope, d. 1666
POPE, MRS. JOSEPH	x	x	x	x	x	x	x							*, Gertrude
Salmon, Samuel														
SHAFFLIN, MICHAEL	x	x	x	x	x	x	x	x	x	x	x	x	x	#
SHATTOCK, SAMUEL	x	x	x	x	x	x	x	x	x	x	x	x	I	*, exile 1659-61
Shattock, Mrs. Samuel	x	x	x	x	x	x	x	I	x	x	x	x	x	
Small, John	x	x	x	x	x	x	x	x	x	x	x	x		#
Small, Mrs. John	x	I	I	I	x	I	I	x	x	x	x			
Smith, John	x	I	I	I	x	I	x	I	x	x	x	x	x	#, Boston jail 1659-61
Smith, Mrs. John	x	x	x	x	x	x	x	x	x	x	x	x	x	nee Margaret Buffum, jailed
Southwick, Daniel							x	I	x	x	x	x	x	*, #
Southwick, Mrs. Daniel							I	x	x	I	x	x	x	nee Esther Boyce
Southwick, John	x	x	x	x	I	x	x	x	x	x	x			
Southwick, Mrs. John	x	x	x	x	x	x	x	x	x	x	x	I		nee Sarah Tidd, d. 1668?
Southwick, Josiah	x	I	I	I	x	x	x	x	x	x	x	x		*, #, exile 1659-61
Southwick, Mrs. Josiah			x		x	x	x	x	x	x	x	x	x	nee Mary Boyce
SOUTHWICK, LAWRENCE	x	x	x											exile 1659, d. 1660
SOUTHWICK, MRS. LAWRENCE	x	x	x											Cassandra, exile 1659, d. 1660
Stone, Robert						I	x	I	x	x	x	x	x	
Stone, Mrs. Robert	I	x	x	x	x	x	x	x	x	I	x	x	I	*, nee Sarah Shafflin
Tompkins, Nathaniel	I	I		I	x	x								
Trask, Henry	x	I	I	I	x	x	x	x						#, see Mary Trask
Trask, Mrs. Henry	x	I	I	I	x	x	x							*, nee Mary Southwick, jailed
VEREN, PHILIP JR.	x	I	x	x	x	x	x							#

Appendix 1 -- Continued

Quakers	Year, 16--	58	59	60	61	62	63	64	65	66	67	68	69	70	
Veren, Mrs. Philip Jr.															
Wharton, Edward		x	x	x	x	x	-	-	x	x	-	x	x	⌐	*, #
Wilson, Robert							-								see Deborah
Wilson, Mrs. Robert						x	x	x	x	x	x	x			nee Deborah Buffum

Notes: Membership in the meeting was determined by the following criteria: (1) specific identification of an individual as a Quaker or confession of being a Quaker by an individual and no retraction of the confession, (2) inclusion in the mass indictments for absence with other known Quakers and citations in two or more years, or (3) strong circumstantial evidence such as a single citation and an active spouse.

    x denotes an indictment or citation for absence from the orthodox church or for Quaker-related offenses during the year indicated.

    - indicates that while the individual was not cited for Quakerism that particular year, I have assumed that the individual was a member of the meeting at that time. The basis for this assumption rests upon the individual's pattern of offenses or upon subsequent identification as a Quaker by other documents. I have not designated anyone a Quaker after his last citation by the county court unless he was listed in the records of the Salem Monthly Meeting or if other evidence revealed Quaker convictions after 1670.

    * designates a reference to the individual as a Quaker after 1670.

    # identifies Quakers who took the oath of allegiance in 1678.

    A name in capital letters indicates a former member of the Salem Church. Other records indicate that Burnell lived in Lynn, the town immediately to the west of Salem, and, in all probability, it was to him that Samuel Sewall referred in his Diary (I, 377).

    + Burnell was identified as a Quaker in Lawrence Southwick's 1660 will.

    Sources: Essex County Court Records, Essex County Court Files, Essex County Court House, Salem, Mass. Salem Manuscript Court Records, Essex County Court House. Salem Monthly Meeting Records, New England Yearly Meeting of Friends Manuscript Collection, Rhode Island Historical Society Library, Providence.

Appendix 2

Fines Assessed Salem Quakers, 1658-70

Quakers	Before 1667 (in Pounds)	Total to 1670 (in Pounds)
Blevin, John	8.00.00	9.00.00
Boyce, Joseph	25.10.00	25.10.00
Buffum, Joshua	5.15.00	8.15.00
Buffum, Mrs. Joshua	24.00.00	25.10.00
Buffum, Tamosin	49.00.00	50.10.00
Burnell, John	--	--
Burton, Hannah	15.02.06	15.02.06
Burton, John Jr.	2.02.06	2.02.06
Burton, John Sr.	11.00.00	14.00.00
Gardner, Demaris	8.02.06	8.19.06
Gardner, Elizabeth	22.17.06	24.07.06
Gardner, Richard	--	--
Gardner, Mrs. Richard	29.15.00	29.15.00
Gaskin, Samuel	32.02.06	34.02.06
Gaskin, Mrs. Samuel	27.15.00	29.15.00
Gray, Robert	1.00.00	1.00.00
Hill, John	2.00.00	2.00.00
Hill, Mrs. John	--	--
King, William	--	--
King, Mrs. William	--	--
Kitchin, John	22.00.00	25.00.00
Kitchin, Mrs. John	33.05.00	35.07.06
Kitchin, Mary	2.00.00	2.00.00
Marston, John Sr.	10.00.00	13.00.00
Marston, William	16.10.00	16.10.00
Needham, Anthony	--	--
Needham, Mrs. Anthony	33.12.06	35.12.06
Phelps, Nicholas	4.02.06	4.02.06
Phelps, Mrs. Nicholas	19.10.00	19.10.00
Pope, Joseph	--	--
Pope, Mrs. Joseph	15.15.00	20.05.00
Salmon, Samuel	12.17.06	12.17.06
Shafflin, Michael	33.10.00	36.10.00
Shattock, Samuel	27.15.00	29.15.00
Shattock, Mrs. Samuel	48.00.00	49.10.00
Small, John	54.00.00	55.00.00
Small, Mrs. John	13.00.00	13.10.00
Smith, John	18.10.00	20.10.00
Smith, Mrs. John	24.00.00	26.00.00
Southwick, Daniel	53.00.00	55.00.00
Southwick, Mrs. Daniel	--	10.00
Southwick, John	9.02.06	9.02.06
Southwick, Mrs. John	38.00.00	38.00.00
Southwick, Josiah	22.10.00	24.00.00
Southwick, Mrs. Josiah	19.15.00	20.05.00
Southwick, Lawrence	4.10.00	4.10.00
Southwick, Mrs. Lawrence	4.17.06	4.17.06

Appendix 2 -- Continued

Quakers	Before 1667 (in Pounds)	Total to 1670 (in Pounds)
Stone, Robert	--	--
Stone, Mrs. Robert	23.07.06	23.07.06
Tompkins, Nathaniel	5.00.00	5.00.00
Trask, Henry	4.00.00	4.00.00
Trask, Mrs. Henry	20.17.06	20.17.06
Veren, Philip	29.15.00	29.15.00
Veren, Mrs. Philip	13.00.00	13.00.00
Wharton, Edward	11.10.00	61.10.00[a]
Wilson, Robert	--	--
Wilson, Mrs. Robert	11.00.00	11.10.00

Notes: [a]Wharton was assessed a fine of fifty pounds for contempt in June 1669. The county court confiscated seventeen pounds of Wharton's goods and requested the constable to find three pounds more to satisfy the court's judgment against Wharton.

Sources: Essex County Court Files, Essex County Court House, Salem, Mass. Salem Manuscript Court Records, Essex County Court House.

Appendix 3

Quaker Probate Records

Name	Date Entered	Value (in Pounds)
Blevin, John	1704	169.12.06
Buffum, Joshua	1705	604.10.00
Buffum, Tamosin	1698	141.12.06
Burnell, John	1692	157.00.06
Burton, John Sr.	1684	lost
Gardner, Elizabeth	1693	lost
Hill, John	1680	312.16.06
Kitchin, John	1676	398.04.00
Marston, William	1672	123.10.00
Pope, John	1666	90.00.00*
Shafflin, Michael	1691	lost
Shattock, Samuel	1689	415.13.08
Small, John	1708	200.13.06
Smith, John	1678	161.15.05
Southwick, Daniel	1719	51.06.00
Southwick, John	1672	601.02.05
Southwick, Josiah	1693	265.03.06
Southwick, Lawrence	1660	196.00.00
Stone, Robert	1690	718.16.00
Tompkins, Nathaniel	1732	821.00.00
Trask, Henry	1694	83.12.06
Wharton, Edward	1678	691.06.11
Wilson, Robert	1681	151.06.00

Notes: *Distribution of cash legacies only.

Sources: Essex Probate Records, Essex Probate Court, Salem, Mass.   George F. Dow, ed., Probate Records of Essex County, Massachusetts, 3 vols. (Salem, Mass., 1916-20).

Appendix 4

Comparative Tax Rates for 1683

Rates (Shillings)	Quaker Taxpayers	% Quaker Taxpayers	Salem Taxpayers	% of all Taxpayers
0	1	6	31	6
1-1/8	0	0	39	7
2	3	18	238	44
2/6-4	9	53	159	30
5+	4	24	74	13

Note: The identification of Quaker taxpayers was derived from those cited in the county court records for failure to attend meetings. See Appendix 1. The tax figures also include two individuals not cited but who were members of the meeting in 1683, Caleb Buffum and Thomas Maule.

Source: "Appendix Tax Lists" in Sidney J. Perley, The History of Salem, Massachusetts, 3 vols. (Salem, 1924-27), 3:419-21. Richard P. Gildrie, Salem, Massachusetts, 1626-1683: A Covenant Community (Charlottesville, N.C., 1975), p. 156.

Bibliography

BIBLIOGRAPHIC NOTE

Most students of early Massachusetts and seventeenth-century Quakerism will be familiar with most of the printed primary materials cited. Any student of early New England legal history should consult David H. Flaherty, "A Select Guide to the Manuscript Court Records of Colonial New England," American Journal of Legal History, 9 (1967):107-26. For a list of the available published materials, one should see William Jeffrey, Jr., "Early New England Court Records--A Bibliography of Published Materials," American Journal of Legal History, 1 (1957): 119-46.

Nathaniel B. Shurtleff, ed., Records of the Governor and Company of the Massachusetts Bay in New England, 1628-1686, 5 vols. (Boston, 1853-54) and the tenth volume of the Massachusetts Archives provided the bulk of the General Court materials dealing with Quakers. Also of importance in any question dealing with law enforcement by the General Court is John Noble, ed., Records of the Courts of Assistants of the Colony of Massachusetts Bay, 1630-1692, 3 vols. (Boston, 1901-28).

The manuscript records and files of Massachusetts county courts are in various locations throughout the commonwealth. The Middlesex and Suffolk records and files are in their respective court houses in Cambridge and Boston. Norfolk and Essex materials are in the Essex Institute. Eventually, all Massachusetts court records for the period 1630-1860 will be placed in the Archives of the Supreme Judicial Court in the new state archives building scheduled for completion in fall, 1985.

Of the county courts, Essex has the most extensive collection of seventeenth-century materials. There are fifty-seven volumes of file papers consisting of depositions, indictments, warrants, and other legal miscellanea.

There are independent record books for the Ipswich and
Salem sessions dating from 1636. In addition, there are
extant "waste books," rough drafts of trial records that
were later copied into the official record books. Anyone
attempting to wade through the handwriting of seventeenth-
century Essex clerks is advised to look first at the WPA
typescripts of the record books and files. These typescripts were completed in 1935-38 under the direction of
Archie Frost.

Middlesex manuscript court records are in the New
County Court House. While the original manuscripts are
reportedly barely legible, the transcriptions completed
by David Pulsifer in 1851 are available and quite readable. Unfortunately, by the time Pulsifer began his
labors, the second volume of records, for the period
1664-70, had disappeared. The file papers appear to be
in good order, though there is no way to tell how much
has been lost because of the ravages of time and the way
in which demands for space prevented close supervision.
Because of the microfilm project of the Church of the
Latter-Day Saints, the file papers have been calendared.

While there are extensive file papers for Suffolk
County, there do not appear to be any record books prior
to 1671. The manuscripts are kept in the Office of the
Clerk in the New Court House. Darrett Rutman thought
that the functions of the Suffolk Court were subsumed by
the General Court; however, file papers on the Quakers
indicate that there was an effective, functioning county
court. The 1671-80 records have been printed in Samuel
Eliot Morison and Zacariah Chaffee, Jr., eds., Records
of the Suffolk County Court, 1671-1680, Publications of
the Colonial Society of Massachusetts, vols. 29-30
(Boston, 1933). The original records for 1680-98 are
illegible; however, there are readable photostatic copies
in the vault of the Old Court House.

Printed court records are available for Essex County,
Maine, and New Hampshire. George F. Dow and Mary Thresher, eds., Records and Files of the Quarterly Courts of
Essex County, Massachusetts, 1636-1692, 9 vols. (Salem,
1911-75) has omitted many file papers to keep the published materials manageable. There are also omissions
in the records. These could prove to be significant.
For example, citations of Salem Quakers after 1663 have
been omitted in the published records. Also, when Dow
included the Norfolk records in these volumes, he gave
the mistaken impression that the county came under the
jurisdiction of Essex. The Maine records have been
printed in Charles T. Libbey, Robert Moody, and Neal
Allen, eds., The Province and Court Records of Maine,
6 vols. (Portland, Me., 1928-75). The New Hampshire
records are to be found in Nathaniel Bouton, et al.,
eds., Documents and Records Relating to New Hampshire,
40 vols. (Concord and Manchester, N.H., 1867-1953).

In addition to the court records, any study of local
life in Massachusetts requires the extensive use of church
and town records. Both Salem and Boston's local records
are in print. The Records of the First Church in Salem
(Salem, Mass., 1974) have benefitted from the experience
gained by its editor Richard Pierce on his previous effort, The Records of the First Church of Boston, 1630-
1686, Publications of the Colonial Society of Massachusetts, vols. 39-41 (Boston, 1961). For the Boston town
meeting records, see the second, seventh, and ninth
Reports of the Record Commissioners of the City of Boston.
The Salem town records may be found in William Upham and
Martha Howes, eds., Town Records of Salem, Massachusetts,
1634-1692, 3 vols. (Salem, Mass., 1868-1934). These
volumes are reprints of the records scattered throughout
the Essex Institute Historical Collections.

Other important manuscript materials regarding Quakers may be found in the New England Yearly Meeting of
Friends Manuscript Collection in the Rhode Island Historical Society Library, Providence. Extant monthly meeting
records are available in manuscript and microfilm. These
records contain birth, death, and marriage records in
addition to the details of the affairs of the monthly
meetings. Of additional importance to students of New
England Quakerism are the various papers in the Buffum
Family Papers in the Essex Institute.

The two most important pamphlets dealing with early
Massachusetts Quakerism are George Bishop, New England
Judged by the Spirit of the Lord (London, 1661) and John
Norton, The Heart of New England Rent (Cambridge, Mass.,
1659). Although both are defenses of their respective
positions, the seeming superiority of Bishop over Norton
as a guide to the events illustrates the Puritan loss of
mastery. Bishop's more modern narrative style has come
to be seen as the more truthful while Norton suffers for
his strident defense of a doctrine that became obsolete
with a generation of his publication. One should keep in
mind that, despite his narrative style, Bishop was trying
to persuade and that he was not above exaggeration.

Other secondary works following Bishop's example also
stressed the persecuting nature of Puritans. These are
important for their preservation and reprinting of many
documents dealing with the subject. Two excellent sources
are James Bowden, The History of the Society of Friends
in America (London, 1854), and William Sewall, The
History of the Rise, Increase and Progress of the Christian People Called Quakers (Burlington, N.J., 1774).

More recently, historians have used Quakers to illustrate the erosion of Puritan communities. The best of
these studies is Richard P. Gildrie, Salem, Massachusetts,
1626-1683: A Covenant Community (Charlottesville, Va.,
1975). Kai T. Erikson, Wayward Puritans: A Study in the
Sociology of Deviance (New York, 1966), attempts to apply
Emil Durkheim's theories of deviance to seventeenth-century Massachusetts and has a major section devoted to

Salem Quakers. Erikson's analysis suffers from his failure to consider the full context of Quakers in the life
of Salem. Marcia Norma Gold, "Sectaries in Puritan
Society: A Study of Seventeenth-Century Quakers" (M.A.
thesis, University of Wisconsin, 1969), tries to extend
Erikson's analysis more fully to Salem. While her treatment of the problem is preferable to Erikson's, she,
understandably in light of the limitations of her thesis,
did not consider the larger implications of central and
local authority.
    Excellent studies on the growth of dissent and the
erosion of Puritan consensus are E. Brooks Holifield,
"On Toleration in Massachusetts," Church History, 38
(1969):188-200, William McLoughlin, New England Dissent,
1630-1833, 2 vols. (Cambridge, Mass., 1971), and Susan
Reed, Church and State in Massachusetts, 1691-1740
(Urbana, Ill., 1914).
    All of the above secondary materials should, of course,
follow the standard works on religion in early America
by Sidney Ahlstrom, Rufus Jones, Edmund Morgan, and Perry
Miller. On Quakers, one should consult Arthur Worrall,
Quakers in the Colonial Northeast (Hanover, N.H., and
London, 1980). Also of critical importance in any understanding of the ways in which religion and society inter-
acted in seventeenth century Massachusetts are the works
of Darrett Rutman, Timothy H. Breen, and Stephen Foster.

MANUSCRIPT SOURCES

Boston Public Library, Boston, Massachusetts
    Chamberlain Manuscript Collection
Essex Institute, Salem, Massachusetts
    Buffum Family Papers
    Essex County Court Files
    Higginson Papers
    Ipswich Court Records, 1636-92
    Ipswich Town Records, 1634-62 (manuscript copy of
       the original)
    Norfolk Court Records, 1648-78
    Records of Chebacco Parish, Ipswich, 1676-1726
       (manuscript copy of the original)
    Salem Court Records, 1636-92
Essex Probate Court, Salem
    Essex Probate Records
Kittery Town Hall, Kittery, Maine
    Kittery Town Records, 1648-1709
Massachusetts Historical Society, Boston
    Miscellaneous Bound Manuscripts
New England Yearly Meeting of the Society of Friends
Manuscript Collection, Rhode Island Historical Society
Library, Providence
    Ancient Epistles, Minutes and Advices on Discipline,
       1672-1735

Minutes of the Yearly Meeting, 1683-1787
Rhode Island Men's Monthly Meeting Records, 1676-1773
   (microfilm copy of the original kept at the
   Newport Monthly Meeting)
Salem, Massachusetts, Birth, Death, and Burial
   Records of the Monthly Meeting, 1645-1819
      Marriage Certificates
      Men's Monthly Meeting Records, 1672-1818
      Monthly Meeting Records, 1672-1945
      Minutes of the Monthly Meeting, 1676-1778
New Hampshire Historical Society, Concord
   Hampton Miscellaneous Town Records
New Hampshire State Library, Concord
   Hampton Town Records
New Middlesex County Court House, Cambridge, Massachusetts
   Middlesex County Court Files
New Suffolk County Court House, Boston, Massachusetts
   Suffolk County Court Files
Old Suffolk County Court House, Boston, Massachusetts
   Suffolk County Court Records, 1680-92
Rhode Island Historical Society Library, Providence
   Moses Brown Papers Regarding the Imprisonment of
      Quakers
   George Selleck Papers
State House, Boston, Massachusetts
   Massachusetts Archives

PRINTED PUBLIC RECORDS

Abstract and Index of the Records of the Inferiour Court
   of Pleas Held at Boston, 1680-1698.   Historical
   Records Survey.   Boston, 1940.

A Collection of Acts of Parliament Relative to Those
   Protestant Dissenters Who Call Themselves Friends.
   London, 1801.

A Representation to King and Parliament of Quakers in New
   England.   London, 1669.

Beverly, Massachusetts First Church Records, 1667-1787.
   William P. Upham, transcriber.   Salem, Mass., 1868.

The Book of the General Lawes and Libertyes Concerning
   the Inhabitants of Massachusetts.   Thomas Barnes,
   ed. 1648; rept. San Marino, Calif., 1975.

Calendar of State Papers: Colonial, 1661-1685.   W. Noel
   Sainsbury and J. W. Fortescue, eds. London, 1880-98.

Documentary History of the State of Maine Containing the
     Baxter Manuscripts, Collections of the Maine Histori-
     cal Society, 2d ser., vols. 1-9. James P. Baxter,
     ed. Portland, Me., 1869-1916.

Documentary History of the State of New York. 4 vols.
     Edmund B. O'Callahan, ed. Albany, N.Y., 1850-51.

Documents and Records Relating to New Hampshire, 1623-
     1800. 40 vols. Nathaniel Bouton et al., eds. Concord
     and Manchester, N.H., 1867-1953.

Ecclesiastical Records of the State of New York. 7 vols.
     Edward Corwin, ed. Albany, N.Y., 1901-16.

Extracts from State Papers Relating to Friends, 1654-1672.
     Norman Penney, ed. London, 1913.

Maine Wills, 1640-1760. William Mitchell Sargent, ed.
     Portland, Me., 1887.

Probate Records of Essex County, Massachusetts. 3 vols.
     George F. Dow, ed. Salem, Mass., 1916-20.

Province and Court Records of Maine. 6 vols. Charles T.
     Libbey et al., eds. Portland, Me., 1928-75.

Quaker Protests, 1659-1675, Proceedings of the Massachu-
     setts Historical Society. Worthington Chauncey Ford,
     ed. 3d ser., 42 (1908):358-81.

Records and Files of the Quarterly Courts of Essex County,
     Massachusetts, 1636-1692. 9 vols. George F. Dow and
     Mary Thresher, eds. Salem, Mass., 1911-75.

Records of the Colony of New Plymouth in New England,
     1620-1692. 12 vols. Nathaniel B. Shurtleff, ed.
     Boston, 1855-61.

Records of the Colony of Rhode Island and Providence
     Plantation in New England, 1636-1782. 10 vols.
     John R. Bartlett, ed. Providence, R.I., 1856.

Records of the County of Middlesex in the Commonwealth of
     Massachusetts. 3 vols. David Pulsifer, Cambridge,
     Mass., 1851.

Records of the Courts of Assistants of the Colony of the
     Massachusetts Bay, 1630-1692. 3 vols. John Noble, ed.
     Boston, 1901-28.

Records of the First Church in Boston 1630-1868, Colonial
     Society of Massachusetts Publications, vols. 39-41.
     Richard D. Pierce, ed. Boston, 1961.

Records of the First Church in Salem, Massachusetts, 1629-
    1736. Richard D. Pierce, ed. Salem, Mass., 1974.

Records of the Governor and Company of the Massachusetts
    Bay in New England, 1628-1686. 5 vols. in 6 parts.
    Nathaniel B. Shurtleff, ed. Boston, 1853-54.

Records of the Suffolk County Court, 1671-1680, Publica-
    tions of the Colonial Society of Massachusetts, vols.
    29-30. Samuel Eliot Morison and Zachariah Chaffee,
    Jr., eds. Boston, 1933.

Second Report of the Record Commissioners of the City of
    Boston Containing the Boston Records, 1634-1661.
    Boston, Mass., 1877.

Seventh Report of the Record Commissioners of the City
    of Boston Containing the Boston Records, 1660-1694.
    Boston, Mass., 1877.

Suffolk Deeds, 1629-1697. 14 vols. Registry of Deeds,
    Suffolk County, Massachusetts. Boston, 1880-1906.

Town Records of Salem, Massachusetts, 1634-1691. 3 vols.
    William P. Upham and Martha Howes, eds. Salem, Mass.,
    1868-1934.

Vital Records of Rhode Island, 1636-1850. 10 vols. James
    N. Arnold, ed. Providence, R.I., 1895.

Vital Records of Salem, Massachusetts to the End of the
    Year 1849. 2 vols. Salem, Mass., 1916.

            OTHER PRINTED PRIMARY MATERIALS

An Answer to a Scandalous Paper Wherein Were Some Scanda-
    lous Queries Given to Be Answered. London, 1656.

Adams, Charles Francis, ed. Antinomianism in the Colony
    of Massachusetts Bay, Publications of the Prince
    Society, vol. 21. 1894; rept. New York, 1967.

Barbour, Hugh, and Roberts, Arthur O., eds. Early Quaker
    Writings, 1650-1700. Grand Rapids, Mich., 1973.

Baxter, Benjamin. Mr. Baxter Baptized in Blood or a Sad
    History of the Unparalleled Cruelty to the Anabaptists
    in New England. London, 1673.

Baxter, Richard. One Sheet against the Quakers. London,
    1657.

_____. The Quaker's Catechism. London, 1655.

Bishop, George. New England Judged by the Spirit of the
     Lord. 1661; rept. London, 1703.

Blome, Richard. The Fanatick History or an Exact Relation
     and Account of the Old Anabaptists and New Quakers.
     London, 1660.

Bond, Sampson. A Publick Tryal of Quakers in Barmudas,
     May 1, 1678. Boston, 1682.

Bugg, Francis. The Pilgrim's Progress from Quakerism to
     Christianity. London, 1698.

Burroughs, Edward. A Declaration of the Sad and Great
     Persecution and Martyrdom of the People of God Called
     Quakers in New England. London, 1660.

Coddington, William. A Demonstration of True Love unto
     You the Rulers of the Colony of Massachusetts in New
     England. London, 1674.

Folger, Peter. A Looking Glass for Our Times. 1676;
     rept. Newport, 1763.

F[ox], G[eorge]. An Answer to Severall Laws and Orders
     Made by the Rulers of Boston in New England. London,
     1678.

_____. Cain and Abel Representing New England's Church
     Hierarchy in Opposition to Protestant Dissenters.
     London, 1675.

_____. Journal of George Fox, Being an Historical Account
     of the Life, Travels, Sufferings, Christian Experi-
     ences and Labours of Love.... 2 vols. London, 1891.

_____. Something in Answer to a Law Lately Made at the
     First Session of the General Court Held at Boston in
     New England. London, 1679.

Fox, George, and Burnyeat, John. A New England Firebrand
     Quenched; An Answer to Roger Williams. N.p., 1678.

Fox, George, et al. The Secret Work of a Cruel People
     Made Manifest. London, 1659.

Hall, David, ed. The Antinomian Crisis, 1636-1638: A
     Documentary History. Middletown, Conn., 1968.

Higginson, Francis. A Brief Relation of the Irreligion
     of Northern Quakers. London, 1653.

Hull, John. "Diaries." Archelogia Americana, 3 (1857):
     113-316.

Hutchinson, Thomas, ed. A Collection of Original Papers
    Relative to the History of Massachusetts Bay. Boston,
    1769.

Johnson, Edward A. Wonder-Working Providence of Sion's
    Saviour in New England. J. Franklin Jameson, ed.
    New York, 1910.

Maule, Thomas. New England Persecutors Mauled with Their
    Own Weapons. Salem, Mass., 1697.

Naylor, James. An Answer to a Book Called the Quaker's
    Catechism. London, 1655.

Norton, John. The Heart of New England Rent. Cambridge,
    Mass., 1659.

Pagitt, Ephraim. Heresiography or a Description of the
    Heretics and Sectaries of These Latter Times. 3d ed.
    London, 1646.

Penney, Norman, ed. The First Publishers of the Truth.
    London, 1907.

Pennington, Isaac, Jr. An Examination of the Grounds and
    Causes which Are Said to Induce the Courts of Boston
    in New England to Make That Order or Law of Banishment
    upon Pain of Death against the Quakers. London, 1660.

Read, Conyers, ed. William Lambarde and Local Government.
    Ithaca, N.Y., 1962.

Sewall, Samuel. Diary, 1674-1729. 2 vols. M. Halsey
    Thomas, ed. New York, 1973.

Stearns, Raymond, ed. "Correspondence of John Woodbridge,
    Jr. and Richard Baxter," New England Quarterly, 10
    (1937):557-83.

Walker, Williston, ed. The Creeds and Platforms of Con-
    gregationalism. New York, 1893.

Walley, Thomas. Balm in Gilead. Cambridge, Mass., 1669.

Ward, Nathaniel. The Simple Cobbler of Aggawam. P. M.
    Zall, ed. Lincoln, Neb., 1969.

Weld, Thomas, et al. A Further Discovery of that Genera-
    tion of Men Called Quakers.... Gateside, England, 1654.

Winthrop, John. History of New England, ed. by James K.
    Hosmer as Winthrop's Journal, 1630-1649 (Original
    Narratives of Early New England). New York, 1908.

Winthrop Papers, <u>Collections of the Massachusetts Historical Society</u>, 4th ser., vols. 6-7. Boston, 1863-65.

SECONDARY SOURCES, BOOKS

Adams, Brooks. <u>The Emancipation of Massachusetts: The
Dream and the Reality</u>. 1887; rept. Boston, 1962.

Allen, David Grayson. <u>In English Ways: The Movement of
Societies and the Transferral of English Local Law
and Custom to Massachusetts Bay in the Seventeenth-
Century</u>. Chapel Hill, N.C., 1981.

Bailyn, Bernard. <u>The New England Merchants in the Seventeenth Century</u>. New York, 1964.

Banks, Charles E. <u>The Planters of the Commonwealth: A
Study of Emigrants and Emigration in Colonial Times</u>.
1930; rept. Baltimore, 1972.

Barbour, Hugh. <u>The Quakers in Puritan England</u>. New
Haven, Conn., 1964.

Battis, Emery. <u>Saints and Sectaries: Anne Hutchinson
and the Antinomian Controversy in the Massachusetts
Bay Colony</u>. Chapel Hill, N.C., 1962.

Besse, Joseph. <u>A Collection of the Suffering of the
People Called Quakers, 1650-1689</u>. 2 vols. London,
1753.

Boorstin, Daniel J. <u>The Americans: The Colonial Experi-
ence</u>. New York, 1958.

Bowden, James. <u>The History of the Society of Friends in
America</u>. 2 vols. London, 1854.

Boyer, Paul, and Nissenbaum, Stephen. <u>Salem Possessed:
The Social Origins of Witchcraft</u>. Cambridge, Mass.,
1974.

Breen, Timothy. <u>The Character of the Good Ruler: A Study
of Puritan Political Ideas in New England, 1630-1730</u>.
New Haven, Conn., and London, 1970.

_____. <u>Puritans and Adventurers: Change and Persistence
in Early America</u>. Oxford, England, 1980.

Brewer, John and Styles, John. <u>An Ungovernable People:
The English and Their Law in the Seventeenth and
Eighteenth Centuries</u>. New Brunswick, N.J., 1980.

Bridenbaugh, Carl. Fat Mutton and Liberty of Conscience:
    Society in Rhode Island, 1636-1690. Providence, R.I.,
    1974.

Brock, Peter. Pacifism in the United States from the
    Colonial Era to the First World War. Princeton, N.J.,
    1968.

Burrage, Henry S. The Beginnings of Colonial Maine,
    1602-1658. Portland, Me., 1914.

Caller, James M., and Ober, M. A. Genealogy of the De-
    scendants of Lawrence and Cassandra Southwick of
    Salem, Massachusetts. Salem, Mass., 1881.

Capp, Brian S. The Fifth Monarchy Men: A Study in Seven-
    teenth-Century English Millenarianism. London, 1972.

Carroll, Kenneth L. John Perrot, Early Quaker Schismatic.
    London, 1971.

Clark, Charles E. The Eastern Frontier: The Settlement
    of Northern New England, 1610-1763. New York, 1970.

Clason, Claus Peter. Anabaptism: A Social History,
    1525-1618. Ithaca, N.Y., 1972.

Cohn, Norman. The Pursuit of the Millenium: Revolution-
    ary Millenarians and Mystical Anarchists of the Middle
    Ages. Rev. ed., Oxford, England, 1970.

Covey, Cyclone. The Gentle Radical: A Biography of
    Roger Williams. New York, 1966.

Daniels, Bruce C., ed. Town and Country: Essays on the
    Structure of Local Government. Middletown, Conn.,
    1978.

Dow, Joseph. History of Hampton. 2 vols. Salem, Mass.,
    1893.

Ellis, George E. The Puritan Age and Rule in the Colony
    of the Massachusetts Bay, 1629-85. Boston, 1888.

Endy, Melvin B., Jr. William Penn and Early Quakerism.
    Princeton, N.J., 1973.

Erikson, Kai T. Wayward Puritans: A Study in the Soci-
    ology of Deviance. New York, 1966.

Felt, Joseph B. A History of Ipswich, Essex, and Hamil-
    ton. Ipswich, Mass., 1834.

_____. Annals of Salem. 2 vols. Salem, Mass., 1845.

Frost, J. William. The Quaker Family in Colonial America:
    A Portrait of the Society of Friends. New York, 1973.

Frothingham, Richard. The History of Charlestown.
    Charlestown, Mass., 1845.

Garrett, John. Roger Williams: Witness beyond Christen-
    dom, 1603-1683. New York, 1970.

Gildrie, Richard P. Salem, Massachusetts, 1626-1683: A
    Covenant Community. Charlottesville, Va., 1975.

Green, M. Louise. The Development of Religious Liberty
    in Connecticut. 1905; rept. New York, 1970.

Greenleaf, W. H. Order, Empiricism, and Politics: Two
    Traditions of English Political Thought, 1500-1700.
    London, 1964.

Gura, Philip F. A Glimpse of Sion's Glory: Puritan
    Radicalism in New England, 1620-1660. Middletown,
    Conn., 1984.

Hall, David D. The Faithful Shepherd: A History of the
    New England Ministry in the Seventeenth Century.
    Chapel Hill, N.C., 1972.

Hall, David D., et al., eds. Saints and Revolutionaries:
    Essays on Early American History. New York, 1984.

Hall, Michael G. Edward Randolph and the American Colo-
    nies, 1676-1703. New York, 1969.

Haller, William. Liberty and Reformation in the Puritan
    Revolution. New York, 1955.

Hallowell, Richard. The Quaker Invasion of Massachusetts.
    Boston, 1883.

Haskins, George Lee. Law and Authority in Early Massa-
    chusetts: A Study in Tradition and Design. New York,
    1960.

Hill, Christopher. Change and Continuity in Seventeenth-
    Century England. Cambridge, Mass., 1975.

_____. The Experience of Defeat: Milton and Some Contem-
    poraries. London, 1984.

_____. Society and Puritanism in Pre-revolutionary England.
    2d ed., New York, 1967.

_____. The World Turned Upside Down: Radical Ideas dur-
    ing the English Revolution. New York, 1973.

Holder, Charles F. The Holders of Holderness: A History
    and Genealogy of the Holder Family with Special
    Reference to Christopher Holder. Pasadena, Calif.,
    1902.

Holdsworth, William G. A History of English Law. 20
    vols. London, 1903-75.

Holifield, E. Brooks. The Covenant Sealed: The Develop-
    ment of Puritan Sacramental Theology in Old and New
    England, 1570-1720. New Haven, Conn., 1974.

Holmes, Oliver Wendall, Jr. The Common Law. Boston,
    1923.

Huehns, Gertrude. Antinomianism in English History with
    Special Reference to the Period 1640-1660. London,
    1951.

Hurd, D. Hamilton. History of Essex County, Massachu-
    setts with Biographical Sketches of Many of Its
    Pioneers and Prominent Men. 2 vols. Philadelphia,
    1888.

Hutchinson, Thomas. History of the Colony and Province
    of Massachusetts Bay. 3 vols. Lawrence S. Mayo, ed.
    Cambridge, Mass., 1936.

James, Sidney V. A People among Peoples: Quaker Benev-
    olence in Eighteenth-Century America. Cambridge,
    Mass., 1963.

Jones, Mary Hoxie. The Standard of the Lord Lifted Up:
    A History of Friends in New England from 1656-1700.
    Providence, R.I., 1961.

Jones, Rufus M. The Quakers in the American Colonies.
    1911; rept. New York, 1962.

_____. Spiritual Reformers in the Sixteenth and Seven-
    teenth Centuries. New York, 1914.

Klein, Randolph S. Portrait of an Early American Family:
    The Shippens of Pennsylvania across Five Generations.
    Philadelphia, 1975.

Konig, David T. Law and Society in Puritan Massachusetts:
    Essex County, 1629-1692. Chapel Hill, N.C., 1979.

Leach, Douglas E. Flintlock and Tomahawk: New England
    in King Philip's War. New York, 1958.

Levy, Leonard W. Origins of the Fifth Amendment: The
    Right against Self-Incrimination. Oxford, England,
    1968.

Lovejoy, David S. The Glorious Revolution in America.
    New York, 1972.

McLoughlin, William G. New England Dissent, 1630-1833:
    The Baptists and the Separation of Church and State.
    2 vols. Cambridge, Mass., 1971.

Miller, Perry. Errand into the Wilderness. New York,
    1964.

_____. The New England Mind: From Colony to Province.
    Boston, 1961.

_____. The New England Mind: The Seventeenth Century.
    Boston, 1965.

_____. Orthodoxy in Massachusetts, 1630-1650. Cambridge,
    Mass., 1933.

Morgan, Edmund S. The Puritan Dilemma: The Story of
    John Winthrop. Boston, 1958.

_____. The Puritan Family: Religion and Domestic Rela-
    tions in Seventeenth-Century New England. Rev. ed.
    New York, 1966.

_____. Roger Williams: The Church and the State. New
    York, 1967.

_____. Visible Saints: The History of a Puritan Idea.
    New York, 1963.

Nuttal, Geoffery F. The Holy Spirit in Puritan Faith and
    Experience. Oxford, England, 1946.

_____. Visible Saints: The Congregational Way, 1640-1680.
    Oxford, England, 1957.

Oberholzer, Emil, Jr. Delinquent Saints: Disciplinary
    Action in the Early Congregational Churches of Massa-
    chusetts. New York, 1956.

O'Callaghan, E. B. The History of New Netherland or New
    York under the Dutch. 2 vols. New York, 1848.

Oliver, Peter. The Puritan Commonwealth: An Historical
    Review of the Puritan Government in Massachusetts in
    its Civil and Ecclesiastical Relations. Boston, 1856.

Parrington, Vernon L. Main Currents in American Thought:
The Colonial Mind. New York, 1927.

Perley, Sidney. The History of Salem, Massachusetts.
3 vols. Salem, Mass., 1924-27.

Phillips, James D. Salem in the Seventeenth Century.
Boston and New York, 1933.

Pope, Robert. The Half-Way Covenant: Church Membership
in Puritan New England. Princeton, N.J., 1969.

Powers, Edwin. Crime and Punishment in Early Massachusetts, 1620-1692: A Documentary History. Boston,
1966.

Reed, Susan M. Church and State in Massachusetts, 1691-
1740. Urbana, Ill., 1914.

Reid, John G. Maine, Charles II, and Massachusetts:
Government Relations in Northern New England.
Portland, Me., 1977.

Robinson, G. Frederick, and Wheeler, Ruth Robinson.
Great Little Watertown: A Tercentenary History.
Cambridge, Mass., 1930.

Rutman, Darrett. American Puritanism: Faith and Practice. Philadelphia, 1970.

_____. Winthrop's Boston: A Portrait of a Puritan Town,
1630-1649. New York, 1965.

Schochet, Gordon. Patriarchalism in Political Thought:
The Authoritarian Family and Political Speculation
and Attitudes Especially in Seventeenth-Century
England. Oxford, England, 1975.

Selleck, George. Quakers in Boston: 1656-1964, Three
Centuries of Friends in Boston and Cambridge.
Cambridge, Mass., 1976.

Sewall, William. The History of the Rise, Increase and
Progress of the Christian People Called Quakers. 3d
ed. Burlington, N.J., 1774.

Shipton, Clifford K. Roger Conant, A Founder of Massachusetts. Cambridge, Mass., 1944.

Shlatter, Richard. Richard Baxter and Puritan Politics.
New Brunswick, N.J., 1957.

Southwick, Henry L. The Policy of the Early Colonies of
    Massachusetts toward Quakers and Others Whom they
    Regarded as Intruders. Boston, 1885.

Spufford, Margaret. Contrasting Communities: English
    Villages in the Sixteenth and Seventeenth Centuries.
    Cambridge, England, 1974.

Stackpole, Everett F. Old Kittery and Her Families.
    Lewiston, Me., 1903.

Strayer, James M. Anabaptism and the Sword. Lawrence,
    Kan., 1972.

Stoever, William B. A Faire and Easie Way to Heaven:
    Covenant Theology and Antinomianism in Early Massa-
    chusetts. Middletown, Conn., 1978.

Tolles, Frederick. The Atlantic Community of Early
    Friends. London, 1952.

VanDeventer, David E. The Rise of Provincial New Hamp-
    shire. Baltimore, 1973.

Vann, Richard T. The Social Origins of English Quaker-
    ism, 1650-1750. Cambridge, Mass., 1969.

Wall, Caleb A. The Puritans vs. the Quakers: A Review
    of the Persecutions of the Early Quakers and Baptists
    in Massachusetts. Worcester, Mass., 1888.

Wall, Robert E. Jr. Massachusetts Bay: The Crucial
    Decade, 1640-1650. New Haven, Conn., 1972.

Walzer, Michael. The Revolution of the Saints: A Study
    in the Origins of Radical Politics. London, 1965.

Watkins, Owen C. The Puritan Experience: Studies in
    Spiritual Autobiography. New York, 1972.

Wertenbaker, Thomas Jefferson. The Puritan Oligarchy:
    The Founding of American Civilization. New York,
    1947.

Windsor, Justin. The Memorial History of Boston Including
    Suffolk County Massachusetts, 1638-1880. 4 vols.
    Boston, 1882-83.

Winslow, Ola Elizabeth. Master Roger Williams, A Biog-
    raphy. New York, 1957.

Winthrop, Robert C. Life and Letters of John Winthrop, Governor of the Massachusetts Bay Company at Their Emigration to New England, 1630. 2 vols. Boston, 1864.

Wood, Nathan E. The History of the First Baptist Church of Boston. Philadelphia, 1899.

Worrall, Arthur. Quakers in the Colonial Northeast. Hanover, N.H., and London, 1980.

Young, Christine. From Good Order to Glorious Revolution: Salem, Massachusetts, 1626-1689. Ann Arbor, Mich., 1980.

Zwierlein, Frederick J. Religion in New Netherland: A History of the Development of the Religious Conditions in the Province of New Netherland, 1623-1664. Rochester, N.Y., 1910.

SECONDARY SOURCES, ARTICLES

Adams, Herbert Baxter. "Allotments of Land in Salem to Men, Women, and Maids." Essex Institute Historical Collections, 19 (1882):167-76.

_____. "Common Fields in Salem." Essex Institute Historical Collections, 19 (1882):241-53.

_____. "Origins of Salem Plantation." Essex Institute Historical Collections, 19 (1882):153-66.

Banks, Charles E. "The West Country Origins of Salem's Settlement." Essex Institute Historical Collections, 46 (1930):317-24.

Beattie, J. M. "Pattern of Crime in England, 1660-1800." Past and Present, 62 (1974):47-95.

Beier, A. L. "Rejoinder." Past and Present, 71 (1976): 130-34.

_____. "Vagrants and the Social Order in Elizabethan England." Past and Present, 64 (1974):3-29.

Brauer, Jerald C. "Puritan Mysticism and the Development of Liberalism." Church History, 19 (1950):151-70.

Breen, Timothy H. "Persistent Localism: English Social Change and the Shaping of New England Institutions." William and Mary Quarterly, 3d ser., 32 (1975):3-27.

_____. "Who Governs: The Town Franchise in Seventeenth-Century Massachusetts." William and Mary Quarterly, 3d ser., 27 (1970):460-74.

Breen, Timothy H., and Foster, Stephen. "The Puritans' Greatest Achievement: A Study of Social Cohesion in Seventeenth-Century Massachusetts." Journal of American History, 60 (1973):5-22.

Brown, B. Katharine. "The Controversy over the Franchise in Puritan Massachusetts, 1954-1974." William and Mary Quarterly, 3d ser., 33 (1976):212-41.

Buckley, Thomas E. "Church and State in Massachusetts Bay: A Case Study of Baptist Dissenters, 1651." Journal of Church and State, 23 (1981):309-22.

Butterfield, Herbert. "Toleration in Early Modern Europe," Journal of the History of Ideas, 38 (1977): 573-84.

Buxton, Bessie Raymond. "The History of the South Church Peabody." Essex Institute Historical Collections, 87 (1951):41-64, 178-207, 341-72.

Cadbury, Henry J. "Early Quakers at Cambridge." Cambridge Historical Society Publications, 24 (1936-37): 67-83.

_____. "Quakers and Their Abettors, Middlesex County, Massachusetts." Quaker History, 27 (1938):9-16.

Camp, Leon R. "Roger Williams vs. the Upstarts: The Rhode Island Debates of 1672." Quaker History, 52 (1963):69-77.

Cohen, Ronald. "Church and State in Seventeenth-Century Massachusetts: Another Look at the Antinomian Controversy," Journal of Church and State, 12 (1970):

Cole, Alan. "The Social Origins of Early Friends." Journal of the Friends' Historical Society, 48 (1957): 117-23.

Cole, W. A. "The Quakers and the English Revolution." Past and Present, 10 (1956):39-54.

Davisson, William I. "Essex County Price Trends: Money and Markets in Seventeenth-Century Massachusetts," Essex Institute Historical Collections, 103 (1967): 144-85.

_____. "Essex County Wealth Trends: Wealth and Economic Growth in Seventeenth-Century Massachusetts." Essex Institute Historical Collections, 103 (1967):291-342.

_____. "Land Precedents in Essex County, Massachusetts." Essex Institute Historical Collections, 106 (1970): 252-76.

Davisson, William I., and Dugan, Dennis J. "Commerce in Seventeenth-Century Essex County, Massachusetts." Essex Institute Historical Collections, 107 (1971): 113-43.

Ditsky, John. "Hard Hearts and Gentle People: A Quaker Reply to Persecution." Canadian Review of American Studies, 5 (1974):47-51.

Dunn, Mary Maples. "Saints and Sisters: Congregational and Quaker Women in the Early Colonial Period." American Quarterly, 30 (1978):582-601.

Emerson, Roger L. "Heresy, the Social Order, and English Deism." Church History, 37 (1968):389-404.

Foster, Stephen. "New England and the Challenge of Heresy, 1630-1660: The Puritan Crisis in Trans-atlantic Perspective." William and Mary Quarterly, 3d ser., 38 (1981):624-60.

Gildrie, Richard P. "Contention in Salem: The Higginson-Nicholet Controversy." Essex Institute Historical Collections, 113 (1977):117-39.

Grimes, Mary Cochran. "Saving Grace among Puritans and Quakers: A Study of Seventeenth- and Eighteenth-Century Conversion Experiences." Quaker History, 72 (1983):3-26.

Henretta, James. "Economic Development and Social Structure in Colonial Boston." William and Mary Quarterly, 3d ser., 22 (1965):75-92.

Holifield, E. Brooks. "On Toleration in Massachusetts." Church History, 38 (1969):188-200.

Hurwich, Judith Jones. "The Social Origins of the Early Quakers." Past and Present, 48 (1970):156-62.

Johnson, George A. "From Seeker to Finder: A Study in Seventeenth-Century Spiritualism before the Quakers." Church History, 18 (1948):299-315.

Jonas, Manfred. "The Wills of the Early Settlers of
    Essex County, Massachusetts." Essex Institute
    Historical Collections, 96 (1960):228-35.

Koch, Donald W. "Income Distribution and Political
    Structure in Seventeenth-Century Salem, Massachu-
    setts." Essex Institute Historical Collections,
    105 (1969):50-71.

Konig, David T. "Community, Custom, and the Common Law:
    Social Change and the Development of Land Law in
    Seventeenth-Century Massachusetts." American Journal
    of Legal History, 18 (1974):137-77.

Lockeridge, Kenneth A., and Kreider, Alan. "The Evolu-
    tion of Massachusetts Town Government, 1640-1740."
    William and Mary Quarterly, 3d ser., 33 (1966):549-
    74.

Lee, Carol F. "Discretionary Justice in Early Massachu-
    setts." Essex Institute Historical Collections, 112
    (1976):120-39.

Lucas, Paul. "Colony or Commonwealth, Massachusetts
    Bay, 1661-1666." William and Mary Quarterly, 3d
    ser., 24 (1967):88-107.

MacLear, J. F. "Popular Anticlericalism in the Puritan
    Revolution." Journal of the History of Ideas, 17
    (1956):443-70.

Manners, Emily. "Elizabeth Hooten, the First Quaker
    Woman Preacher, 1600-1672." Journal of the Friends
    Historical Society, supplement no. 12 (1914):

Mosse, George L. "Puritanism and Reason of State in Old
    and New England." William and Mary Quarterly, 3d
    ser., 9 (1952):67-80.

_____. "Puritan Radicalism and the Enlightenment." Church
    History, 29 (1960):424-40.

Park, Charles E. "Puritans and Quakers." New England
    Quarterly, 27 (1954):53-74.

Perley, Sidney. "Beverly in 1700." Essex Institute
    Historical Collections, 56 (1920):209-20.

_____. "Center of Salem Village in 1700." Essex Insti-
    tute Historical Collections, 44 (1918):115, 225-89.

_____. "Northfields, Salem in 1700." Essex Institute
    Historical Collections, 48 (1912):173-84, 260-62; 49
    (1913):186-92.

_____. "Rial Side, Part of Salem in 1700." Essex Institute Historical Collections, 45 (1919):49-55.

Pestana, Carla Gardina. "The City upon a Hill under Siege: The Puritan Perception of the Quaker Threat to Massachusetts Bay, 1656-1661." New England Quarterly, 56 (1983):323-53.

Phippen, George D. "The Old Planters." Essex Institute Historical Collections, 1 (1859):97-111, 145-53, 185-200.

Pound, J. F. "Debate: Vagrants and the Social Order in Elizabethan England." Past and Present, 71 (1976): 126-29.

Reay, Barry. "The Quakers, 1659, and the Restoration of the Monarchy," History, 63 (1978):193-213.

Schochet, Gordon. "Patriarchalism, Politics, and Mass Attitudes in Stuart, England," Historical Journal, 12 (1969):413-41.

Simmons, Richard C. "The Founding of the Third Church in Boston." William and Mary Quarterly, 3d ser., 26 (1969):241-52.

_____. "Godliness, Property, and the Franchise in Puritan Massachusetts." Journal of American History, 55 (1968):495-511.

Solt, Leo. "The Fifth Monarchy Men: Politics and the Millenium." Church History, 30 (1961):314-25.

Thomas, Keith. "Women and the Civil War Sects." Past and Present, 13 (1958):42-62.

Tolles, Frederick B. "A Quaker's Curse--Humphry Norton to John Endecott, 1658." Huntington Library Quarterly, 14 (1951):415-21.

_____. "The Transatlantic Quaker Community in the Seventeenth Century." Huntington Library Quarterly, 14 (1951):239-58.

Vann, Richard T. "From Radicalism to Quakerism: Gerrard Winstanley and Friends." Quaker History, 43 (1969): 71-91.

_____. "Quakerism and the Social Structure of the Interregnum." Past and Present, 43 (1969):71-92.

_____. "The Social Origins of the Early Quakers, a Re-
joinder." Past and Present, 48 (1970):162-64.

Wall, Robert E., Jr. "Decline of the Massachusetts Franchise, 1647-1666." Journal of American History, 54
(1972):303-10.

_____. "Massachusetts Bay Colony Franchise in 1647."
William and Mary Quarterly, 3d ser., 27 (1970):136-44.

Weeks, Louis. "Cotton Mather and the Quakers." Quaker
History, 59 (1970):24-34.

Willauer, G. J., Jr. "First Publishers of Truth in New
England: A Composite List, 1656-1775." Quaker
History, 65 (1976):35-44.

Worrall, Arthur J. "Persecution, Politics, and War:
Roger Williams, Quakers, and King Philip's War."
Quaker History, 66 (1977):73-86.

UNPUBLISHED THESES AND PAPERS

Dailey, Barbara. "John Cotton's Abstract of the Laws of
New England." Seminar paper, Boston University, 1977.

Gold, Marcia Norma. "Sectaries in Puritan Society: A
Study of Seventeenth-Century Quakers." Master's
thesis, University of Wisconsin, 1969.

Moody, Robert. "The Maine Frontier, 1607-1763." Ph.D.
dissertation, Yale University, 1933.

Pope, Robert G. "Society, Security, and Persecution."
Paper presented at Thomas More College, Fort Mitchell,
Ky., 1975.

Wall, Robert E., Jr. "The Membership of the Massachusetts
General Court, 1634-1686." Ph.D. dissertation, Yale
University, 1965.

Index

About the Author

JONATHAN M. CHU is Associate Professor of History at the University of Massachusetts, Boston. He has written for the *New England Quarterly* and the *Essex Institute Historical Collections.*